PATRIOTISM AND PIETY IN ARMENIAN CHRISTIANITY

ST VLADIMIR'S SEMINARY PRESS
ST NERSESS ARMENIAN SEMINARY
AVANT Series

Series Editor
MICHAEL DANIEL FINDIKYAN

Patriotism and Piety in Armenian Christianity

The Early Panegyrics on Saint Gregory

Abraham Terian

ST VLADIMIR'S SEMINARY PRESS
ST NERSESS ARMENIAN SEMINARY
Crestwood, New York 10707
www.svspress.com

2005

Library of Congress Cataloging-in-Publication Data

Terian, Abraham, 1942–
  Patriotism and piety in Armenian Christianity : the early panegyrics on Saint Gregory / Abraham Terian.
     p. cm. — (Avant, ISSN 1536–2752 ; no. 2)
  Includes bibliographical references and index.
  ISBN 0–88141–293–7 (hardcover : alk. paper)
  1. Gregory, the Illuminator, Saint, ca. 240–ca. 332. 2. Armenian Church—Biography. 3. Armenian Church—History. 4. Armenia—Church history.
I. Title. II. Avant (New Rochelle, N.Y.) ; no. 2
  BX129.G697T47 2005
  270.1'092—dc22

                               2005000481

AVANT: Treasures of the Armenian Christian Tradition – Number 2

The **AVANT** Series, an undertaking of St Vladimir's Seminary and St Nersess Armenian Seminary, aims to bring to light the riches of the Armenian Christian tradition by providing annotated English translations of Armenian patristic, dogmatic, liturgical and other early religious literature with a view toward revealing the distinct witness of Armenian Christianity and its significance today.

ISBN: 0–88141–293–7
ISSN: 1536–2752

Si parva licet componere magnis

Preface

THE START OF THIS BOOK goes back a decade, when I began translating the text of the panegyric on St. Gregory by Yovhannēs Erznkats'i instead of filling crossword puzzles on long flights. Later, when His Holiness the late Karekin I invited some fifty Armenologists to meet with him in Paris on June 13–15, 1996, to lay down plans for the celebration of the 1700th anniversary of the proclamation of Christianity in Armenia (whereby Armenians became the first nation to embrace Christianity), I thought of producing a commentary on the text I had more or less translated—perhaps providentially. The first part of the introduction appeared shortly thereafter as an article in *St. Nersess Theological Review* I (1996) 117–144, under the title "Surpassing the Biblical Worthies: An Early Motif in Armenian Religious Literature." Nearer the end of the present work, a sample of it appeared in the same periodical under the title "The Ancestry of St. Gregory the Illuminator in the Panegyrical Tradition" (7 [2002] 45–65).

Much has transpired since the memorable meeting in Paris. His Holiness Karekin I did not live to see the realization of the plans for the commemoration of the auspicious event. While committees were formed to plan for pilgrimages, exhibitions, scholarly conferences, etc., His Holiness kept pleading for the publication of books as permanent markers of the commemoration. It was in keeping with the wish of His Holiness that St. Nersess Armenian Seminary launched its AVANT series, to perpetuate the significance of the celebrated event. This volume is a fitting sequence to the inaugural volume of the series, *The Teaching of St. Gregory* by Professor Thomson, who chaired the ad-hoc committee on prospective publications at the Paris meeting.

The blend of patriotism and piety in Armenian Christianity needs no substantiation. My purpose in this book is to show that this phenomenon is not a late development but one born in the very cradle of Armenian Christianity and nurtured from the inception of the Armenian letters early in the fifth century. After nearly a millennium of growth as a motif in Armenian literature, the phenomenon reached its highest point in the medieval panegyrics on St. Gregory, foremost of which is that by Yovhannēs Erznkats'i (*ca.* 1230–1293), who chose for its setting the summit of Mount Sepuh, not far from his birthplace, where St. Gregory spent the closing years of his life. Speaking of this panegyric, Bishop Karekin Sruandziants' (1840–1892), himself a man of letters, remarks on its author: "He sang the praises of the Superior Sepuh and elevated the Armenian Church above the sun and made her shine brighter" (*T'oros Aghbar,* 2 vols. [Constantinople: Paghtatlean, 1879–85] 2:50: «Որ Սեպուհ Գերազանց նուազեր էր եւ Հայաստանեայց եկեղեցին քան զարեւն ի վեր բարձրացուցեր եւ փայլեցուցեր էր...»). This spirit of patriotism and piety is alive and well in modern Armenian literature, seen in the works of Alishan, Khrimian, Varoujan, Yeghivard and several others where patriotism often surpasses piety. Alishan may well be responsible for its transmission from ancient to modern Armenian literature. *Patriotism and Piety in Armenian Christianity* is a reminder of the early history of this religio-literary tradition.

I am grateful to the trustees of the Bishop Zgon Hagopian Memorial Fund not only for underwriting the publication expenses of this volume but also for the generous grants subsidizing my salary over the last five years of my tenure at St. Nersess as Professor of Armenian Patristics. This was in keeping with the will of the late Bishop who had a profound love for the writings of the Armenian Church fathers. No less gratitude is due the Primate of the Eastern Diocese of the Armenian Church in America, His Eminence Archbishop Khajag Barsamian, who as President of St. Nersess Armenian Seminary made it possible for me to be associated with the school. The generosity of the grants along with the possibilities at St. Nersess brought the present work to fruition.

On a more personal note, I wish to thank my wife, Dr. Sara Kärkkäinen Terian, for being my first critical reader and for her perceptive observations. I could not have done this work without her help. I also wish to thank my colleagues at St. Nersess, the V. Rev. Dr. Daniel Findikyan, Dean of the Seminary, and Dr. Roberta Ervine for reading earlier drafts of the manuscript and for making valuable suggestions. Responsibility for the contents of this book is ultimately mine.

A.T.
Thanksgiving Day 2002

Contents

Transcription of Armenian

Based on the Library of Congress System

ա	բ	գ	դ	ե	զ	է	ը	թ	ժ	ի	լ	խ
a	b	g	d	e	z	ē	ĕ	t'	zh	i	l	kh

ծ	կ	հ	ձ	ղ	ճ	մ	յ	ն	շ	ո	չ	պ
ts	k	h	dz	gh	ch	m	y	n	sh	o	ch'	p

ջ	ռ	ս	վ	տ	ր	ց	ւ	փ	ք	օ	ֆ	ու
j	ṙ	s	v	t	r	ts'	w	p'	k'	ō	f	u

Introduction

Through conversion to Christianity early in the fourth century and the subsequent translation of the Bible into their language a century later, Armenians found a new identity. Not that they were in search of an identity, for their national identity must have preceded the early days of the Achaemenids of the Old Persian Empire. The rock-cut Behistun inscription of Darius I (dated 518 BC) bears witness to this, as does the history of their pre-Christian past in other non-Armenian sources, such as Herodotus and Xenophon.[1] However, as a result of the cultural revolution that accompanied their conversion, and in their overwhelming Christian piety, Armenians began to redefine themselves in scriptural terms vis-à-vis ancient Israel, as did nearly all early Christian communities. This effort was stretched to zealotic proportions among medieval Armenians whose literary heritage was a product of Christian times. The early writers went on to extol their spiritual leaders as equal to—or even surpassing—the biblical worthies in piety. As we shall see, the tendency is well attested in the earliest Armenian writings, and because of its prevalence, it evolved into a literary motif. The motif reached its climactic point in the medieval panegyrics on St. Gregory the Illuminator, especially in the one by the thirteenth-century rhetor and grammarian, hymnographer and theologian Yovhannēs Erznkats‘i, whose life and work are discussed in the third part of the Introduction and to whose panegyric much of the remainder of this book is assigned.

The line of demarcation between the historical and the religious in early Armenian literature is blurred by the fact that all known authors were clerics and the extant writings abound with scriptural allusions and quotations from the Armenian Bible, the product of the vision of St. Mashtots‘ (called Mesrop by writers after his own time) and the administrative sagacity of St. Sahak, the Catholicos of the day (in office 387–438). Their dream of having Moses with the Prophets and Paul with the Apostles to be read in Armenian or, as Koriwn puts it, to become "Armenian-speaking," came admirably true. Koriwn gives us the following dramatic picture of the far-reaching effect of this great undertaking:

> At that time our blessed and pleasant land of Armenia became truly wonderful, where at the hands of two associates, as if suddenly, Moses the teacher of the Law with the prophetic order, progressive Paul with the whole apostolic group, along with the world-sustaining Gospel of Christ, came to be found in the Armenian tongue, became Armenian-speaking. What heart-warming joy existed there from that time on, and what a pleasant sight for the eyes of the beholder! For a land unfamiliar even with the fame of those regions where all the miracles wrought by God had been performed, soon learned all the things that had taken place: not only those that had been venerated through time, but also those that were long before, from eternity, and those that are to come later—the beginning and the end and all the God-given traditions (11 [56.10–15]).[2]

Besides hastening the transition to Christianity, the expeditious translation of the Bible had an immediate and overwhelming influence on the ensuing Armenian literature.[3] The writers of the fifth and later centuries adorned their works with countless quotations from Scripture and often incorporated its language into their prose.[4] They went on to compare their religious founders and leaders with the foremost biblical characters, at times flagrantly.[5] This tendency, as stated, evolved into a discernible literary motif, beginning with Koriwn's *Life of Mashtots'* and followed by the pseudonymous Agat'angeghos, the author of the *History of the Armenians* with his focus on the life and teaching of St. Gregory the Illuminator. The motif is detectable in the anonymous author or compiler of the *Buzandaran Patmutiwnk'*, in Ghazar and Eghishē, the exponents of the wars of St. Vardan, in Khorenats'i, the elusive "father of [Armenian] history," and others thereafter—especially the medieval panegyrists on St. Gregory.

Moreover, the early Armenian writers drew on a wide range of Early Christian works dependent on the Classical tradition, and were well acquainted with their style, their apologetics, and their explicit and implicit purpose. Rhetorically, most of these writings are persuasive literature, documents for reinforcing the Christian faith primarily, but not devoid of other aims underlying their literary intentions. On their part, Armenian writers were able to utilize powerful and proven symbols as they dwelt on native heroes, producing works evocative of strong religious and patriotic ideals, the dynastic propaganda for their patrons notwithstanding. They provided icons of identification for future generations and succeeded in leaving a permanent imprint on the way in which later generations viewed their faith. More importantly, the scrupulously devout and patriotic orientation of the early Armenian writers imprinted itself indelibly on the Armenian literary tradition.

Comparing a eulogized hero with renowned persons from the past is an encomiastic or panegyrical requirement in the rhetorical literature ever since Classical times, popularized through the *Progymnasmata,* the widespread guidelines for writers in Late Antiquity and the early Byzantine period. Aristotle, for example, has this rule in his *Rhetoric* (1368a11–25): "Point out . . . that he has done it better than anyone else"; "the comparison should be with famous men; that will strengthen your case; it is a noble thing to surpass men who are themselves great" (lines 12, 21).[6] Maintaining the Classical tradition in Late Antiquity, Aphthonius has this admonition in his *Progymnasmata:* "add comparison, in order to infer a greater position for the one being praised."[7] Such comparison becomes a recurring motif in early Armenian literature, and it is in suchlike instances of encomiastic comparison in Koriwn's *Life of Mashtots‘* that the pattern is set for subsequent Armenian authors to follow.[8]

Biblical precedents, especially from the New Testament, could be cited among the factors contributing to similar developments in the Early Church. The following saying attributed to Jesus and addressed to the disciples, the future Apostles, regarding their standing vis-à-vis the Prophets, of whom St. John the Baptist was considered the last and the greatest, is noteworthy: "Among those born of women there has not arisen anyone greater than John the Baptist; yet he who is least in the kingdom of heaven is greater than he" (Matt. 11:11; cf. vs. 13). This was to further depreciate Mosaic authority in the early Christian disputes with Judaism so as to extol the Messianic. There is also St. Paul's admonition to become imitators of him as he is of Christ (1 Cor. 11:1), and to follow the example of others praised by him.[9] The formal praise of a long line of biblical worthies in the Epistle to the Hebrews (ch. 11) further justifies the praising of the saints early in the history of Christianity, following similar praise of "famous men" in one of the acclaimed books of the Old Testament Apocrypha, Ecclesiasticus, or the Wisdom of Jesus Son of Sirach (Ben Sira for short, chs. 44–50). Early Christian hymns, the emerging liturgical literature, and early hagiography dealing with the lives and legends of the saints are other major elements in this development. Moreover, there can be no doubt about an excessive Christian exegetical understanding of the Old and New Testaments of which early Armenian writers were aware, as seen in their reliance on a vast array of patristic translations.[10] These writings tend to heighten the distinction between the dominance of the Law in the so-called "old dispensation" of Patriarchs and Prophets and the perceived superior role of the Spirit in the New Testament era or the Apostolic age.[11]

Precedents aside, there seems to be a particular self-definition emerging in the early Armenian writers, surveyed below, beginning with Koriwn's *Life of Mashtots'*. This self-definition is somewhat akin to that in early Christianity and its relation to Judaism ever since the emergence of Christian distinctiveness in the first century, when there was a strong consciousness among early Christians of their being the people of God.[12] By the fifth century Christians had already established, to their own satisfaction, that they were the true heirs of ancient Israel. The way early Armenian writers expressed this consciousness of their Christianity calls for a more exhaustive study, employing for its method principles of phenomenology and sociology of knowledge. Suffice it to say that the initial inroads made by Christianity must have been socially and politically far more painful and destabilizing than the picture presented by the historians of the early church.[13] Circumstances in Armenia during the period of the Christian Arsacids were probably similar to those elsewhere in the fourth and early fifth centuries. It was a time of uneasy change in the self-consciousness of the Armenian people, and vestiges of Zoroastrianism lingered on for centuries among the Arewordik', the "Children of the Sun."[14] Yet from that time onward, as the writings of the ecclesiastic spokesmen indicate, Armenians had acquired a new identity and no longer defined themselves by their pre-Christian past. They had become closely associated with the commonwealth of the New Israel or the people of God; they had become a distinct entity whose religion was neither Iranian nor Greco-Roman but "biblical."

A substantial part of the early authors' intent, like that attributed by them to their respective heroes, was to heighten this self-consciousness among the people, to condition the new identity based on the new faith. There were also political corollaries to their intent: to distance themselves from the super-powers of the day and possibly to unite—on the basis of the new faith—the sovereign principalities ruled by the dynastic princes or feudal lords, the Nakharars of Arsacid society, within both the struggling kingdom to the north and the autonomous territories to the south and to the west. Their efforts may be deemed significant in view of prevailing conditions in the much fragmented land with its constantly shifting boundaries, not only between the threatening Byzantines and Sasanians but also among the feuding Nakharars. The religious and conceivably no less political consolidation at the capital Vagharshapat invokes a theophany for its legitimacy, the descent of the apocalyptic Christ to establish His church at Ejmiatsin, acccording to a vision attributed to St. Gregory by Agat'angeghos. This was a decisive departure from the old religious center at Ashtishat in Tarōn, in Western Armenia, with certain of its Christian monuments built there earlier by St. Gregory himself.

The very high esteem for the native heroes of faith in early Armenian literature, as being no less honorable than the biblical worthies, may suggest dire socio-political realities and trying times when the newly acquired faith and the new identity that came with it had to be reaffirmed. This was done repeatedly, especially when facing foreign invaders, and more so when the enemy threatened the faith. Within a few generations the new faith had become the historic faith of the fathers, a faith worth dying for as the Jewish zealots of Maccabean and subsequent times did for theirs. The Armenian martyrs for the faith in the AD 451 war against the Persians partake of the covenantal Eucharist on the eve of the decisive battle, after they are admonished by the priest Ghevond to resist to death—in a speech modeled on that of the dying Mattathias, the leader of the Maccabees (1 Macc. 2:49–68).[15] Reciting the Nicene Creed and partaking of the Eucharist when besieged by the enemy seem to have been among the more prevalent expressions of faith in the face of calamities. This kind of history is repeated at various times and in different parts of historic Armenia. A later example of it is found in Kirakos Gandzakets'i's account of the surrender of the clergy at Lorunt, near his native Gandzak, to the Tatars in 1236.[16] Hope of deliverance is introduced by turning to the supernatural at times, such as at the height of the Arab domination of Armenia in the late seventh century, when the apparition of the cross on Mount Varag was claimed with the discovery there of a relic of the cross of Christ.[17]

What is conspicuous about early Armenian Christianity is that it did not dwell on defining itself in terms of "orthodoxy" and "heresy," even though the Church adhered to Athanasian orthodoxy at the height of the Arian controversy.[18] Nor did it assert a separate identity among fringe-groups or sects within the early Church, even though the ruling Arsacids from the accession of Tiran in 339 to that of Arshak III in 379 aggressively pursued an Arianizing policy.[19] Notwithstanding the unique historical circumstances that seem to have influenced the shape of the Armenian ethos, the confluence of patriotism and piety in the literature of the fifth century is indicative of a self-understanding similar to the two most prevalent and related self-definitions in primitive Christianity: (1) its continuity with ancient Israel, and (2) its willingness for martyrdom as the persecuted yet faithful remnant of God's people. As for the first self-definition, there was a strong sense of apostolic tradition in Armenian Christianity, seen in the assumption of continuity with the Prophets and the Apostles, in being part of salvation history—thanks to the traditions associated with Sts. Thaddaeus and Bartholomew (one derived earlier from Edessa and the other later, possibly from Pontic Caesarea) and, especially, to St. Gregory, the acclaimed "Prophet" and "Apostle" of the Armenians, a Parthian by birth, begotten as "the spiritual child of St. Thaddaeus."[20] As for the second self-definition, early Armenian writers had a strong penchant for martyrdom not simply because they were the spiritual successors of the Maccabees but because the reward of those who thus bear witness for Christ, those who do not abandon His "covenant," is all the greater.

The early and distinct events in Armenian history, namely, the conversion to Christianity, the invention of the alphabet, and the battle for the faith, had a strong, determining impact on the confluence of patriotism and piety in Armenian Christianity. These consequential events, along with their respective heroes, were viewed from a biblical standpoint and were treated by the early writers following the Classical literary-rhetorical requirements mandated in the early Byzantine period. Thus was laid the foundation for a literary tendency and one with considerable longevity, affecting the national ethos for generations thereafter.

I. Patriotism and Piety in Early Armenian Literature

Koriwn is one of the two earliest Armenian authors whose identity is known and whose authorship is undisputed; the other is his fellow disciple and co-worker among the "Holy Translators," Eznik of Koghb, of whom more shall be said later. For several reasons, not the least of which are his subject matter and gripping style, Koriwn became the standard bearer of early Armenian literature, whereas Eznik had little or no influence on Armenian writers after his own time. This is demonstrated by the fact that subsequent Armenian authors of the fifth century and others thereafter were dependent upon Koriwn's brief yet significant, consequential work. It is appropriate therefore to begin with him, and the more so since all indicators are that he is the progenitor of the motif under consideration.

The motif begins with the comparative description of the profound joy of St. Mashtots' on his way back to Greater Armenia with the newly finalized alphabet. Koriwn compares the joyous Saint bearing the Armenian letters with the despondent Moses on his way down from Mount Sinai bearing the Decalogue (*Life of Mashtots'*, 9 [52.1–8]). Koriwn's comparison, in spite of his apology for it, is to show that his teacher fared better with his anticipation for the Armenian people than did the lawgiver of Israel upon seeing the idolatry of the Golden Calf in the Hebrew camp (alluding to Ex. 31:18–32:19; 34:29–35). Koriwn writes:

> Even the magnificent Moses was not as joyous during his descent from Mount Sinai. We cannot say that his [joy] was greater, for it was far less. For when the man who had seen God was descending from the mountain with the commandments inscribed and given by God in his arms, the vengeful people—who had turned their backs to divine things and had corrupted the earth by rejecting the Lord and by bowing down to their molten idols—caused the bearer of His commandments to weep bitterly with a broken heart. For the despair of the bearer became visibly apparent in the shattered tablets. But as for this blessed one, concerning whom our oration is composed, he did not act in that manner as had transpired there. On the contrary, being filled with spiritual consolation, he was thinking of the eagerness of those who were to be the recipients . . .

Koriwn continues:

> Let no one consider us very bold for what we have said, for which we may be censured. How could a very modest man be compared with the magnificent Moses, be made equal to the one who had spoken with God and had

done wonders? But we can, more so in the belief that whether in revealed or in hidden things there is nothing to fault the Deity for, since it is the grace of the one omnipotent God that is distributed to all earth-born nations (9 [52.1–19]).

This is followed by comparing the ongoing scribal and evangelistic activities with those mandated by Moses in the Law, David in the Psalms, and Christ in the Gospel (11 [54.18–56.9]). Finally, the deeper sorrow of the ever-active St. Mashtots' over the death of his associate St. Sahak is compared with the sadness, loneliness, and relative inactivity of the Apostle Paul because of the temporary absence of his associate Timothy (25 [90.2–11]).[21] Koriwn observes:

> Inasmuch as the holy Apostle, upon temporarily not finding his partner, Timothy, says that his soul was restless, how much more intense is deemed the survivors' grief over those who are altogether departed? Whereas the sadness caused by loneliness would not allow [Paul] to be cheerful, [Mashtots'] carried out fully, with the grace of God, the course of evangelism and administration of the holy church and strove even more, trying harder, exhorting everyone to be undaunted in goodness (lines 4–11).

Earlier, however, Koriwn had indicated that the concern of St. Mashtots' for his people is no less than that of the Apostle Paul for his people (2 [30.18]).[22] Still, the two persons with whom St. Mashtots' is laudably compared are the first of the Prophets and the last of the Apostles: Moses and Paul, the two most accomplished biblical characters from the Old and New Testaments respectively. Beginning with Koriwn's introductory analogy between his praise of St. Mashtots' and the Bible's treatment of its worthies, the masterful use of the Scriptures to compare, to restate, and to reaffirm faith is noteworthy.

More importantly, Koriwn had placed his writing in line with the biblical tradition (2 [30.17–34.24]), much as his contemporary and associate among "the holy translators," Eznik Koghbats'i, had done. The latter, as "a worthy narrator" of God, associates himself with the biblical writers, "the friends of God," a privileged group which also included those who were martyred for his sake (*Refutation*, 355).[23] This self-understanding expressed by the earliest known Armenian writers, beginning with Koriwn's presentation of their master, Mashtots‘, was well understood by Vardan Vardapet Arewelts‘i, a thirteenth-century sage and hymnographer. In his "Hymn to the Holy Translators" Arewelts‘i speaks of them as inspired apostles and prophets "like unto Saint Moses the Great," who established "the living script to shepherd the flock of New Israel."[24] Interestingly, in the hymnal of the Armenian Church, this hymn follows the "Hymn to the Holy Prophets," an arrangement further implying that the holy translators are for the Armenian people what the Hebrew prophets are for their people.

The immediate influence of Koriwn's *Life of Mashtots‘* is seen in the *History of the Armenians* by the shadowy author Agat‘angeghos ("good messenger" in Greek), the most widely held primary source on the life and teaching of St. Gregory and the conversion of Armenia to Christianity.[25] The fifth-century Armenian author, writing in about 460, purports to be a Roman scribe and an eyewitness of the conversion of King Trdat or Tiridates IV the Great (298–330),[26] at whose command he writes the *History* (12–13). His use and adaptation of various sources, including Greek and Syriac hagiographical writings in the first part (1–258, i.e., before the insertion of *The Teaching of St. Gregory*, 259–715) and Koriwn's *Life of Mashtots‘* in the second part (716–900), have long been demonstrated in critical scholarship.[27] The importance of this work is attested by early translations, partially or in full, into several languages: Greek, Arabic, Georgian, Syriac, Latin, and Ethiopian, with two distinct recensions discernible among them.[28] Regardless of the stylized hagiography, the mythical elements, and the embellishments seen in the variants to the story in the various versions that comprise the two recensions, the seminal tradition regarding St. Gregory in the *History* of Agat‘angeghos is deemed trustworthy.

Agat‘angeghos punctuates his work with numerous biblical allusions and comparisons, such as the skin condition of St. Gregory on his emergence from the pit and that of Job in his misery (Job 30:30; cf. *History*, 217). Far more noteworthy, however, is the description of the return of St. Gregory to Armenia as bishop. Agat‘angeghos uses a substantial part of the above-quoted passage from Koriwn, transferring to St. Gregory much of what Koriwn had said of St. Mashtots‘ on his way to Greater Armenia with the new script. Note the similarities in this description:

> At this time our land of Armenia was blessed, envied and truly admired.
> Like Moses, who suddenly became a teacher of the law to the Hebrew

camp with all the ranks of the Prophets, or like the outstanding Paul with the entire group of the Apostles, with the gospel of Christ that brings life to the world, so too did he come and appear and speak Armenian to the Armenians (854).

This section is from the middle of the ample borrowings from Koriwn, especially from the latter's description of the missionary activities of St. Mashtots', appropriated for St. Gregory by Agat'angeghos (818–900).[29]

Moreover, when commenting on the ascetic life of St. Gregory, Agat'angeghos compares him with Elijah the Prophet and St. John the Baptist (848). Before the epilogue, he concludes the historical narrative with this statement on his hero: "So in this fashion he spent all the days of his life in acts like those of the Apostles" (891). The epilogue itself is a chain of scriptural citations that draw a parallel between the royal command to Agat'angeghos to chronicle the life of St. Gregory on the one hand and on the other hand the divine mandate in the Scriptures to write down the Law and the prophetic books (892–900). Thus in the epilogue Agat'angeghos places his writing in line with the Scriptural tradition, in keeping with Koriwn, who, in his prologue, claims continuity between his writing of the *Life of Mashtots'* and the apostolic writings of New Testament times (2 [30.17–34.24]). The very last words in Agat'angeghos underscore the new identity the Christian faith has brought to the Armenian people, who address God in the covenantal words of the Prophet Jeremiah: "'You are our Lord God.' And he will say to them: 'You are my people' [Jer. 3:22; 7:23; 11:4; 31:33]" (900). Here we see a likely parallel to Koriwn's quotation from the Psalms in the following: "He distanced them so much from their ancestral [traditions] and made them lose their recollection to such an extent that they said, 'I forgot my people and my father's house' [Ps. 45:10 (44:10 LXX)]" (15 [62.27–28]).

Because of these and other striking parallels between Koriwn's *Life* and the *History* of Agat'angeghos—*The Teaching of St. Gregory* included, as well as similarities of vocabulary, style, and other factors between them, Archbishop Norayr Bogharian (Pogharean) and others before him have long held that Koriwn is also the author of the latter two works. Noting similar features also in the *Buzandaran Patmut'iwnk'*, Bogharian hastens to add this work as well to Koriwn's repertoire.[30] Although the distinct authorship of the latter work is demonstrable, as shall be pointed out at the conclusion of our discussion of the work, the arguments regarding the common authorship of the *Life* and the *History* that bears the name of Agat'angeghos cannot be ignored.[31] These arguments, at best, seem to underscore the dependence of the latter upon the former and the beginnings of emerging literary motifs.

The *Buzandaran Patmout'iwnk'*, a collection of oral histories of Greater Armenia during the fourth century, was compiled by an anonymous author about the year 470. In a way it chronicles the history of Armenia during the long reign of Shahphur II of Persia (309–379) and concludes with the official partition of the already fragmented land under his successor, Shahpuhr III, in 387.[32] The bereaved author laments the end of the period he chronicles: "And the kingdom of Armenia was diminished, divided, and scattered. And it declined from its greatness at that time and thereafter" (6.1).[33] Through his compilation he attempts to fill the historical gap between Agat'angeghos' history of the conversion of Armenia at the hand of St. Gregory and Koriwn's account of the invention of the alphabet at the hand of St. Mashtots'. Clearly, the author utilizes the work of Koriwn and shows awareness of the traditions about St. Gregory—though not the entire received tradition as in the Armenian version of Agat'angeghos (*Aa*). He is also well immersed in the Armenian version of the Scriptures. All his other sources seem to have been oral traditions, reflecting the rich oral heritage of early Christian Armenia.[34] He appears to have been a churchman familiar also with liturgical practices and the lives of saints, with which he punctuates the otherwise gloomy history.[35]

Of the several lives of saints contemplated in the *Buzandaran* is that of St. James of Nisibis or Mtsbin, a much venerated saint in the Eastern churches and especially by Armenians, in whose tradition he appears as a cousin of St. Gregory the Illuminator and a sojourner in Armenia.[36] While on the slopes of the mountains of Urartu, in the district of Korduk' or Qardû in the Assyrian March of southern Armenia, this "apostle of Christ" prayed that God would allow him to see Noah's Ark.[37] His prayer, however, was answered differently. In his sleep an angel alerted him to a piece of wood from the Ark lying near his head. Taking it, he descended from the mountain, and we are told that "not even the great Moses on his descent from the Sainaitic mountain exulted with such utter joy" (3.10).[38] Earlier, in the same chapter, a spring had gushed forth for him and for his companions while on that mountain, just as a spring had gushed forth for

Moses and the Israelites at Rephidim and at Meribah (Ex. 17; Num. 20). The rest of the description of St. James' descent closely follows Koriwn's description of the return of St. Mashtots' to Greater Armenia with the new alphabet (9 [52.1–19]). The author of the *Buzandaran* seems to have made a play on his Scriptural analogy derived from Koriwn, an interesting leap from one ark to the other: from a piece of wood from Noah's Ark to Moses and the Decalogue, the prime object later placed in the Ark of the Covenant.

Early in the next chapter (3.11) the author laments the deaths of the commander-in-chief Vach'ē Mamikonean and his companions who fell in the war of about AD 338 between the Persians and the Armenians. Perpetual commemorative services were instituted for the fallen martyrs by the patriarch Vrt'anēs who, in a sermon attributed to him, eulogized the "pious martyrs," likening them to the Maccabees and applying to the Armenian experience the vulnerability as well as the aspirations of the Jewish people under the tyrannical Seleucids. Here no doubt the author is reflecting the influence of the relatively recent martyrdom of St. Vardan and his companions and the overwhelming impact it must have had on their contemporaries. Thus the *Buzandaran* anticipates the martyrological sentiments and the Maccabean connection in Ghazar and, especially, in Eghishē, the exponents of the AD 451 war.

One further passage in the *Buzandaran* ought to be underscored as it relates to the motif under consideration and also shows the extent of the author's dependence on Koriwn. The passage in question recounts the Bible-laced admonitions of St. Nersēs the Great (4.4), which follow Koriwn closely, maintaining the very sequence of his Scriptural citations (2 [32.5–34.18]). Throughout, St. Nersēs is referred to as an apostle, on whose head the Holy Spirit descended bodily as a dove at the time of his consecration as Patriarch of Greater Armenia—just as the Spirit descended upon the Lord Himself at the time of His baptism.[39]

Again, the similarities between Koriwn's *Life* and the *Buzandaran* compelled Archbishop Bogharian to speculate on Koriwn's authorship of the latter work as well. We ought to grant the influence of style and other similarities between the two resulting from the dependence of the author of the *Buzandaran* on Koriwn; however, the idea of identical authorship has to be rejected because of the far greater differences between them.[40] As for the relation obtaining between the *Buzandaran* and the *History* of

Agat'angeghos, I agree with Thomson and Garsoïan that while the author of the *Buzandaran* may show familiarity with the received text of Agat'angeghos, *The Teaching of St. Gregory* especially, he opts for a divergent tradition, perhaps an earlier oral one pertaining to St. Gregory.[41]

We shall pursue our motif in the *History* of Ghazar P'arpets'i which covers the period 387–485. Ghazar names Koriwn and leaves no doubt about his familiarity with the latter's work, acknowledges the works of the shadowy Agat'angeghos and the *Buzandaran,* and considers his own contribution as the third historical writing (Koriwn's work, while conveying ample historical information, is considered a hagiographical encomium). We are thus compelled to relegate the popular histories of Eghishē and Khorenats'i to later times and to consider Ghazar the first Armenian historian of the fifth century whose identity is known.[42] The focus of his *History* is on the revolt of 451. In beautiful imagery and in keeping with the motif under consideration, Ghazar describes the popular response to the battle-cry sounded by St. Vardan when Armenia was invaded by the Persians:

> On hearing this, the lovers of the truth and of immortality were stirred up, vying with each other like flocks who at the sound of the flute hasten after the shepherds. It seems to me that Abraham did not run so fast to bring the calf to the angels who promised to give him his son (Gen. 17–18), as the Armenian army hastened to follow the blessed Vardan, Sparapet of Armenia, in order to go to Christ's banquet and to eat the bread of angels (p. 68).[43]

Ghazar refers frequently to St. Gregory. In the prayer of repentance which he attributes to the Armenian nobility, St. Gregory is deemed equal to the Twelve Apostles: "Grant us through the intercession of the illuminating Apostles and through the labors of the holy martyr Gregory, their equal and coworker, forgiveness for our sins" (p. 62). The equation of St. Gregory with the Apostles is not uncommon in these early writings; however, the unusually high frequency of references to him in the extant *History* of Ghazar is surprising.[44] This may be explained by the fact that "the relics of the holy, apostle-like martyr, Gregory" were newly discovered, possibly during the reign of Emperor Zeno (474–491),[45] and have come to acquire cultic significance in Ghazar's heyday; they were used in processions and ceremonial blessings (pp. 55, 176). In the speeches attributed to the priest Ghevond and the saintly commander Vardan Mamikonean, St.

Gregory is upheld as the foremost martyr for the Armenian warrior martyrs who are summoned to the heavenly Jerusalem in his name (pp. 70–71).

Ghazar's martyrological sentiments vis-à-vis those of the Books of the Maccabees are not as pronounced as those in Eghishē; however, there is no need to repeat them all here except to point out that for Eghishē the Armenian martyrs fare no less well than these biblical worthies—considering the canonical place of 1–2 Maccabees in the Septuagintal and early Christian tradition. Eghishē uses the word "covenant" *(ukht)* precisely in its Judaic sense of Intertestamental times (Heb. *berith*): not as one of the Scriptural Testaments of the Christian Canon *(ktakaran)* but as a reference to the community of God's people—now applied to the Armenians who like the Maccabees face an enemy that comes to forcefully alter their faith.[46] Moreover, Eghishē reflects the predominant esteem of martyrs in the early Church, that not only do they imitate the suffering of Christ, but that their death is a testimony to Christ's achievement. To shrink from martyrdom is therefore tantamount to denial of Christ. This notion is based on the fact that the word for witnessing and/or martyrdom is the same *(vkayut'iwn)*;[47] hence, true witnesses for Christ did not shrink from martyrdom for His sake. Death by martyrdom was the Christian's highest achievement, the standard against which all others were to be judged. The cardinal virtue which Eghishē upholds throughout his work is the virtue of martyrdom. The passionate author must have been familiar with the ordeals of the early martyrs, of which there were several compilations in his time.[48] He employs well established literary forms and features when depicting martyrdom, especially in the speeches he attributes to the priest Ghevond and to St. Vardan just before the battle. This virtue is upheld along with its attendant virtue of zeal for the faith, "pious heroism," as gathered from the several examples of biblical warriors especially in the speech attributed to Ghevond: Abraham, Moses, Phinehas, Joshua, Gideon, Jephthah, and David (pp. 107–109). These warrior worthies are referred to as "our forefathers" who are excelled by their spiritual descendants, who are "truly born of the Holy Spirit, are sons of God and heirs of Christ," and who thus "have attained an even greater fate."[49]

What we have in Eghishē's *History of Vardan and the Armenian War* is a reinterpreted history, an event interpreted by Ghazar prior to being reinterpreted and expanded along the same martyrological lines by Eghishē, but without any reference to St. Gregory (since the latter did not die a martyr's death—however much tortured, thus falling short of the kind of martyrdom upheld by this author; hence his silence about St. Gregory). There are other, numerous differences between the two accounts, beginning with the circumstances leading to the conflict that led to the revolt and to war. Differences aside, Eghishē's more passionate retelling has endeared his version to readers since its publication, to the point of allowing little hearing for the other. Questions persist, however, about Eghishē's claim to have been an eyewitness to the events recorded by him, since in its present form the *History of Vardan* appears to be a sixth-century redaction drawing on existing Armenian sources, including the *History* of Ghazar as found in a text different from that known later, and on Armenian translations that could not have existed before the sixth century, such as those of certain works of Philo of Alexandria. These observations do not, in any way, diminish its significance; it remains "a carefully constructed piece of literary work."[50]

Eghishē is not only an impressive writer but also a skilled theologian. With very moving words he narrates the experiences of the imprisoned Armenian nobles who were sacrificing themselves and their families like Abraham's sacrifice of Isaac (Gen. 22:9; pp. 48–49). He details the encounters between St. Vardan and the Persians, and the last encounter in particular—as though he were on the front lines of that fateful battle. With words reminiscent of the battle by the Pool of Gibeon, between David's men and those of Abner (2 Sam. 2:13), Eghishē writes: "For neither side was victorious and neither side was defeated; but heroes attacked heroes and both sides went down to defeat" (p. 119). His overriding purpose, however, is to show that St. Vardan and his associates in martyrdom, like the Apostles of old, bore the ultimate witness to Christ by shedding their blood for His sake. This was their supreme testimony for the Christian faith. The author's descriptive skill is sustained to the very end, where he speaks of the sorrowful widows and the wives of the nobles imprisoned in Persia and goes on to extol their virtues:

> The delicate women of Armenia, who had been coddled and pampered in their private litters and couches, daily attended the houses of prayer without shoes and on foot, tirelessly entreating with oaths that they might be able to endure their great tribulation. Those who from their childhood were nourished with marrow of steers and the best of the game, lived a

herbivorous life, like wild animals, receiving their food most joyously and without any thought of the customary delicacies. The color of their skin turned black, for by day they were scorched by the sun, and the whole night they lay on the ground.

Drawing on liturgical imageries, Eghishē continues:

Psalms were the perpetual murmur on their lips and readings from the Prophets were their utmost consolation. They were joined in couples like willing and equally yoked pairs, plowing straight the furrow of the King-dom so that they might arrive at the haven of peace without losing their way. . . . By their prayers they opened the closed gates of heaven, and by their pious supplications brought down angels for salvation. From afar they heard the good news, and they glorified God on high . . . (pp. 201–202).[51]

Without employing any direct comparison in this exordium, Eghishē sustains a lengthy analogy between "the delicate women of Armenia" and the worthies of the New Testament church: like Anna the widowed prophetess (Luke 2:36–38) and those gathered daily in prayer in the upper room at Pentecost (Acts 1:13–14; 2:1), they attended daily the houses of prayer; like those being persecuted in the Apocalypse (Rev. 7:14), they were able to endure their great tribulation; like the church symbolized as a woman who survives in the wilderness (Rev. 12:14), they lived a life of utter austerity;[52] like those who follow Paul's admonition to make the most of one's time when days are evil (Eph. 5:15–20), they consoled themselves with recitations from the Psalms and readings from the Prophets; like the seventy other disciples in Luke (10:1), they were to be found in companies of two; like worthy disciples who place their hands on the plow and press forward without looking back (Luke 9:62), they plowed straight the furrow of the Kingdom; like the Prophets Elijah and Elisha in prayer (1 Kgs. 18:37–46; 2 Kgs. 6:15–17), they opened the gates of heaven and summoned angels; and like the great worthies, the champions of faith in the Epistle to the Hebrews (ch. 11), from afar they greeted and embraced the promised salvation. The way Eghishē weaves together all these biblical examples and applies them with liturgical overtones to the sorrowful women is noteworthy.

In a lesser known work attributed to Eghishē, *Meknut'iwn Araratsots'* (Commentary on Genesis, the authorship of which is unresolved and which survives in excerpts in Vardan Arewelts'i's commentary on the same Pentateuchal book), he compares the Armenian language with other known languages of the time. His admiration of the native tongue is unambiguous in his remarks on the confusion of the tongues at Babel:

> The following is well said of what became of that one great language: Greek is smooth, Latin is rough, Hunnish is harsh, Syriac is plaintive, Persian is pleasing, Albanian is affable, Gothic is funny, Egyptian is haunting, Indian is shrilly, but Armenian is delightful and capable of containing all the languages in it.[53]

We shall take but a brief look at Khorenats'i. He favors the biblical chronology over and above other ancient chronologies and thus endeavors to synchronize certain legendary Armenian ancestors with biblical characters: Aram and his son Ara with Abraham, and Sur with Joshua (1.19).[54] Yet in keeping with his declared interest in history rather than theology, he gives much more attention to the secular than to the religious. His exaltation of the exploits of King Artashēs I of Armenia (190–159 BC), whom he proclaims "superior to Alexander the Macedonian" for ruling distant lands without leaving his country (2.13), and his portrayal of King Tigran the Great (95–55 BC) as "supreme among men" (1.24), are but examples of the secular reverberations of the motif under consideration. However, more veritable echoes of the motif are found in other chapters of the *History*. With reference to the unmarked, primary burial of St. Gregory, Khorenats'i remarks that the Saint's relics were hidden for many years by divine providence, "like [those of] Moses of old" (2.91; cf. Deut. 34:6). Likewise, when describing the indignant departure of St. James of Nisibis (purportedly a cousin of St. Gregory) from the court of Prince Manach'ihr of the Rshtunis, following the Saint's failed pleading with the prince to release certain innocent captives, Khorenats'i remarks: "[St. James] returned to his own see full of anger, like Moses leaving the presence of Pharaoh" (3.7; cf. Ex. 11:9). More of this motif is discernible in the concluding chapter of the *History*, where Khorenats'i laments the fortunes of the Armenian people following the death of their fifth-century leaders, especially of St. Sahak the Great and of the blessed St. Mashtots', both of whom are referred to as the author's "fathers" responsible for his spiritual birth and education abroad. Their death is like that of Moses who has been removed, but without a Joshua to succeed them (3.68).[55] Here Khorenats'i seems to rely on the threnody upon St. Nersēs the Great in the *Buzandaran* (5.30).

The motif is discernible in subsequent writers, such as Yovhannēs Mamikonean, the tenth-century pseudonymous author and continuator of the history he attributes to Zenob Glak, who describes Armenia as the Promised Land flowing with honey and where the heavenly manna never ceases to fall.[56] So too the last anonymous continuator (eleventh-twelfth centuries) of the early tenth-century history by T'ovmay Artsruni, who declares that "the staff of the all-powerful right hand [of our Holy Illuminator Gregory] which tended the Lord's people was superior to the two staffs of the great prophets Moses and Aaron."[57] In his "Ode to Saint Gregory the Illuminator," St. Grigor Narekats'i (951–1003) praises the Illuminator as a universal mediator (trans., Selection IV), and considers his own *Girk' Aghot'its'* (Prayerbook) as a new Psalter (Prayer 3b) and its rewriting as that of the Decalogue written and rewritten by the finger of God (Prayer 34j).[58] When recording his ancestral history in *Vipasanut'iwn Haykazants'* (Epic History of the Descendants of Hayk), Catholicos St. Nersēs Shnorhali (in office 1166–1173) establishes his kinship to St. Gregory and refers to the literary works of his great-grandfather Grigor Magistros (*ca.* 990–1059), comparing them with the works of Homer and Plato.[59] Similarly, Step'anos Ōrbēlean, bishop and historian of Siwnik' (*ca.* 1260–1304), praises the literary output and especially the biblical commentaries of his contemporary Esayi Nch'ets'i, the great scholar of Gladzor (*ca.* 1255–1338), by claiming that Esayi has outdone his namesake the prophet Isaiah: for while Isaiah's fame rests on a single book, Esayi's fame rests on his profound knowledge of all the books of the Bible.[60] More examples could be cited, such as Vanakan Vardapet's (1181–1261) *Govest Hayots' Azgi* (In Praise of the Armenian Nation), where he exalts the faith and the virtues of the Armenians as Christians.[61] Given the limits of this study, however, it is not necessary to prolong the investigation of the motif beyond the panegyrical compositions in medieval Armenian literature dedicated to St. Gregory.[62] These panegyrics on the Illuminator reflect more than the popular sentiments regarding him in later times, the times in which they were written; they mirror better than anything else the blend of patriotism and piety among the Armenian people ever since their adoption of Christianity.

II. The Motif in the Medieval Panegyrics on the Illuminator

The laudatory tradition in the medieval Armenian panegyrics on St. Gregory and the higher esteem in which he is held in comparison with biblical worthies in these later writings could be traced to the already established tendency in the surveyed sources. Other sources of influence could be cited, such as the other versions comprising the Agatʻangeghos cycle, certain Greek panegyrics on various saints, especially those by the Cappadocian Fathers,[63] and two panegyrics on our Saint in particular, said to have been translated from Greek into Armenian and traditionally attributed to St. John Chrysostom (*ca.* 350–407) and to his disciple Theophilos, respectively. The traditional authorship and date of these two works, which came to be known since the twelfth century, cannot be supported. While Greek as the original language of their composition is likely, there can be no doubt about their Armenian patronage—if not authorship—given the overly patriotic elements in them and the apparent influence of Narekatsʻiʼs poetic discourse on St. Gregory.

The first, *Srboyn Yovhannu Oskeberani Nerboghean Asatsʻeal yaghags Varutsʻ ew Nahatakutʻean Srboyn Grigori Hayotsʻ Metsatsʻ Hayrapeti* (Panegyric Recited by St. John Chrysostom upon the Life and Martyrdom of St. Gregory the Patriarch of Greater Armenia), was translated in 1141 by Abraham Gramatikos, a Greek rhetor, upon the request of the Catholicos Grigor III Pahlawuni (in office 1113–1166) and revised by St. Nersēs Shnorhali, his brother and successor to the Catholicosate (in office 1166–1173), according to a colophon by the latter at the end of the text.[64]

In the year 590 [of the Armenian Era = AD 1141], this oration was translated from Greek into ours at the hand of Abraham Gramatikos from old and faded copies, though certain words were emended by me, the humble [servant] Nersēs, given my scholarship and vocabulary, upon the request of my lord and kin, Gregory [III], Catholicos of the Armenians; and it was penned by the scribe Stepʻanos. Those who read or copy it, remember by name before Christ Jesus the above mentioned individuals who labored on it, and copy the few words of this colophon with every copying; that a permanent memorial may be written for you in the living registers of Christ.

The second, *Eranelwoyn Tʿēovpʿilosi asatsʿeal nerboghean patmagrabar surb hōrn meroy ew lusaworchʿi, kʿahanayapetin Kʿristosi ew vkayi, Metsin Grigori Arkʿepiskoposi Hayotsʿ Metsatsʿ ashkharhi* (Narratively Recited Panegyric by the Blessed Theophilos on Our Holy Father and Illuminator, the High Priest of Christ and Martyr, Gregory the Great, the Archbishop of Greater Armenia), was translated earlier by another Greek rhetor, Theopistos.[65] This was done upon the request of Catholicos Grigor II Vkayasēr (in office 1066–1105), according to a twelfth-century colophon appended to certain manuscripts of this panegyric:[66]

> This brilliant and beautifully composed oration was translated from Greek into our language by order of the thrice-blessed patriarch, Lord Gregory [II], Catholicos of Greater Armenia, by the wise and ingenious translator Theopistos. Until now this lamp was hid under a bed and was covered under a bushel.[67] However, by God's command, it was brought to light at the holy monastery of Arkʿaykaghni.[68] I, Paul, the unworthy, grievous sinner and useless cleric, strongly desired to place a copy of it in the glorious, capital-city-like [and] holy solitude of Arkʿaykaghni, as a memorial for my sinful self and for my parents. Thus its fame, like that of a crown-adorned king, reached the heaven-like solitude of Akner, where God dwells, to the holy and blessed father Stepʿanos who is draped in light. And he sent an official note and ordered to have a copy made and deposited at the door of the Church of Astuatsamayr,[69] for the glorious celebration of the feast of our Illuminator, and as a memorial for himself, his parents, and myself, the altogether sinful. And I, within my ability, made a copy and sent it. And I plead with you, O seraphic choirs grouped in the light, that you remember in your prayers the Abbott of the holy order at the solitude of Akner, father Stepʿanos, the one honored by God, and his parents, and the wise musician Manuēl, who brought on his shoulder this oration to the monastery, and me, Paul, the toiling scribe, and our parents, and all who believe in Christ. And may Christ have mercy on you who do remember habitually and on us who are remembered. Glory to Him, always. Amen.

Grigor II Vkayasēr commissioned Armenian-speaking Greek rhetors to translate St. John Chrysostom's commentaries *On the Acts of the Apostles* and *On the Gospel of John*, as well as *The Life of St. John Chrysostom* by St. Proclus of Byzantium among other Greek hagiographies.[70] Theopistos, the named translator of the *Panegyric,* is also the translator of *The Life of St. John Chrysostom,* according to another colophon.[71]

It must be remembered that upon his appointment as Catholicos in 1066, Vkayasēr (Vahram Pahlawuni) took the name of St. Gregory because of ancestral kinship to him and thus revived the long-lost hereditary Gregorid succession.[72] Maksoudian rightly observes:

> At the time of Nersēs Shnorhali's death in 1173 there was no longer any doubt that the Catholicate was considered to be the hereditary office of the Pahlawuni clan, since by that time members of that family had held the position for more than a century—since 1066. There is also reason to believe that the same principle of hereditary succession was also the tradition in the see of Aght'amar where the presiding anti-catholicoi were related to the minor branches of the Artsruni clan.[73]

The renewed interest in the traditions surrounding St. Gregory at this time and the production of panegyrics on him in the twelfth-thirteenth centuries are largely due to the succession of the Pahlawuni Catholicoi, from Grigor II to Grigor VI (1066–1203). Translated among the Selections are odes on St. Gregory by Grigor III Pahlawuni (in office 1113–1166) and by his brother and successor, St. Nersēs IV Klayets'i, known also as Shnorhali (in office 1166–1173). To this period belong also the panegyrics on the descendants of St. Gregory, such as those by Vardan Arewelts'i (on Sts. Aristakēs and Vrt'anēs and their descendant successors; on St. Grigor Vkayasēr and his descendant successors) and by Yovhannēs Erznkats'i (on St. Nersēs the Great).

In the panegyric attributed to St. John Chrysostom, St. Gregory is ranked with the angelic hosts, the Prophets, and the Apostles in heaven; he is most accomplished in heavenly virtues (pp. 7, 9; cf. p. 74: he combines in himself all the virtues of all the eternal saints). Like Abraham he was called from paganism to God's light; like David he is an exemplary shepherd, unmoved by the flood of grief; like Moses he ascended the mountain to receive the spiritual law; like Joshua he brought the people not to the Promised Land but to heaven itself; like the Prophets he made predictions, and like the Apostles he presented many souls to God (pp. 12–13). Like St. Paul he received a direct call from heaven and endured humanly unbearable pains; even more: Isaiah the Prophet was sawed asunder, St. John the

Baptist beheaded, St. Stephen stoned, St. Peter crucified, and St. Paul also beheaded, yet the martyr St. Gregory appropriated the suffering of them all in the pain he endured (pp. 14–15). While in the pit, St. Gregory was like the Prophet Jonah in the belly of the fish and like St. Paul when saved from the depths of the sea (alluding to the shipwreck at Malta, Acts 27); his coming out of the pit is like being called from the grave to resurrection (quoting Eph. 5:14; pp. 28–29). The divine promises once made to Abraham are here repeated to St. Gregory (Gen. 12:2; 17:4; 22:17; 32:12; *ibid.*). In his virtue St. Gregory participated with the Prophet Elijah in the heavenly ascent. In his suffering he was with the Prophet Jonah in the harshest isolation and with St. Paul in the bonds of imprisonment. As an equal to St. Peter in apostolic authority, he shares "the keys of the Kingdom" with him (referring to Matt. 16:19; p. 30). Whereas the Apostles divided the world among themselves for mission,[74] St. Gregory was given more than the Apostles' share, for he alone was privileged to preach universally. For this reason he is called "Sun of Righteousness" by the Lord himself, who passes on the title to him (p. 31; trans., Selection II).

The pseudonymous author is not slow to ascribe to St. Gregory some of the attributes and epithets of Christ, such as "Sun of Righteousness," as he does above. Earlier, when describing St. Gregory's deliverance from the pit, he claims for the Saint the triumph of Christ over the forces of evil, that there he trampled upon Beliar—the name given to Satan in Jewish apocalyptic writings of the Intertestamental period (p. 29). Like Christ in Hebrews 4:14 and elsewhere in the Epistle, St. Gregory is a high priest who has ascended to heaven (p. 46). And finally, as on Christ, so also on St. Gregory at the time of his consecration, the Spirit descended as a dove (p. 68).[75]

Through the conversion of King Trdat, whose dramatic experience is here compared with that of the Apostle Paul (p. 38), "a special people" is presented to God. This happens even as the Saint concludes his prayer for the healing of the king (p. 34).[76] To St. Gregory are applied the words spoken of St. John the Baptist: "You, child, shall be called a prophet of the One on high" (Luke 1:76; p. 44). In the afflictions that the Saint endured patiently, he is like David and Job (63–64);[77] in his solitary confinement he is like Elijah the Prophet and St. John the Baptist (p. 69); in his purity he is like Elijah, united with God (p. 74). Although Abel is much praised for his perfect sacrifice (Gen. 4:4; Heb. 11:4), St. Gregory surpassed him in that he offered himself daily as a rational offering; although Enosh hoped for God

(Gen. 4:26), the Saint continues to demonstrate that hope; although Enoch was taken from earth to heaven (Gen. 5:24), the Saint had his soul contemplatively and completely translated to heaven; although Noah saved the animals from the flood by bringing them into the ark (Gen. 6–8), the Saint built a better ark—the church—and saved people from the perils of paganism by bringing them to God; although Abraham excelled in his love for God, hospitality, and even willingness to offer his son Isaac (Gen. 17–18, 22), the Saint surpassed him in that he welcomed Christ not once but daily while in the pit and sacrificed not a ram in place of Isaac but himself as a rational offering;[78] although Isaac is glorified for his righteousness and exemplary life (Gen. 24–26), the Saint set a standard of righteousness and exemplary purity; although Jacob is wonderful in his simplicity of spirit, in begetting many children, and in seeing the ladder that reached from earth to heaven (Gen. 27–30), the Saint begot many shepherds and flocks for the Chief Shepherd, set his mind to be elevated from earth to heaven over an intelligible ladder, and begot many children of light;[79] although Job is most renowned for bearing afflictions patiently (Job 1–3; 7:5), the Saint's suffering is no less, for instead of sitting on a heap of ashes outside the city he went farther away, into hellish solitude, and coped with snakes instead of worms (pp. 74–77). And the comparison continues in like manner, comparing the Saint with Joseph, Moses, Samuel, David, Elijah, and Sts. John the Baptist, Peter, and Paul—with St. Gregory surpassing them all (pp. 77–81).

There are fewer comparisons in the panegyric attributed to Theophilos, a disciple of St. John Chrysostom. The focus, throughout, is on the imprisonment of St. Gregory in the deep pit or dungeon at Khor Virap, the survival of this man of God who at the beginning of the document is declared an equal to Sts. Peter and Paul since he evangelized the East as they evangelized the West (p. 92) and who at the end of the document is referred to as "second Paul," "second Moses," and "new Daniel" (p. 122; trans., Selection III).[80] Though ranked among the Apostles, St. Gregory is "a twofold apostle who preached the word of truth to a proud nation" (p. 123: *krkin aṙakeal, or kʻarozetsʻer zbann chshmartutean yazg hpartatsʻeal*). The Saint's condition in the pit is compared with that of Lazarus in the grave (John 11), yet unlike Lazarus the Saint's pit had no stench but smelled like the Garden of Eden (p. 98; cf. p. 108, for further Edenic description of the place).[81] Unlike Adam, St. Gregory did not succumb to the serpents there (Gen. 3; p. 101; cf. p. 109, where these serpents are said to be descended from the one that deceived Eve). He is like the three Hebrew youths in the fiery furnace: Hananiah, Azariah, and Mishael (Dan. 3:19–27; cf. 1:7 for the names; p. 103). St. Gregory's fourteen-year survival in the deep pit is said to be a greater miracle than that of the Prophet Daniel in the lions' den (Dan. 6), since snakes are considered deadlier than lions (p. 104).[82] There he was fed like the Prophet Elijah in the wilderness (1 Kgs. 17:1–7; p. 116). In most of these examples, as in those preceding them, the Illuminator fares better than the biblical worthies.

These two "Chrysostomian" panegyrics said to have been translated from Greek had profound influence on all subsequent Armenian panegyrics on St. Gregory, especially those of Yovhannēs Sarkawag, Vardan Arewelts'i, and Yovhannēs Erznkats'i—the latter in particular.[83] Before surveying their works, however, I wish to account briefly for the work of Grigor Sarkawagapet Erusaghēmats'i, an otherwise obscure writer were it not for his panegyrical discourse entitled *Khosk' i Surb Grigor Lusaworich'* (Discourse on St. Gregory the Illuminator).[84] Given the relatively minor influence of the "Chrysostomian" panegyrics on his work, there are grounds to believe that he lived before the twelfth century. His work is the most subdued of these compositions. While it begins and ends with panegyrical overtones, it is for the most part a homiletical text. At its beginning St. Gregory, the most beloved of Christ, is said to be a greater miracle-worker than the Prophets and the Apostles; for he was able to transform a boar, King Trdat, to a human being. Because of the baptisms that followed, the Euphrates became no less significant than the Jordan, and divine favor was manifested in greater measure in the land of Armenia. Like Jesus, St. Gregory kept forgiving his persecutors, and like Moses he ascended the mountain (i.e., Mount Sepuh) to converse with God continually (pp. 132–136; trans., Selection V). At the end, Sarkawagapet repeats his appeal to the reader to accept St. Gregory as one equal to the Prophets and the Apostles and to adhere to his equally authoritative teachings (pp. 156–157).

Yovhannēs Sarkawag (*ca.* 1050–1129) begins his *Nerboghean i Surbn Grigor* (Panegyric on St. Gregory) by remarking that Armenian martyrs, such as the Illuminator, manifest far greater zeal for God than that manifested by Phinehas (Num. 25:6–8; cf. Ps. 106:30 [105:30 LXX]); their testimony is much more effective than the word of Elijah when he spoke against iniquity and thereupon brought drought upon the land (1 Kgs. 17:1; 18:1; cf. Luke 4:25; James 5:17); their inspired messages that have been transmitted to the faithful are comparable to the sayings of the biblical worthies, those well known to God and familiar to us in the Old and New Testaments (pp. 6–7). Near the end of the panegyric Sarkawag systematically compares St. Gregory with Moses. He draws analogies between Moses' encounter with God at the burning bush, where the prophet was unable to see God when told to deliver the Israelites from Egypt (Ex. 3:1–12), and St. Gregory's encounter with the "Bridegroom" in Roman territory and his return to the native land to deliver his people (pp. 28–30).[85] He then turns to the miracles wrought by the rod of Moses, the rod by which he turned the Nile water to blood, the rod which turned into a serpent, and by which he led the Israelites to the Promised Land (Ex. 4:1–9; 7:8–25), comparing them with what the Illuminator accomplished by the Word of the Lord and the sign of the Cross: taming the serpents in the pit, transforming the very person of the king, and bringing the Northern tribes from darkness into God's light (pp. 30–31). Whereas Moses inflicted ten plagues upon the Egyptians at the time of the Exodus (Ex. 7:14–11:10), St. Gregory delivered and lifted up his people through the suffering inflicted upon himself. Whereas Moses used his rod when crossing the Red Sea, causing Pharaoh to drown (Ex. 13:20–14:31), the Saint turned the tide at his crossing of the Euphrates by baptizing the masses, and in so doing he crushed the head of "the invisible Pharaoh" once crushed at the Jordan (p. 32).[86] Whereas Moses fed the people with manna (Ex. 16:13–35), St. Gregory fed them with the true Bread from Heaven (alluding to John 6:25–59). Whereas Moses hit the rock, causing a spring to gush forth for the people to drink (Ex. 17:5–7), St. Gregory activated the spring of the Water of Life to quench their spiritual thirst (alluding to John 7:37–39). Whereas Moses with his outstretched arms helped Joshua carry a victory over the Amalekites (Ex. 17:8–16), St. Gregory carried victories with the sign of the Cross and destroyed the sanctuaries of demons, chasing them out to the Caucasus. And whereas Moses led the Israelites to the Promised Land, the Saint brought his people into "the world to come"; even to see God (pp. 33–34). Sarkawag has come full circle in his systematic comparison between Moses and the Illuminator by repeating the notion that Moses was unable to see God: whether at the burning bush or, presumably, when he asked to see God's face (Ex. 33:21–23; cf. John 1:18). Moreover, he has pursued the motif under consideration near the beginning and near the end of his composition, thus creating a larger literary frame or an *inclusio*. Of his panegyric, the overwhelming comparison between St. Gregory and Moses (pp. 27–34) is translated here (Selection VI).

In his *Nerboghean yErits's Eraneal Part'ewn Grigorios Lusaworich' Hayastan Ashkharhis* (Panegyric on the Thrice Beatified Parthian, Gregorios the Illuminator of Armenia) Vardan Arewelts'i (*ca.* 1200–1271) carries the motif a step further. In the dedicatory preface to his patron, Tēr Hamazasp, Bishop of Haɫbat (1243–1261), he refers to St. Gregory as "your Abraham" and our spiritual ancestor (p. 40).[87] He then equates St. Gregory and King Trdat with the two anointed leaders, the "two branches" in the book of Zechariah: Joshua the high priest and Zerubbabel, the would-be-king of Davidic descent (Zech. 4:3, 11–14; pp. 51–52). He follows with another pair of different sort: the plains of Ararat are graced with the glory and grace of Mounts Sinai and Horeb (alluding to the twin peaks of Ararat, p. 54; a significant remark given the fact that Arewelts'i flourished at Khor Virap, the site of St. Gregory's pit near the foot of the mountain). Elsewhere, St. Gregory is the "new Joshua," the high priest who ushers in Trdat, the "new Zerubbabel" (pp. 55–56). Moreover, the Saint holds the two sticks mentioned in Ezekiel (37:16–23): with one he leads the flock and with the other he wards off the wolves (p. 52). These two sticks become the one rod of a walnut tree mentioned in Jeremiah (1:11),[88] identified here with the Saint himself (p. 53). The plains of Ararat are graced with the glory of Mount Horeb and of Mount Sinai, since that which St. Gregory saw in the vision of Shoghakat' is the pillar of light and of cloud that led the Israelites through their wanderings in the Sinai (Ex. 13:21; p. 54).[89] St. Gregory is the "new Jacob" who likewise had a vision of a heavenly ladder and saw the Only-begotten descend to earth (alluding to Ējmiatsin) and who, like Jacob, obtained a flock of bright-striped sheep (Gen. 28:12; 31:8; p. 55). These are the great Armenian people whom he begot for God through his suffering (pp. 56–57, 61). St. Gregory's descent into the pit is like Christ's descent into the world at His incarnation and into hell following His resurrection (John 1:14 and 1 Pet. 3:19; cf. 4:6), and like Daniel's into the lions' den (Dan. 6); and his fifteen years there are more severe than Jonah's three days in the belly of the fish (Jonah 1:17; p. 62; cf. p. 71). God went down with him into the pit, just as when He told Jacob He would go down with him into Egypt and would bring him out of there (Gen. 46:4–5; p. 64).[90] St. Gregory rejoiced in the presence of the Lord as David did before the Ark of the Covenant (2 Sam. 6:14–15; p. 72); and on Mount Sepuh the Saint was like Elijah on Mount Carmel (1 Kgs. 18:16–46; p. 74). The only two analogies between St. Gregory and Moses are found at the beginning and at the end, respectively: in one, St. Gregory with his two sons, Sts. Aristakēs and Vrt'anēs, are the counterparts of Moses, Aaron and Joshua (p. 44); in the other, St. Gregory's death on Mount Sepuh is compared with that of Moses on Mount Nebo; however, upon the Saint's death his kin did not lament over him as the Israelites did for thirty days upon the death of both Moses and Aaron (Num. 20:29; Deut. 34:8; pp. 73, 75–76).[91] As in the panegyric by Sarkawag, the references to Moses in this panegyric serve as a literary frame.[92] His short description of Mount Sepuh (pp. 73–76) is translated here (Selection IX).

The panegyric by Yovhannēs Erznkats'i, *Asats'uats Nerboghakan Govesti i Surb Lusaworich'n Hayots' Grigorios* (Panegyric Recited in Praise of St. Gregorios the Illuminator of the Armenians; hereinafter, *Panegyric on St. Gregory the Illuminator*) has been acclaimed as the best of these medieval compositions because of its artistic creativity seen in rich imageries and associations.[93] It is in the work of this thirteenth-century prolific author where the ultimate development of the motif is to be seen; consequently, it is translated here in its entirety and with ample annotation, a full commentary. For Erznkats'i Mount Sepuh, the place where St. Gregory retired for ascetic solitude in his ancestral domain, also considered the site of his death and burial after the miraculous discovery of his remains, is superior to all the biblical mountains—including Ararat, Sinai, Zion, and even Golgotha (pp. 123–139 [§§29–40]). Repeatedly in this panegyric, St. Gregory, the most radiant among the saints in heaven, is compared with Moses (pp. 99, 113, 124, 130, 138, 145 [§§13, 22, 29, 33, 39, 44]) and several other biblical worthies whose names are associated with one mountain or another; they are: Noah, Abraham, David, Solomon, Elijah, Elisha, and Isaiah.[94] Even the Caves of Manē, where St. Gregory sought shelter on the mountain, and which were named after one of the associates of Sts. Hṙipsimē and Gayanē who had separated herself from the soon to be martyred virgins so as to end her life in seclusion, are compared with the Cave of the Nativity in Bethlehem (pp. 139–140 [§41]).[95] Moreover, St. Gregory is said to be a prophet and an apostle not just to the nations that dwell in the North but to all nations (pp. 110–113 [§§21–22]). He is also the new Aaron, the new Bezalel, and the new Jacob of the Armenian people (pp. 145, 149 [§§44–45, 49]). On the whole, this work brings to a climax the blend of patriotism and piety that characterizes early Armenian Christianity.[96]

The motif under discussion persists in the works of subsequent writers, such as in the eulogy on St. Gregory and King Trdat by Aṙakʻel Baghishetsʻi (*ca.* 1390–1454), the abbot of the monastery of Erkayn-Erkuzeatsʻ in the region of Chʻmshkatsak,[97] and in the "Ode Representing the Prophets and Christ and the Illuminator" by Mkrtichʻ Naghash (*ca.* 1400–1469), the archbishop of Amid.[98] It is rather curious that there is no mention of the Apostles in the latter ode. The succession of "flowers" is as follows: "The flowers were the prophets, patriarchs and first saints [i.e., Noah and certain of his predecessors]. The flower which came after them was Jesus, only-begotten of the Father." As for St. Gregory, he is "the flower at the foot of the cross." These lines are doubly significant in light of the fact that the disciples of Jesus were absent at the time of the crucifixion according to the Synoptic Gospels.

III. THE PANEGYRIC ON THE ILLUMINATOR BY YOVHANNĒS ERZNKATSʻI

A. *The Author and His Other Works*

Yovhannēs Erznkatsʻi, known also by his nickname "Pluz" either because of his blue eyes or, more likely, because of his short stature, was one of the most prolific Armenian authors of his time (*ca.* 1230–1293).[99] More than a hundred prosaic and poetic works dealing with religious as well as secular subjects have reached us under his name, ranging from books to tracts— from organizational manuals and grammars to hymns and homilies.[100] He was born either in Erznka or in one of its surrounding villages in the district of Ekegheatsʻ and was educated in the nearby monastic solitude (*anapat*) of St. Minas, not far from Mount Sepuh in the district of Daranaghikʻ, the site of St. Gregory's seclusion for nearly thirty years and of his death and primary burial. We meet the author first in 1266 as a deacon and scribe at the newly built church of Surb Pʻrkichʻ (Holy Savior) in Erznka, copying works of St. Gregory of Nyssa (*ca.* 335–*ca.* 395). In his colophon to the manuscript, his first attempt at copying, he mentions his parents, father Shirin and deceased mother Sapʻira; his brothers, Awetshah

and Shahĕnshah; a classmate at St. Minas, Sargis, as his "spiritual brother";
and his teachers there, Yakob, whom he calls his "spiritual father," and
Yovhannēs, who was recently "slain with the sword, by the lawless ones."[101]
The family seems to have had the means to afford his education, wishing
that he would return to secular life, but was disappointed by his decision to
follow the monastic life instead.[102] He was ordained to the priesthood at
St. Minas, receiving the title *Vardapet* ("Teacher") in 1268.[103] The exact
period of his study with Vardan Arewelts'i at St. Andrēas in Kayeni Dzor,
where the renowned teacher of Khor Virap had moved to the peaceful valley between Haghbat and Sanahin, is not known. This could have been in
the years immediately before Arewelts'i's death in 1271, whereupon
Erznkats'i returned to his native city.

By this time his poetic and musical skills must have been well known.
For when the remains of Catholicos St. Nersēs the Great (in office 353–373;
great-great-grandson of St. Gregory) were discovered beneath the rubble
of the church in T'il, three miles west of Erznka, in 1273, and removed for
secondary burial at the newly built church of Surb P'rkich' in Erznka, our
author was commissioned by Archbishop Sargis to compose a hymn for the
occasion. Erznkats'i was able to express profoundly the feelings surrounding the event, in which he became a participant, in the hymn *"Or zloys
anchar shnorhats'* . . ."* (Who [caused] the light of indescribable graces
. . .),[104] as well as in a panegyric recounting the whole event, *"Patmut'iwn
yaytnut'ean nshkharats' srboyn Nersisi"* (History of the Discovery of the
Remains of St. Nersēs).[105]

Erznkats'i is a well known hymnographer, often employing the customary acrostics, such as seen in the initial letters of the first seven sections or
strophes of the panegyric, spelling out his name. The opening words of the
panegyric are reminiscent of two of his hymns found in the hymnal of the
Armenian Church.[106] The first hymn, in alphabetical acrostic, *"Aysōr zuarchats'eal ts'ntsay ekeghets'i* . . ."* (Reveling today the Church rejoices . . .), is
likewise dedicated to St. Gregory and was later designated for the feast-day
commemorating his commitment to the pit.[107] A comparable composition
in alphabetical acrostic, with considerably common contents, is found at §18
of the panegyric.[108] As for the arrangements in alphabetical acrostic, like
several such compositions in the Armenian hymnal, they are inspired not
only by certain of the biblical Psalms (e.g., Pss. 9–10, 25, 34, 37, 111–112, 119,
145) but also by the first and foremost of these hymns, that for St. Hŕip'simē

and her companions who were martyred not long after St. Gregory was committed to the dungeon: *"Andzink' nuirealk' siroyn K'ristosi . . ."* (Souls devoted to the love of Christ . . .).[109] The hymn was composed by Catholicos Komitas I (in office 615–628) on the occasion of the transfer of the martyrs' relics from their secondary burial—at the hands of St. Gregory upon his release—to the magnificent church built for St. Hr̄ip'simē near Ējmiatsin in 618. The second hymn of which one is reminded in the opening line of the panegyric is the above mentioned hymn dedicated to Catholicos St. Nersēs the Great, *"Or zloys anchar̄ shnorhats' . . ."* (Who [caused] the light of indescribable graces . . .), which has a couple of sections or strophes beginning with similar words: *"Aysōr tōnē ekeghets'i . . ."* (Today the Church celebrates . . .), and *"Aysōr zuarchats'eal tōnen erknayink'n . . ."* (Reveling today the heavenly beings celebrate . . .). Moreover, the praise of Mount Sepuh at §29 of the panegyric recalls yet another hymn by our author, on the same subject and likewise dedicated to St. Gregory: *"Lerink' amenayn . . ."* (All [you] mountains . . .).[110] Our author also has a hymn dedicated to the Saint's release from the pit: *"Tagh Srboyn Grigori Lusaworch'in Hayots'"* (An Ode to St. Gregory the Illuminator of the Armenians) in onomastic acrostic, yielding the name "Grigorios Lusaworich' Hayots'."[111] This, however, was not included in the official hymnal perhaps because of its criticism of the hierarchs.

The Armenian city or town with which he is associated, Erznka or Erzinçan in the district of Ekegheats' (ancient Acilisene, between Erzrum to the East and Sivas to the West) and just over a mile north of the Euphrates, was on a vital trade route within the Anatolian networks of roads. An estimate of the city's size in Erznkats'i's day may be gathered from William of Rubruck's travel accounts of 1253–1255, where he reports that an earthquake in 1254 killed more than 10,000 people there.[112] Even with a likely exaggeration, the figure indicates a mid-size city or a typical town of the period.[113] The city's boundaries were probably the same in earlier times, when it was called Celtzene. In much earlier times, in the Hellenistic and Roman periods, the region of Ekegheats' was a center for the cult of Anahit, with a temple for the goddess within the city. The temple was destroyed during the establishment of the new faith at the turn of the fourth century, and the place was converted to a church dedicated to the Blessed Virgin Mary. Ghevond Alishan surmises that the feast day of Anahit, the 15th of Navasard (August 25), became the day to celebrate the Assumption of the Blessed Virgin.[114]

The commercial advantages of this trading post, along with the tradition associated with the Gregorid domains nearby, allowed monasteries to thrive in the region—including a Jacobite Syrian monastery.[115] Thus, the town came to be known as a fledgling scholarly center. It was better known however for its industry, even through a treatise by Erznkats'i himself: *Kanonk' ew Sahmank' Miabanut'ean Eghbarts' Erznka K'aghak'i* (Canons and Regulations of the Community of Brothers in the City of Erznka).[116] In it he spells out the rules of fairness governing a guild of unmarried craftsmen who have committed themselves to a spiritual bond of relationship. The organization of the young "brothers" in thirteenth-century Erznka has much in common with the Muslim *"Futuwwa"* institutions or the *"Akhiyyah"* fraternities that played an important role in the economic and political life of Anatolian towns at this time.[117] There is good reason to believe that Erznkats'i was instrumental in founding this analogous Christian brotherhood, headed by the elderly *Vardapet* and former classmate at St. Andrēas, Grigor Sanahnets'i, in 1280.[118] Perhaps more than its industry, especially fabrics[119] and metal utensils,[120] Erznka was known for the frequency of earthquakes in the region. It was rebuilt by the Emperor Justinian (527–565) after a devastating earthquake early in the sixth century. A similar earthquake occurred in 1045. The city was rebuilt only to be destroyed by Turkish conquerors in 1057. It was repeatedly rebuilt and destroyed by successive earthquakes, as in 1066 and 1068. Several local earthquakes with devastating effects are mentioned by ancient chroniclers, including several that occurred during Erznkats'i's lifetime: in 1236, 1246, 1254, 1268, 1281, 1287, and 1290.[121] At about the time of Erznkats'i's birth, in 1230, the city was taken by the Tatars and later governed for them by Baron Yovhannēs and his father Archbishop Sargis (1250–1279).[122] The two, relatives and local patrons of our author, were killed during a failed Turkish attempt to recapture the city from the Tatars in 1279.

Further autobiographical information is found in Erznkats'i's own preface to his *Hawak'umn Meknut'ean K'erakani* (Compilation of Commentary on Grammar). The text of the preface is given in its entirety in the *Grand Catalogue* of the St. James manuscripts collection: it is that of manuscript 1311, pp. 58–69, a miscellany dated 1602 and containing several other grammatical and orthographical works attributed to various authors from before and after Erznkats'i.[123] In it he relates his activities and accounts for several grammatical works known to him. His indebtedness to his predecessors constitutes much of the reason for the preface entitled "A foreword to the *Compilation of Commentary on Grammar* and an address by Yovhannēs, who has labored on this subject, to the steward(s) of the word."[124] After an elaborate commendation to the readers of his work and a disclamatory statement about his mastery of the subject (a rhetorical element), Erznkats'i cites the circumstances that led to his involvement in that work. He had been on a pilgrimage to Jerusalem in the year 1281.[125] Upon his return through Cilicia, the Catholicos Yakob I Klayets'i (in office 1267–1286), nicknamed *Gitnakan* (Scholar) and known for his command of the Scriptures and patronage of learning, prevailed on him to teach grammar to fellow ecclesiastics at the See of Hṙomklay (1281–1283) and this, eventually, led to his *Compilation of Commentary on Grammar*. Equally instrumental in persuading him to undertake this project was a written request by a certain Yovhannēs Vardapet who once served at the church of St. Karapet in Tarōn and who had afterwards become a renowned teacher and interpreter of the Scriptures. To complete his task, Erznkats'i resorts to the solitude of St. Minas, the very place where he had received his early education and ordination.

Our author must have been reputed for his oratory as well, for while at Hṙomklay he delivered the oration on the induction of the princes Het'um and his brother T'oros, the sons of Levon II (1270–1289), into chivalry (1283).[126] Equally noteworthy is the author's dedication of the *Compilation of Commentary on Grammar*, in a colophon at the end of the book (dated 1293, the year of the author's death), to King Het'um II (reigned intermittantly, 1289–1306, murdered in 1307 with his nephew, Levon III [1301/6–1307], by a Mongol general in Anazarba).[127] There too, in a brief encomium to the king, he reveals his thorough familiarity with the encomiastic or panegyrical rules derived from the rhetorical tradition of Classical times. The same proficiency in rhetorical or oratorical writing is evident—albeit on a larger scale—in the panegyric on St. Gregory, and to a certain extent in the less known paraenetical or hortatory writings of the author.[128] It is conceivable that the bulk of his prosaic works, which are the largest contribution by a single author to the genre of hortatory (*khratakan*) writings in Armenian, was likewise written at St. Minas and near the end of the author's life.

It was at the same solitude of St. Minas—if not at one of the monasteries on Mount Sepuh—where he also composed his *Asats'uats Nerboghakan Govesti i Surb Lusaworich'n Hayots'* (Recitative Panegyric on St.

Gregory the Illuminator of the Armenians), hereinafter abbreviated *Panegyric on St. Gregory the Illuminator*, in 1288. The patriotic sentiments expressed in this work, acclaimed as the best of his poetic output,[129] reflect his yearning for the historically renowned region where he was raised physically and spiritually, where his priesthood began, and to which place he had finally returned. Erznkats'i drew his inspiration for the work from the immediate vicinity. As a prominent place for pilgrimage until the Genocide of 1915, Mount Sepuh, the resting-place of St. Gregory, attracted worshipers from among the clergy and the laity. It is to such a mixed audience—though more to the clergy—that the work is addressed. The author's attachment to the site, so vividly described in the panegyric, seldom allowed him to leave the region thereafter. He was there when an earthquake shook the area in 1287. He died in 1293, while on a visit to the monastery of Akner in Cilicia. His remains were later transferred to his native town of Erznka, and his tomb was preserved for some time in the Church of St. Nshan.[130]

B. *The Occasion for the Panegyric and the Times*

Erznkats'i begins his panegyric with a common, early Christian notion that the Church is a symbolic representation of heaven, and that the departed saints constitute the constellation of stars in this new firmament. Therefore, the everpresence of St. Gregory, especially in the Armenian Church, is a reality for worshipers. This is more true at the Church of the Illuminator's Resting Place (*Hangist Lusaworch'i*) on Mount Sepuh, marking the place where St. Gregory spent the closing years of his life in seclusion, where he died and where he was buried unrecognized by shepherds who happened to find his body. His remains were apparently undisturbed until an ascetic named Gaṙnik was miraculously led to the spot and had them removed for burial in T'ordan in the district of Daranaghik' sometime before 341.[131] Pilgrims flocked to the medieval monasteries on the mountain, which for the author is the most prominent place on earth because of its linkage with the closing years of the Saint's life.

From its outset the panegyric indicates a festal occasion (§§1–3; cf. 9, 11, 15), and there are clear and recurring rhetorical pointers to a recitation at a solemn gathering. The unspecified yet special feast mentioned in §§1, 9 and 15, the seasonal reference in §11, and the recurring references and allusions

to John 10 (§§16, 24, 52, 55–57), especially verses 11–16, "The Good Shepherd," which is the Gospel reading in the Lectionary for the feast-day of
the discovery of St. Gregory's remains, are noteworthy. So also are the
opening words of the panegyric, which like the hymn *Aysōr zuarchats'eal
ts'ntsay ekeghets'i...*" (Reveling today the Church rejoices ...), seem to have
been inspired by Psalm 132:9 (131:9 LXX), another of the readings in the
Lectionary for the feast-day of the discovery of the saint's remains. Moreover, the repeated references to the place, "the resting place" of St. Gregory
(§§6, 10, 12, 21, 28, 39, 42), leave no doubt that the composition was intended
for the foremost of the annual feasts of St. Gregory in the Armenian
Church: that commemorating his death and the discovery of his remains
(*Giwt nshkharats'*), celebrated at the very site of these events.

In the thirteenth century this feast was celebrated on the sixth Saturday of the Lenten period, this according to the testimony of Erznkats'i's
contemporary Kirakos Gandzakets'i.[132] Nowadays, it is celebrated on the
third Saturday after Pentecost.[133] Of the two other feast-days of the Saint,
his descent into the dungeon (*Mutn i virap*) and his release from the dungeon (*Eln i virapē*), the former is commemorated on the fifth Saturday of
the Lenten period and the latter on the first Saturday after Pentecost. But
these were not as much in vogue at this site as they were at Khor Virap,
where the Saint was confined for some fifteen years. These latter feast-days
gained added prominence in the eighteenth century, during the reforms of
Catholicos Simēon Erewants'i (in office 1763–1780), who advocated their
observance on Saturday with all the elevated deportment of Sunday.[134]
So was also the feast of Shoghakat' (lit., "effusion of light"), commemorating the building of the first three chapels by St. Gregory in the capital
Vagharshapat, over the respective sites where Sts. Hṙip'simē, Gayanē, and
the unnamed virgin at the vat-store were martyred. Named for the initial
light emanating from the third site and culminating with the Saint's
mystic vision of the church, the feast of Shoghakat' was celebrated on the
Saturday before the Assumption of the Blessed Virgin (celebrated on
the Sunday nearest to August 15). The feast anticipates that of the founding of the Armenian Church at the capital Vagharshapat, with its cathedral named for the Blessed Virgin, *Surb Astuatsatsin* (Holy Bearer of
God); hence the consecutive feast days.[135] As for the somewhat redundant
and later feast commemorating the founding of Holy Ējmiatsin (a later
name given to the cathedral of *Surb Astuatsatsin*), based on St. Gregory's

vision—the descent of the heavenly "man, tall and fearful" with a golden hammer to mark the site of the cathedral to be built in the capital, it is celebrated on the Sunday after the feast of the Saint's release from the dungeon. These last feasts, more feasts of the founding of the Armenian Church at Vagharshapat than feasts of St. Gregory, were of lesser interest at Mount Sepuh, and less so since Ējmiatsin was not the See of the Catholicosate from 484 to 1441.[136]

There are ample grounds to suppose that in addition to the major feast early in the Spring, the entire month after Pentecost (roughly the whole of June) was a long festal season at Mount Sepuh, when the various saints associated with the life of St. Gregory were commemorated (nowadays culminating with the feast of the discovery of his remains). This second festive season began with the feast of St. Hṙip'simē and her companions on the first Monday, that of St. Gayanē and her companions on Tuesday, and that of St. John the Baptist and St. Athenogenes—whose relics were enshrined at Ashtishat by St. Gregory—on Thursday.[137] In the second week after Pentecost, on Tuesday, are commemorated Sts. Nunē and Manē, who separated themselves from the band of the soon to be martyred virgins, the former to evangelize the Georgians and the latter to spend the rest of her life in seclusion in the caves on Mount Sepuh, where she died. Her remains were found and buried by St. Gregory when he came there for the same purpose, just as his own remains were later found and buried, first by shepherds who were unable to identify him and later by an ascetic named Gaṙnik (lit., "little lamb") who was led in a vision to retrieve the remains for secondary burial at T'ordan.[138] The tradition regarding St. Manē helped tie the two festal seasons at Mount Sepuh into a prolonged feast, from early Spring to early Summer.

Presumably, the Church of the Illuminator's Resting Place (*Hangist Lusaworch'i*) within the Great Monastery of the Holy Illuminator (*Mets Surb Lusaworch'i Vank'*) was the gathering place on Mount Sepuh. An appeal is made to those who have come there to cleanse themselves in preparation for celebrating the Saint's memorial day and, as they enter the various edifices, to consider entering also the spiritual quarters of his life (§§4–5). Judging from the closing sections of the *Panegyric*, it would seem that a considerable part of the audience consisted of clergy. The entire address to the heads or bishops of the Church, marking a formal and lengthy appeal (§§52–57), is significant. The addressees are referred to with a variety of related ecclesiastical terms: high priests and heads of the Church, presiders for justice, and guides along the heavenly path (§52); and again with another trilogy, as sailors, husbandmen, and healers (§53).

The times were difficult. Turkic and Mongol invasions came with such intensity and frequency as to keep the population of Armenia and Cilicia off-balance much of the time during the eleventh to thirteenth centuries. Chroniclers and literary historians lamented their times, puzzled as to where these conquests would lead and how these might square with the grandeur suggested by Armenia's past. The thirteenth century was particularly turbulent. After the initial shock of the Seljuk and Tatar attacks (often ending with enslavement of the young, massacre of the elderly, and devastation of the land) came the heavy taxations imposed by the Mongols, the constant despoilings and trade disruptions by Turkmen raids, and then defeats by the Egyptian Mamluks. Moreover, the process of Islamization was on the rise while questions of orthodoxy and heresy from the Christian West were unrelenting despite the cecession of Armenian lands to Byzantium, the conciliatory efforts of the Armenian Catholicoi, and the royal ties with the Crusader principalities. Yet the crises were not of such an enormity as to threaten the continuity of Armenian religious culture. Unlike the Greek neighbors and the Latin intruders, the Asiatic conquerors were not bearers of a sophisticated civilization prior to their conversion to Islam and there were no attempts to implant any of their culture within the conquered lands.

The unidentified foreign oppressors in the panegyric (§48) were primarily the Mongol and Mamluk conquerors. The Cilician Armenian King Het'um I (1226–1270) journeyed to Karakorum in 1253–1256 to acknowledge the rule of the Mongol khan Monghu, and shortly thereafter his troops accompanied the ilkhan Hulagu on the campaign that destroyed Baghdad in 1258. The defeat of the Mongols two years later at 'Ayn Jalut made Armenian Cilicia the object of the fury of the victorious Mamluks. Consequently, they plundered Cilicia in 1266, under Baybars (1260–1277), and again in 1292, under Sultan al-Ashraf (1291–1293), at which time Hr̄omkla was sacked and the Catholicos Step'annos IV (in office 1290–1292) taken captive to Egypt, where he died a year later (the year of Erznkats'i's death, 1293).[139] This catastrophe necessitated the move of the Catholicosate to Sis. Armenian sentiments toward the Mongols varied with circumstances, yet the Cilician kings remained loyal to their Mongol overlords until these converted to Islam at the turn of the fourteenth century. The references to the invaders as "malicious beasts" (§49, where more difficult times for the nation are prophesied in an oracular manner) and "wild boars: Satan and evil-loving demons" (§50) agree with other contemporary descriptions of the Asiatic and other raiders and conquerors.[140] Desecration of churches by the enemy, abduction and martyrdom of monks, and looting of precious objects with total disregard to anything sacred are reported lamentingly by nearly all Armenian chroniclers of the thirteenth century. There was a sense that the momentous events of destruction, pillage, and even enslavement could well be divine visitations of judgment: that God had punished the people for their departure from religious traditions, the more so since the clergy have been negligent.[141]

A certain incident reported from thirteenth-century Erznka is noteworthy. An official of the Seljuk sultanate of Konya (Iconium) attempted to halt an Armenian religious procession which involved the parading of crosses and the ringing of church bells. The Mongol envoy of Hulagu stopped the Seljuk attempt.[142] However, at about this time or shortly thereafter, the Tatars of Keul (Kelü), who had settled around Erznka, embraced Islam.[143] But even after the latter development, the city continued to experience its share of plunder and destruction like most other towns and villages of eastern Asia Minor, and eventually succumbed to the inevitable process of Islamization that swept the region.

As is often the case in times of national crisis, strength and inspiration are drawn from the past. The heroes of the past are evoked especially when leadership and guidance appear to be lacking in the present; their guidance and help are sought in the face of the besetting challenges and confusion. Speaking as it were with his patron Saint, Erznkats'i begs: "Gregory, likeness to the heavenly Father and image of parental compassion: Would you speak to your erring children . . . For we have no one to counsel us again with yearning compassion . . . Behold, it is time for war, gathering of masses. But your ready soldiers are deserted and have become weary. We have no brave and ingenious captain to rally the soldiers for battle on the frontline" (§49). The spiritual warfare notwithstanding, the author is pointing to ecclesiastical negligence of the masses in trying times. The turbulent decades at the close of the thirteenth century are clearly contemplated here, perhaps also the ill-fated military exploits of King Levon II of Cilicia (1270–1289), who with the Mongol ilkhans of Persia invaded the

Syrian city of Homs in 1280 and ended up agreeing to a very costly settlement with the victorious Mamluks in 1285.[144]

C. St. Gregory and the Sites on Mount Sepuh

The primary source on the life of St. Gregory, the *History of the Armenians* by Agat'angeghos, as pointed out earlier, is relatively late. It was written some 150 years after the events it describes, and not without anachronisms, contradictions, and occasional expansions especially in the surviving Armenian version (*Aa*). So as to highlight the work of St. Gregory, the latter version is silent about the Apostle Thaddaeus and the Syriac or Edessene phase of Christianity in Armenia that claims to have its beginnings in Apostolic times. The essential kernel—the sum of the common elements in the various versions—is nevertheless reliable:[145] after much suffering and tribulation, St. Gregory was able to convert the king to Christianity and to establish the first organized Armenian bishoprics, the patriarchal see being at Ashtishat in Tarōn.[146]

The received Armenian version (*Aa*) can be summarized as follows: St. Gregory, of Parthian descent and noble birth, was the son of Anak who upon the instigation of the Sasanian usurpers of the Iranian Arsacid throne murdered the Arsacid king of Western Armenia, Khosrov or Chosroes (II K'aj, 279/280–287).[147] During the ensuing blood feud, Gregory was whisked off to Caesarea of Cappadocia where he was educated and converted to Christianity. He returned to Armenia as a missionary cloaked in royal service. Once his true faith became known, for refusing to venerate the statue of Anahit in the famous temple at Erēz (Erznka or Erzinçan), King Trdat (IV the Great, 298–330)[148] subjected him to various tortures to force him to revert to paganism. The identity of the unyielding Saint was discovered during these ordeals, and he was thrown into a snake-infested pit and left for dead. Miraculously, he survived for some fifteen years; a woman kept him alive by dropping bread to him. Meanwhile the Emperor Diocletian (284–305) fell passionately in love with Hŕip'simē, a Christian virgin living in a convent in Rome, who refused to marry him. Fearing the consequences, her superior Gayanē led her and seventy-odd companions to seek refuge in Armenia, and eventually in the vineyards of the capital Vagharshapat. At the emperor's request the fugitive nuns were found by King Trdat, who also fell madly in love with Hŕip'simē. Failing to pursuade her to marry him, he commanded that she and her companions be killed. Thereupon the king was visited by divine retribution and was struck with insanity, with the whole city suffering because of him. He is described as "being transformed into a wild boar," as was Nebuchadnezzar in the book of Daniel. It was repeatedly revealed to his sister Khosrovidukht, in dreams, that only St. Gregory's intercession could heal him. Rescued from the pit after much doubt about his survival for these fifteen years,[149] the Saint hastened to bury the martyred nuns at a revealed place in the capital city—thus anticipating the establishment of the new religious center[150]— and to heal the king. The pagan shrines were overthrown, and St. Gregory was sent to be consecrated at Caesarea. Upon his return he built the first churches in Armenia, baptized the king, and converted the entire realm (of course, the country as a whole was by no means converted overnight).

Agat'angeghos has very little about St. Gregory's last years, a subject which looms large in our panegyric. After telling about the Saint's missionary activity in Armenia, he concludes: "The king greatly implored Gregory to remain with him continually and to travel around with him, but he did not agree; he rather preferred to live in desert places, suppressing himself by fasts . . . until the day of his death when summoned by Christ to rest" (858). The king then sent for St. Gregory's sons "and in person went out with them to seek St. Gregory, wherever he might find him. And they came and found him in the province of Daranaghik', on the mountain called the Caves of Manē, in the wilderness" (861).[151] After a likely interpolation narrating Emperor Constantine's conversion and St. Gregory's and King Trdat's purported visit to Rome with a considerable entourage, the author refers to the Council of Nicaea, attended by Aristakēs, the younger son of St. Gregory, as the Armenian Church representative. He brought over the Nicene canons, to which the aging Saint made some additions. Agat'angeghos then returns to St. Gregory's ascetic solitude on Mount Sepuh and concludes with these words reminiscent of the *Buzandaran* and Koriwn: "Day and night, with fasting and prayers and ardent requests and strong words he commended the divine commandments to everyone. 'He gave no sleep to his eyes, no respite to his eyebrows, no rest to his limbs' [Ps. 132:4 (131:4 LXX)] until he attained the rest of the Lord" (888).[152]

Mount Sepuh, with its Caves of Manē to which St. Gregory retired, is also known as Mount Gohanam and, by the name of the district, the Mount of Daranaghik'. It is identified with today's Kara Daghi, height 3,030 meters, in the north-eastern Taurus chain. The mountain seperated two ancient districts: Daranaghikʻ to the west and Ekegheatsʻ to the east. These adjacent districts in westernmost Armenia have long been associated with the hereditary domain of the Gregorid house, with its ancestral village and necropolis at Tʻordan in the district of Daranaghikʻ and another ancestral necropolis at Tʻil in the district of Ekegheatsʻ.[153] According to Agatʻange-ghos, the ordination of Aristakēs, the younger son of St. Gregory, as bishop by his elderly father took place where the Saint was found: "in the province of Daranaghikʻ, on the mountain called the Caves of Manē" (861–862). Manē was one of the virgins or nuns traditionally associated with Sts. Hṙipʻsimē and Gayanē. She was believed to have taken refuge in these caves prior to the martyrdom of her companions.[154] Later in this panegyric, the author draws upon subsequent tradition whereby St. Gregory is credited with burying her remains when he came to the same region for his ascetic withdrawal (§41). There he died and his unrecognized body was buried by shepherds, and the burial site remained unknown until the ascetic named Gaṙnik was divinely led to discover it for secondary burial at Tʻordan.[155]

The proximity of these historic and venerated sites to the author's birthplace is a substantial reason for his devotion to the area and to Mount Sepuh in particular, for which he claims what the Scriptures hold for Mount Zion: "this mountain where God dwells" (§12; cf. §§29, 34: "Rejoice, Mount Sepuh, and exult in majestic glory alongside Zion"). His panegyric, especially §§28–43, is a primary source when it comes to establishing the major edifices on Mount Sepuh in the thirteenth century.[156]

Foremost of the sites was the Great Monastery of the Holy Illumina-tor (*Mets Surb Lusaworchʻi Vankʻ*). There, the Church of the Illuminator's Resting Place (*Hangist Lusaworchʻi*), to which were attached the Chapel of the Holy Bearer of God (*Surb Astuatsatsin*) to the north and later the Chapel of St. James of Nisibis (*Mtsbnay Surb Yakob*) to the south, was the main attraction to pilgrims (§§6, 12, 21). This was the site of St. Gregory's primary burial, his first grave, marked with a tombstone (§§21, 43). On the remains of these and other venerated sites in the area, the archaeological survey and report by Thierry is indispensable.[157] Necessarily, some corre-lation must be established between the archaeology of the place and this text, which is unaccounted for by Thierry.

There is some uncertainty regarding the exact number of chapels in the immediate vicinity of the Great Monastery of the Holy Illuminator (*Mets*

Surb Lusaworch'i Vank'). Our text mentions but one, "the holy shrine resembling the Wood," named for Christ, "the Sun of Righteousness, the Morning Star," and for His "Forerunner," St. John the Baptist (*Surb Karapet*, §38).[158] This is an unmistakable reference to the cruciform Church of the Holy All-Savior (*Surb Amenap'rkich'*), said to have been built by the Illuminator himself.[159] There was yet another chapel dedicated to the "Forerunner" (*Surb Karapet*), at the Main Monastery (*Awagavank'*), located some seven kilometers south-east of the Great Monastery of the Holy Illuminator, at the foot of Mount Sepuh, and likewise said to have been built by the Illuminator.[160] Erznkats'i follows the local tradition that claims too much for the place, for the shrine built by St. Gregory for the Forerunner (*Surb Karapet*) is invariably linked with that for St. Athenogenes (*Surb At'anakinēs*), the burial of their relics at Ashtishat in Tarōn and Bagawan in Bagrewand.[161] The claim that St. Gregory built places of worship on the mountain where he retired must belong to a much later tradition. It may be gathered from §37, as also from the author's hymn to Mount Sepuh, that the cross believed to have been used by St. Gegory was probably kept in one of the chapels there.[162]

A passing reference is made to the monuments for the "Seraphim" (*Serovbēk'*) at the foot of the mountain (§36). According to a local tradition, detailed in the panegyric by Vardan Vardapet Arewelts'i and translated here (Selection IX), St. Gregory wanted to make a pilgrimage to Jerusalem on his knees and to die there. When he thus descended from his seclusion on the mountain, he was met by two angels in the valley who told him that Christ had considered the extent of his devotion and that he should return to his mountain to die there. The Saint did accordingly, but not before erecting crosses at the site where he was met by the angels; wherefore the village there is called Serovbēk' (Seraphim) "to this day."[163]

Among "the numerous streams of water" two fountains in particular, "the Fountain of Light and the Sweet-tasting Water," had healing powers attributed to them (§39).[164] Pilgrims apparently took of the soil of the site for healing purposes (§32), and salt from the region of Daranaghik' was a prized gift (§43). Certainly, the mineral waters and the salt deposits of the region were well known in antiquity.[165]

D. *The Structure and Text of the Panegyric*

St. Gregory is the acknowledged source of inspiration for our author. In the proemial adulation Erznkats'i attributes his goodness to his parents and his rationality to the intercession of St. Gregory: "According to my parents' hope, you mediated my coming into being from nothing and became the cause for this useless fruit to exist blessedly, [giving] opportunity to my rational part to be active and prompting it to remain constant in the same. Accept now this obligation in words, [written] with your help" (§6). Similarly, in the concluding prayer to St. Gregory he exclaims: "I am talking with you as I would with someone truly living" (§58), and goes on to refer to his panegyric as "this gift of rational offering" dedicated to his patron Saint (§60).

The author's thorough familiarity with the panegyrical tradition is evident from the outset and is apparent in some of his other works. In the above cited remarks on himself and his present work, Erznkats'i is fulfilling yet another important panegyrical requirement: self-effacement or minimizing one's own role so as to further underscore the greatness of the one praised.[166] He is not slow, however, to declare his knowledge of "panegyrical principles" (§19). Most evidently, this is to be seen in his use of comparison, especially in his praise of St. Gregory and Mount Sepuh (§§19–25 and 28–42).[167]

Except for the poem in alphabetical acrostic (§18), the author employs the lofty, poetic prose befitting his panegyric. His composition is replete with literary devices like alliteration and chiasmus that add to the rhetorical effects of the recitation. One also senses occasional hymnic drifts, even a suggestion that he wanted to sing certain parts (§47). Obviously, the hymns in praise of the saints antedate the more formal and lengthier panegyrics. Of such early hymns in the *Sharakank'*, one composed by Movsēs Bishop of Siwnik' (in office, 725–731) to commemorate St. Gregory's release from the pit must have been well known.[168]

Erznkats'i is cognizant of the entire tradition about St. Gregory, even beyond that given in the Armenian version of Agat'angeghos (*Aa*), including elements such as the Saint's providential relation to St. Thaddaeus as found in the Karshuni version and in Khorenats'i.[169] Yet he relies on documentary sources, Agat'angeghos and the earlier panegyrists on St. Gregory. At times he follows the text of Agat'angeghos verbatim, as when he sets out to recount but a few of the twelve tortures of the Saint (§§24–26).[170] He leaves no question about having a manuscript before him. Note the following affinities:

Agat'angeghos 69	*Erznkats'i 25*
[Թագաւորն] եւ	[Թագաւորն] հրամայէր
կապել զնա ձեռս յետոս,	կապել գձեռան յետոս,
եւ արկանել զայլ ի բերան նորա,	եւ Հարկանել զայլ ի բերանն,
եւ եւս կախել շառաչեզս ադի	եւ կախել շառաչեզս ադի
ի վերայ ոդին նորա,	ի վերայ ոդանն,
եւ տալ զելոգս կրծից նորա,	եւ տալ զելոգս կրծիցն,
եւ արկանել առասանս ի կապս	եւ արկանել առասանս ի կապս
կրծից զելարանացն,	զելարանաց կրծիցն,
կապել եւ Համբառնալ	եւ վերամբարձ կախել
ի բարձրաւանդակ տանիս	ի բարձրաւանդակ տանիս
ապարանից որմոյն մենքենայիւք:	ապարանից որմոյն մեքենայիւք:
Եւ կայր այրեցալ կապեալ այնպէս	Եւ կայր այնպէս
զաւուրս եօթն:	զեօթն օր:

At times Erznkats'i introduces the special units of his overall composition:

§10   Introduction of four topics of immediate concern

§17   Introduction of a poem in alphabetical acrostic to St. Gregory

§19   Introduction of an encomium on St. Gregory

§26   Introduction of an oracle to King Trdat

§28   Introduction of an encomium on Mount Sepuh

§47   Introduction of a lament over the land, the people, and the Church of Armenia

§54   Introduction of an appeal to the hierarchs

Beyond these introductions, the panegyric consists of several distinct units, marked by varying features. The first unit (§§1–7) is at once a preface, an ode to St. Gregory, and an autograph, with the author's name (ՅՈՀԱՆԷՍ) obtained through the initial letters of the respective strophes or sections comprising the unit. The next unit (§§8–10) consists of three sections beginning with the words "And now" (*Ew ard . . .*), a recurring phrase at the start of several other sections (§§21, 26, 28, and 47; cf. the corresponding final appeal in §§55–57). Here the author declares his three-fold intent: to draw a portrait of St. Gregory, for which task he prays a three-part prayer to the most blessed Trinity (§8), to pursuade pilgrims to prepare themselves for the celebration "on this memorial day of the confessor of Christ" (§9), and to introduce four short sections by title (§10) which, in effect, provide a rough outline of the work as a whole: (A) "This time and day of joyous festivity," (B) "The resting place of St. Gregory," (C) "His most praiseworthy and laudable image," (D) "And the things pertaining to this time and place" (§§11–14). Two sections, one on the place of St. Gregory in history (§15) and the other on the attributes of the Saint (§16), along with the special poem in alphabetical acrostic (§18, introduced at §17), function as a prelude to the encomium on St Gregory (§§20–25, introduced at §19). This is followed by an oracular address to King Trdat (§27, introduced at §26). Half-way into his composition—measured in manuscript length, the author begins a second encomium: this one on Mount Sepuh, complete with a prelude and a postlude (§§29–42, introduced at §28). There follows a three-part praise of the land, people, and Church of Armenia, including the hierarchs (§§43–46), all beginning with the word "Rejoice" (*Tsʻntsay . . .*), balanced with a three-part lament over the land, people, and Church of Armenia (§§48–50, introduced at §47) and a three-part admonition to the hierarchs (51–53). Each of the three parts of the lament begins with the word "Weep" (Oghba / Oghbatsʻēkʻ). The composition concludes with a three-part appeal to the hierarchs (§§55–57, introduced at §54) and a three-part prayer to St. Gregory (§§58–60). Each part of the appeal begins with the word "Now" (*Ard . . .*), and each part of the prayer has the vocative "O" (*Ov . . .*) in the first line. The following outline or synopsis should be helpful for a consideration of the composition as a whole:

I.   §§1–7   **Proemial adulation**
            Prefatory, seven-strophe praise to St. Gregory, in
            onomastic acrostic, yielding the name of the author:
            Yohanēs (1–7)

II. §§8–14 **Invocations**
Three invocations, each beginning with
"And now . . ." (8–10)
> Three-part prayer to Father, Son, and Spirit (8)
> Call to celebration (9)
> *Introduction of four subjects of concern* (10)
> The four subjects considered (11–14)

III. §§15–18 **Prelude to an encomium on St. Gregory**
The place of St. Gregory in history (15)
The attributes of St. Gregory (16)
Introduction of a special poem (17)
A poem in alphabetical acrostic (18)

IV. §§19–25 **Encomium on St. Gregory**
Introduction of an encomium on St. Gregory (19)
Birth and upbringing, in three parts:
> ancestral, physical, and spiritual (20–22)
Accomplishments in virtue, in three parts:
> marriage, mission, and forbearance (23–25)

V. §§26–27 **Oracle to King Trdat**
Introduction of an oracle to King Trdat (26)
Oracular address to the king (27)

VI. §§28–42 **Encomium on Mount Sepuh**
Introduction of an encomium on Mount Sepuh (28)
Prelude to the praise (29)
Twelve-part praise to Mount Sepuh,
> each beginning with "Rejoice . . ." (30–41)
Postlude to the praise (42)

VII. §§43–46 **Praise to the land, the people, and the Church**
Three-part praise, each beginning with "Rejoice . . .",
> to the land, the people, and the Church of
> Armenia—the latter in two segments:
> the Church and her hierarchs (43–46)

VIII.   §§47–50   **Lament over the land, the people, and the Church**
Introduction of a lament (47)
Three-part lament, each beginning with "Weep . . .",
over the land, the people, and the Church of
Armenia (48–50)

IX.   §§51–53   **Admonition to the Church**
Three-part admonition to the Church and her
hierarchs (51–53)

X.   §§54–57   **Appeal to the hierarchs**
Introduction of an appeal (54)
Three-part appeal to the hierarchs,
each beginning with "Now . . ." (55–57)

XI.   §§58–60   **Prayer to St. Gregory**
Three-part prayer to St. Gregory,
each beginninng with the vocative (58–60)

Although the structure of the composition is elaborate, it is by no means complex. The above outline is inherent in the text and lends itself conveniently to delineation, without being forced into a mold at any point. One can see that the formal introductions of special units are important elements that function as subheadings of a sort in the overall composition. More importantly, our author seems to be fond of tri-partite divisions, as is noticeable throughout: his invocations (§§8–10), prayers (§§8, 58–60), the birth and upbringing of St. Gregory (§§20–22), his accomplishments (§§23–25), the praise of Mount Sepuh with prelude and postlude (§§29–42), the praise of the land, people, and Church of Armenia (§§43–45), the corresponding parts of these three in the lament (§§48–50), and the three-fold appeal to the hierarchs (§§55–57). This outline has been incorporated into the translation as subheadings.

The translation is based on the two published texts: the Venice 1853 edition[171] and the Erevan 1986 edition by Srapyan.[172] The numerous typographical errors in the latter edition are glaringly apparent vis-à-vis the text published by the Venetian Mekhitarists. There are, nonetheless, hitherto unnoticed textual corruptions that call for necessary emendations in both editions. I have noted in the Appendix all the recognizable errors in these editions, including the emended corruptions. While neither of the editions is a critical text, a reliable reading is obtained between them. Still, I am not fully convinced about Srapyan's versification of the entire text. Except for the unit which the author himself introduces as a poem (§18), I prefer to see the entire text as a composition in poetic prose rather than in free verse.[173] However, given the oratorical and recitative nature of the text, Srapyan's free-verse arrangement may be deemed justifiable. And although her general arrangement of the text may be acceptable, certain of her divisions of sections and lines are not; in fact, at times they are not even logical. These also I have noted in the Appendix. Obviously, I have readjusted the section divisions. The numbers and subtitles given to sections are supplied for convenience, to help guide the reader and also to facilitate cross-references throughout the Commentary.

The translation posed no serious difficulties beyond the usual translational problems, necessitating occasional insertion of conjunctions, prepositions, and pronouns, besides auxiliary verbs. All other additions are enclosed in brackets. A somewhat unusual problem had to do with rendering the inconsistent use of the Saint's name throughout the panegyric. The most frequent form of the name is Grigorios, transliterated from the Greek, Grēgorios (Latin, Gregorius). Occasionally, the more common Armenian name Grigor is used. For consistency, I have rendered both forms of the name as Gregory. By its very frequency, Grigorios appears to be the original reading, following the form of the name in Agat'angeghos and in the early panegyrics on St. Gregory, especially those said to have been translated from Greek and with which our author was familiar—as the references in the Commentary indicate. A unique case is the *hapax legomenon* «ապեւեւկի», a botanical term which occurs only in this panegyric (§20; rendered "pine") and nowhere else in published Classical Armenian texts.

A translation never supercedes the original of a comprehensible text, especially when the text is rhetorical or recitative—as is this panegyric. Inevitably, the translation loses not only the occasional rhyme (rare in this case), but also the oratorically significant acrostics and alliterations, such as those found in §§4 and 7, for example. No compensation could make up for these losses.

The Commentary is not exhaustive. For the most part it is an annotation and elucidation of the text, with references to other ancient Armenian writings where some of the author's thoughts have parallels. There are scores of references in the Commentary to the other medieval panegyrics on St. Gregory, those published in the Sop'erk' Haykakank' series. For example, Erznkats'i's oracular address to King Trdat (§27) has its parallels in similar but shorter addresses to the king in the two "Chrysostomian" panegyrics said to have been translated from Greek (*Sop'erk'*, 4:25–26, 111–113). The exaltation of Mount Sepuh (§§30–41) has a lesser parallel in a hymn by the author (trans., Selection XII), and the veneration of the site is attested in the panegyric by Vardan Vardapet Arewelts'i (*Sop'erk'*, 5:73–76; trans., Selection IX). Similarly, the addresses to the bishops and heads of the Armenian Church (§§52–57) have parallels in other works by Erznkats'i (as in Selection XI) and in works by several of his contemporaries. Thus, the Commentary on the ultimate of these medieval panegyrics on St. Gregory the Illuminator may be considered a commentary on them all.

Notes

[1]For a definitive edition of the text of the Behistun inscription, which names the Urarteans and the Armenians interchangeably, see L. W. King and R. C. Thompson, *The Sculptures and Inscriptions of Darius the Great on the Rock of Behistun of Persia* (London: British Museum, 1907); for a bibliography, A. T. Olmstead, *History of the Persian Empire* (Chicago: University of Chicago Press, 1948), p. 118 n. 39. For Greek and Latin authors on Armenia(ns), see R. W. Thomson, "The Armenian Image in Classical Texts," in R. G. Hovannisian, ed., *The Armenian Image in History and Literature* (Malibu, CA: Undena Publications, 1981), pp. 9–25. See also P. Z. Bedoukian, *Coinage of the Artaxiads of Armenia*, Royal Numismatic Society Special Publication 10 (London: RNS, 1978). For the earlier periods, see I. M. Diakonoff, *The Prehistory of the Armenian People*, trans. from the Russian (*Predystoriia armianskogo naroda* [Erevan: Arm. Academy of Sciences, 1968]) by L. Jennings, with revisions by the author (Delmar, NY: Caravan Books, 1984), and the brief discussions by J. [R.] Russell, "The Formation of the Armenian Nation," and N. [G.] Garsoïan, "The Emergence of Armenia," both in R. G. Hovannisian, ed., *The Armenian People from Ancient to Modern Times. Vol. I: The Dynastic Periods: From Antiquity to the Fourteenth Century* (New York: St. Martin's Press, 1997), pp. 19–36 and 37–62, respectively.

[2]Translations from Koriwn are mine. For the text, see M. Abeghyan, ed., *Vark' Mashtots'i* (Erevan: Haypethrat, 1941); Eng. trans., B. Norehad, *Koriwn: The Life of Mashtots* (New York: AGBU, 1965); both repr. with introduction by K. H. Maksoudian (Delmar, NY: Caravan Books, 1985).

[3]The literary sway of the Scriptures extends far beyond the early catechetical and homiletical writings, on which see K. Sarkissian, *A Brief Introduction to Armenian Christian Literature* (London: Faith Press, 1960); A. Oghlugean, "Hamaṙot Aknark Hay Ekeghets'woy Vardapetakan Astuatsabanut'ean Grakanut'ean" (A Brief Survey of the Doctrinal-Theological Literature of the Armenian Church), *"Gandzasar" Theological Review* 4 (1993) 45–71; for a broader survey, see C. A. Renoux, "Langue et littérature arméniennes," in M. Albert et al., eds., *Christianismes orientaux: Introduction à l'étude des langues et des littératures*, Initiations au christianisme ancien (Paris: Cerf, 1993), pp. 107–166.

⁴Illustrative of this is "Appendix IV: Scriptural Quotations and Allusions" as well as "Appendix V: Epic and Scriptural Formulae" in N. G. Garsoïan, *The Epic Histories Attributed to P'awstos Buzand (Buzandaran Patmut'iwnk')*, Harvard Armenian Texts and Studies 8 (Cambridge, MA: Harvard University Press, 1989), pp. 577–596. The religious overtones of these historical yet somewhat apologetic writings by clerics are quite evident. These histories emerged from dire times extending from the periods accounted for to the very times of the respective authors; hence, an element of hope—at times profound—could be detected in all of them. On the complex geopolitcal and religious situation during these crucial centuries see Garsoïan's collected articles in *Armenia between Byzantium and the Sasanians*, Collected Studies Series 218 (Aldershot: Variorum, 1985) and N. Adontz, *Armenia in the Period of Justinian*, N. G. Garsoïan, ed. and trans. (Lisbon: Calouste Gulbenkian Foundation, 1970), pp. 7–74. Note also the following assessment by R. W. Thomson: "The self-avowed purposes of the Armenian historians were basically two: to present an ordered narrative of the worthy and glorious deeds of past generations, and to offer their readers an edifying narrative which would deter men from following impious ways and show them the eventual blessings that are enjoyed by those who suffer for the sake of Christ and his church." "The Fathers in Early Armenian Literature," *Studia Patristica* 12 (=Texte und Untersuchungen 115; Berlin: Akademie Verlag, 1975) 469; repr. in *idem, Studies in Armenian Literature and Christianity*, Collected Studies Series 451 (Aldershot: Variorum, 1994), pp. 457–470.

⁵For the predominantly biblical orientation in Armenian historiography, see J.-P. Mahé, "Entre Moïse et Mahomet: Réflexions sur l'historiographie arménienne," *Revue des études arméniennes*, n.s. 23 (1992) 121–153.

⁶Cf. Cicero *De Oratore* 2.85.348: "A splendid line to take in a panegyric is to compare the subject with all other men of high distinction."

⁷From the trans. by R. Nadeau, "The Progymnasmata of Aphthonius in Translation," *Speech Monographs* 19 (1952) 273; for the entire trans., see pp. 264–285.

⁸See my essay, "Koriwn's *Life of Mashtots'* as an Encomium," *Journal of the Society for Armenian Studies* 3 (1987–1988) 1–14.

⁹Cf. 1 Cor. 4:16; Phil. 3:17; 4:9; 1 Thess. 1:6–7; 2 Thess. 3:9; 1 Tim. 4:12; Titus 2:7; see also 1 Clement 31:2; Ignatius *Eph.* 2:1; Justin Martyr *Dial.* 125:5.

¹⁰See, e.g., Thomson, "The Fathers in Early Armenian Literature," 457–470.

¹¹St. John Chrysostom, e.g., observes that the prophetic witness was less than that of the apostolic, since the Prophets were geographically limited, but not so the Apostles, whose witness is universal (*In Mat. Hom.*, 15.6, quoting Matt. 5:13; a similar argument was made earlier in Hellenistic Judaism, that the Hebrew Prophets surpass the Greek philosophers since the former spoke universally, whereas the latter spoke to a select few—Josephus *Contra Apionem* 2.168–169). Similar sentiments regarding the Apostles, and by extension regarding St. Gregory, are common in Armenian sources.

¹²A consciousness already reflected in the Epistle of James (1:1; cf. Luke 22:30; Acts 26:7). For this rather widespread identity, extending to Christians in neighboring Iran of the fourth-fifth centuries, see S. Brock, "Christians in the Sasanian Empire: A Case of Divided Loyalties," in Stuart Mews, ed., *Religion and National Identity*, Studies in Church History 18 (Oxford: Blackwell, 1982), pp. 1–19, note especially the references to Aphrahat and the synod of 410, p. 13; repr. in Brock's *Syriac Perspectives on Late Antiquity*, Collected Studies Series 199 (London: Variorum, 1984), ch. VI. A prayer said silently by the celebrant priest just before "The Lord's Prayer" in the Divine Liturgy of the Armenian Church has these words: "God of truth and Father of mercy, we thank you, who have exalted our nature, condemned as we were, above that of the blessed Patriarchs [of the Old Testament]; for you were called God by them, whereas in compassion you have been pleased to be called Father by us."

¹³For a general assessment, see R. L. Fox, *Pagans and Christians* (San Francisco: Harper and Row, 1986), pp. 293–335.

¹⁴J. R. Russell, *Zoroastrianism in Armenia*, Harvard Iranian Series 5 (Cambridge, MA:

Harvard University Press, 1987), pp. 515–528. Remnants of the Arewordik' in Samosata were admitted into the Armenian Church in the twelfth century, according to a letter of St. Nersēs Shnorhali, *Ĕndhanrakan T'ught'k' S. Nersisi Shnorhalwoy* (General Epistles of St. Nersēs Shnorhali) (Jerusalem: St. James Press, 1871), pp. 223–229.

[15]Ghazar and Eghishē, the exponents of that war, borrow from the books of the Maccabees not only to exhort to endurance based on faith in Christ but also to enhance their descriptions of battle scenes. For more, see R. W. Thomson, "The Maccabees in Early Armenian Historiography," *Journal of Theological Studies*, n.s. 26 (1975) 329–341.

[16]Kirakos Gandzakets'i, *History of the Armenians*, 24; Arm. text: K. A. Melik'-Ohanjanyan, ed., *Kirakos Gandzakets'i: Patmut'iwn Hayots'* (Erevan: Arm. Academy of Sciences, 1961), p. 247; Eng. trans., R. Bedrosian, *Kirakos Gandzakets'i's History of the Armenians* (New York: Sources of the Armenian Tradition, 1986), p. 209.

[17]This event is memorialized in a hymn by Catholicos Sahak Dzorop'orets'i (in office 677–703/4), for which see *Sharakan Hogewor Ergots' Surb ew Ughghap'aṙ Ekeghets'woys Hayastaneayts'* (Hymnal of Spiritual Songs of the Holy Orthodox Armenian Church) (Jerusalem: St. James Press, 1936; repr. New York: St. Vartan Press, 1986), pp. 671–675. The much popularized oral epic of *David of Sasun* is of later derivation.

[18]The pre-Chalcedonian Armenian sources, especially those attributed to St. Gregory (on which more shall be said shortly), are indicative of this development; see L. Ter Petrosyan, *Daser Hay Ekeghets'akan Matenagrut'yunits' (E Dar)* (Lessons from Armenian Ecclesiastical Bibliography [5th Century]) (Soch'i: Armenian Diocese of Nor Nakhijewan and Russia, 1993), especially pp. 22–23, 35–38. In Eznik Koghbats'i, in whose untitled work (dubbed *Eghts aghandots'* [Refutation of the Sects] by Armenian editors and *De Deo* by French editors; see below, n. 22), the Church appears to begin to define itself by denouncing "heresy." Of the Christian movements Marcionism alone is condemned; others denounced by Eznik are non-Christian religious systems or philosophies. The Church adhered to a broadly defined "orthodoxy," owing perhaps to the influence of St. Irenaeus (d. *ca.* 200), who defines Orthodoxy in terms of Apostolicity (a considerable part of his writings survives in Armenian only). On the subsequent anti-Chalcedonian posture of the Armenian Church, see K. Sarkissian, *The Council of Chalcedon and the Armenian Church* (London: SPCK, 1965), and more recently, N. Garsoïan, *L'Église arménienne et le grand schisme d'Orient*, Corpus Scriptorum Christianorum Orientalium 574, sub. tom. 100 (Leuven: Peeters, 1999).

[19]As for church-state relations under the Arsacids, see N. G. Garsoïan, "Politique ou Orthodoxie? L'Arménie au quatrième siècle," *Revue des études arméniennes*, n.s. 4 (1967) 297–320; repr. in *eadem, Armenia between Byzantium and the Sasanians*, ch. IV.

[20]At the extreme end of this self-definition, and for political expediency in the Armenian dynastic rivalries, there were claims to Hebrew ancestry or even descent from the Hebrew kings—however unfounded. For the Bagratids' claim, see Movsēs Khorenats'i, *Patmut'iwn Hayots'*, 1.22; 2.33; M. Abeghean and S. Yarut'iwnean, eds. (Tiflis: Martiroseants', 1913; repr. Delmar, NY: Caravan Books, 1981, and Erevan: Arm. Academy of Sciences, 1991); Eng. trans., R. W. Thomson, *Moses Khorenats'i: History of the Armenians*, Harvard Armenian Texts and Studies 4 (Cambridge, MA: Harvard University Press, 1978). Yovhannēs Kat'oghikos Draskhanakertts'i goes a step further by claiming that the Bagradits are descended from King David, *Patmut'iwn Hayots'*, 4.10; M. Emin, ed. (Moscow: Vladimir Gotie, 1853; repr. Tiflis: Aghaneants', 1912, and Delmar, NY: Caravan Books, 1980); Eng. trans. and commentary, K. H. Maksoudian, *Yovhannēs Drasxanakertc'i: History of Armenia*, Scholars Press Occasional Papers and Proceedings: Columbia University Program in Armenian Studies 3 (Atlanta: Scholars Press, 1987), see especially pp. 40, 73. See also C. Toumanoff, *Studies in Christian Caucasian History* (Washington, DC: Georgetown University Press, 1963), pp. 327–334, for such a claim by the Iberian or Georgian Bagratids as well. For the Pahlawuni-Kamsareans' (Neo-Kamsarakans) claim to Abrahamic ancestry through the patriarch's wife Keturah, see the eleventh letter in *Grigor Magistrosi T'ght'erĕ* (The

Epistolary of Grigor Magistros); K. Kostaneants', ed. (Alexandropol: Gēorg Sanoyeants', 1910), pp. 36–44 and xii–xiv, quoting later affirmations from the first epic by St. Nersēs Shnorhali, *Vipasanut'iwn Haykazants'* (Epic History of the Descendants of Hayk); text in *Tn. Nersesi Shnorhalwoy Hayots' Kat'oghikosi Bank' Ch'ap'aw* (Words in Verse by Lord Nersēs Shnorhali, Catholicos of the Armenians), 2nd ed. (Venice: S. Ghazar, 1928), pp. 548, 588.

²¹Judging from the context, there seems to be a conflation, if not confusion, between 1 Thess. 3:1–6 (cf. Acts 17:14–16a) and 2 Cor. 2:13 (cf. 8:23). If the allusion is more to the Corinthian passage, as it seems to be, then the reference would be to Titus and not Timothy. An early scribal error could be suspected here.

²²Alluding to Rom. 9:1–3.

²³Eznik Koghbats'i, *Eghts aghandots'* (Refutation of the Sects), 355; Arm. text with French trans. in *Eznik de Kołb: De Deo*, L. Mariès and C. Mercier, eds., *Patrologia Orientalis* 28, fascs. 3–4 (Paris: Firmin-Didot, 1959); Eng. trans., M. J. Blanchard and R. D. Young, *Eznik of Kołb. On God*, Eastern Christian Texts in Translation 2 (Leuven: Peeters, 1998); see also T. Samuelian, *Refutation of the Sects: A Retelling of Yeznik Koghbatsi's Apology* (New York: St. Vartan Press, 1986). Regardless of its title, Eznik's treatise deals with the problem of the origin of evil and attacks on four fronts the wrong understanding of God as responsible for evil. Cf. this line of Koriwn from the quotation before the preceding: "But we are quite persuaded in the belief that there is nothing to fault God for, whether in the realm of things manifest or in the realm of secret things."

²⁴*Sharakan*, p. 692. This new identity is often repeated by Armenian authors and is a recurring theme in the liturgy, e.g., Step'anos Siwnets'i (d. 735) in his *Meknut'iwn Zhamakargut'ean* (Commentary on the Daily Office) 7.8: «ԵԼ Եղեալ ազգ սուրբ եւ անունն կոչեցեալ Նոր Իսրայէլ՝ այսինքն Քրիստոնեայք» ("And we became a holy nation and are called 'New Israel,' that is, 'Christians'"). For text and translation, see M. Findikyan, "The Commentary on the Armenian Daily Office by Bishop Step'anos Siwnec'i: Edition and Translation of the Long and Short Versions with Textual and Liturgical Study," Diss., Pontificum Institutum Studiorum Orientalium, Romae, 1997.

²⁵Unless otherwise indicated, all references to Agat'angeghos in this study are to the surviving or "received" Arm. text (*Aa*), *Agat'angeghay Patmut'iwn Hayots'*, G. Tēr Mkrtch'ean and S. Kanayeants', eds. (Tiflis: Martiroseants', 1909; repr. Delmar, NY: Caravan Books, 1980); Eng. trans., R. W. Thomson, *Agathangelos. History of the Armenians* (Albany, NY: State University of New York Press, 1976). On the complicated textual history of the work, see Thomson's introduction and the references below, n. 27.

²⁶On the hitherto problematic years of his reign and the emerging consensus in scholarship, see P. Ananean (Ananian), "S. Grigor Lusaworch'i dzeṙnadrut'ean t'uakanĕ ew paraganerĕ," *Bazmavep* 117 (1959) 9–23, 129–142, 225–238; 118 (1960) 53–60, 101–113 (= *S. Grigor Lusaworch'i dzeṙnadrut'an t'uakanĕ ew paraganerĕ* [Venice: S. Ghazar, 1960]; Italian trans., *idem*, "La data e le circostanze della consecrazione di S. Gregorio Illuminatore," Le Muséon 74 [1961] 43–73, 319–360); C. Toumanoff, "The Third-Century Arsacids," *Revue des études arméniennes*, n.s. 6 (1969) 233–281; R. H. Hewsen, "The Synchronistic Table of Bishop Eusebius (Ps. Sebēos): A Reexamination of its Chronological Data," *Revue des études arméniennes*, n.s. 15 (1981) 59–72; N. G. Garsoïan, "The Aršakuni Dynasty (A.D. 12–[180?]–428)," in R. G. Hovannisian, ed., *The Armenian People from Ancient to Modern Times*, 2 vols. (New York: St. Martin's Press, 1997) 1:63–94.

²⁷On the sources used by Agat'angeghos, see the survey of scholarship by Thomson, *Agathangelos*, pp. lxxv–xciii; for an Eng. trans. of the catechism attributed to St. Gregory, see *idem*, *The Teaching of St. Gregory*, rev. ed., AVANT: Treasures of the Armenian Christian Tradition 1 (New Rochelle: St. Nersess Armenian Seminary, 2001); the Arm. text (*Vardapetut'iwn*) is an integral part of Agat'angeghos (*Aa* 259–715), for which see above, n. 25. On the questionable ascription of the *Teaching* to St. Gregory, see the introduction by Thomson, especially pp. 41–49, where he invites attention to its likely Greek sources, particularly the first eighteen homilies of the *Catecheses* of St. Cyril of Jerusalem—homilies delivered at the Holy Sepulchre in 348 or 351, long after

the death of St. Gregory in 328. Much of the same criticism applies also to the other work attributed to St. Gregory, the homiliary known as *Yachakhapatum* (Arm. text, *Srboy Hōrn Meroy Eranelwoyn Grigori Lusaworch'i Yachakhapatum Chaṙk' Lusawork'* [Often-repeated and Enlightened Homilies of Our Blessed Father St. Gregory the Illuminator], A. Tēr Mik'elean, ed. [Ējmiatsin: Mother See Press, 1894]). Their pre-Chalcedonian date, however, is certain.

[28]For the recensions, see Thomson, *The Teaching of St. Gregory*, pp. 3–5; cf. G. Winkler, "Our Present Knowledge of the History of Agat'angełos and its Oriental Versions," *Revue des études arméniennes*, n.s. 14 (1980) 125–141. The various versions suggest that the existing Armenian text (*Aa*) is a reworking of a lost Armenian version closer to one of the two Greek versions (*Vg*): G. Garitte, ed., *Documents pour l'étude du livre d'Agathange*, Studi e Testi 127 (Vatican City: Biblioteca Apostolica Vaticana, 1946).

[29]See the numerous references to Koriwn in Thomson's notes to these sections, *Agathangelos*, pp. 492–503; cf. pp. lxxxviii–lxxxix. Equally noteworthy are sections 774–776, which correspond with our first quotation from Koriwn, above.

[30]N. Tsovakan (Pogharean), *Koriwn Vardapeti Erkerě* (The Works of Koriwn Vardapet) (Jerusalem: St. James Press, 1984; repr. of his articles in *Sion* 56 [1982] 191–193; 57 [1983] 38–40, 87–90, 152–155, and 211–214, with an added index of the special terms considered). See further G. Fntglean, *Koriwn, Vark' Mashtots'i, Ughgheal ew Lusabaneal* (Koriwn, Life of Mashtots': Emended and Annotated) (Jerusalem: St. James Press, 1930), p. ii, who insists that *The Teaching of St. Gregory* is the *magnum opus* of Koriwn. In earlier scholarship, see N. Biwzandats'i, *Koriwn Vardapet ew Norin T'argmanut'iwnk'* (Koriwn Vardapet and His Translations) (Tiflis: Martiroseants', 1900), who, marshalling similar data, concludes that Koriwn was the translator of the Books of the Maccabees, Euthalius of Alexandria, Agat'angeghos, and the *Buzandaran* (see the next note for a related view in more recent scholarship).

[31]In an insightful article J. R. Russell suggests convincingly that the very name Mashtots' means "bearer of good news or reward," on the basis of an Iranian form, *mwjdg* or *mozhdag*, attested in Manichaean texts in Middle Parthian of Turfan, and thus identical in meaning to Agat'angeghos, the purported author of the *History* of Armenia's conversion to Christianity. Russell goes so far as to suggest, following Pogharean, that "Koriwn was in all events the author of the Agat'angeghos, and that the mythic scribe at the court of Tiridates is certainly modelled— and possibly named—after Koriwn's own teacher" ("On the Name of Mashtots," *Annual of Armenian Linguistics* 15 [1994] 67–78, especially 72–78). However, the adoption of the name Agat'angeghos could also be traced to an anonymous early Armenian source, conveniently called *Primary History* (from *Nakhneats'n Patmut'iwn*, lit., History of the Ancestors), used by Khorenats'i (beginning at 1.9) and found as a preliminary to the anonymous seventh-century history attributed (wrongly it seems) to Bishop Sebēos (chs. 1–6): G. V. Abgaryan, ed., *Patmut'iwn Sebēosi* (Erevan: Arm. Academy of Sciences, 1979), pp. 47–64. Elsewhere, Abgaryan ascribes the larger work that bears the name of Sebēos to the monk Khosrovik: *Sebēosi Patmut'yuně ev Ananuni aṙeghtsvatsě* (The *History* of Sebēos and the Enigma of the Anonymous) (Erevan: Arm. Academy of Sciences, 1965); however, he retains the name of Sebēos in both titles out of deference to past scholarship. French trans. of this so-called short version of the *Primary History* (chs. 1–4), under the title "Le Pseudo-Agathange: histoire ancienne de l'Arménie," is found in V. Langlois, *Collection des historiens anciens et modernes de l'Arménie*, 2 vols. (Paris: Firmin-Didot, 1867–1869) 1:195–200 (the so-called long version, under the title "Mar Apas Catina: histoire ancienne de l'Arménie," in *ibid.*, pp. 18–53, is the expanded version found in Book I of Khorenats'i). Thomson provides an annotated translation of the *Primary History* (chs. 1–4) as an "Appendix" in *Khorenats'i*, pp. 357–367, with an analysis on pp. 53–56. (Far less is said about the *Primary History* and no trans. of the document is provided in *The Armenian History Attributed to Sebeos*, trans. with notes by R. W. Thomson, historical commentary by J. Howard-Johnston, assistance from T. Greenwood, 2 pts., Translated Texts for Historians 31 [Liverpool: Liverpool University Press, 1999] 1:xxxii–xxxiii; the trans. begins with ch. 7 of Abgaryan's edition [p. 64]). This short account

contains a brief reference to "Mar Abas, the philosopher of Mtsurn," who found in the ruins of that city built on the Euphrates by King Sanatruk (an Arsacid king of Armenia, possibly first century AD) a stele inscribed in Greek with this title: "I Agatʻangeghos the scribe wrote on this stele with my own hand the years of the first Armenian kings, taking them from the royal archive at the command of the valiant Trdat." The anonymous author of the *Primary History* then adds: "A little later you will see the content thereof in its [appropriate] place." As Thomson observes, this presumably refers to the end part of the *Primary History* containing the list of Armenian kings (*Khorenatsʻi*, p. 358 n. 9). It is conceivable that this story in the *Primary History* inspired the adoption of the name Agatʻangeghos for the anonymous author of the work which bears the title *History of the Armenians* and accounts for Armenia's conversion to Christianity—unless one would go so far as to argue the point of adoption the other way around (see Thomson, *Agathangelos,* p. xxv, for when the name was first associated with the received history of St. Gregory and the conversion of Armenia [*Aa*]). On the impertinence of this document for a reconstruction of the early history of Armenia, see R. H. Hewsen, "*The Primary History of Armenia:* An Examination of the Validity of an Immemorially Transmitted Historical Tradition," *History in Africa* 2 (1975) 91–100.

32The treaty of Theodosius in 387 divided the Armenian territories into vassal states subject to either Byzantine or Sasanian rule, with the latter extending over the larger part of the land of Armenia. Thus ended the centuries-old conflict between Rome and Persia.

33For the text, see *Pʻawstosi Buzandatsʻwoy Patmutʻiwn Hayotsʻ i chʻors dprutʻiwns* (Pʻawstos Buzandatsʻiʻs History of the Armenians in Four Registers) (4th ed., Venice: Mekhitʻarists, 1933); Eng. trans., Garsoïan, *The Epic Histories (Buzandaran Patmutʻiwnk');* quotations are from her translation. In the absence of any critical edition of the text, the following edition may also be consulted: *Pʻawstosi Buzandatsʻwoy Patmutʻiwn Hayotsʻ,* Kʻ. P[atkanean], ed. (St. Petersburg: Kayserakan Chemaran Gitutʻeantsʻ, 1883; repr. Delmar, NY: Caravan Books, 1984, and Erevan: [State] University of Erevan, 1987, with a modern translation). Cf. the concluding laments in Khorenatsʻi, *History,* 3.67–68.

34As for the lost Books I-II, like much of Book I of Khorenatsʻiʻs *History,* they could have been inspired by the anonymous *Primary History,* on which see above, n. 31.

35On the author's familiarity with contemporary hagiography, see Garsoïan's introduction to *The Epic Histories,* pp. 26–30. He is one of the primary sources of such popular stories as that of the lion with the wounded paw healed by an anchorite and the flight of snakes away from islands where Christians have been banished.

36On his alleged relation to the Illuminator, see (Ps.) Yovhannēs Mamikonean, Patmutʻiwn Tarōnoy, A. Abrahamyan, ed. (Erevan: Haypethrat, 1941), pp. 70–71; Eng. trans., L. Avdoyan, *Pseudo-Yovhannēs Mamikonean: The History of Tarōn,* Scholars Press Occasional Papers and Proceedings: Columbia University Program in Armenian Studies 6 (Atlanta: Scholars Press, 1993), p. 72.

37Clearly, the *Buzandaran* does not associate the place with the present-day Mount Ararat to the north, but follows earlier tradition as in Theodoret of Cyrrhus, *Religious History,* q.v. *Life of St. James,* Eng. trans., R. M. Price, *A History of the Monks of Syria,* Cistercian Studies Series 88 (Kalamazoo, MI: Western Michigan University Press, 1985), pp. 12–20; Theodoret, however, is silent about the Saint's adventures in Armenia; cf. P. Peeters, "La légende de Saint Jacques de Nisibe," *Analecta Bollandiana* 38 (1920) 285–373. See also Garsoïan, *The Epic Histories,* pp. 252–253, 431, 474–475, 489.

38The heavy dependence on Koriwn's *Life* is evident (9 [52.1–2]).

39In a panegyric on St. Gregory attributed to St. John Chrysostom and translated from Greek, *Nerboghean Asatsʻeal yaghags Varutsʻ ew Nahatakutʻean Srboyn Grigori Hayotsʻ Metsatsʻ Hayrapeti* (Panegyric Recited upon the Life and Martyrdom of St. Gregory the Patriarch of Greater Armenia), the Spirit as a dove descended on St. Gregory at the time of his consecration (*Sopʻerkʻ Haykakankʻ* [Armenian Writings], [Venice: S. Ghazar, 1853] 4:68). For more on this panegyric, and another attributed to a disciple of Chrysostom, Theophilos, see further below.

[40]Despite Tsovakan (Poghatean), *Koriwn Vardapeti Erkerĕ*, pp. 37–47, et al. (see above, nn. 30–31).

[41]Thomson, *Agathangelos*, pp. lxxv–lxxvii; Garsoïan, *Epic Histories*, pp. 24–26.

[42]In a letter (appended to the *History*, pp. 185–204) to an old friend and dynast, the *marzpan* Vahan Mamikonean, he defends himself against rival and malicious clergy because of whom he had sought exile in Amid (modern Diyarbakir). Thereupon, he was called by Vahan to head the monastery at Vagharshapat and was commissioned to write the *History*.

[43]Quotations from Ghazar are from R. W. Thomson's translation, *The History of Łazar P'arpec'i*, Scholars Press Occasional Papers and Proceedings: Columbia University Program in Armenian Studies / S. D. Fesjian Academic Publications 4 (Atlanta: Scholars Press, 1991); see p. 111. Arm. text, *Patmut'iwn Hayots'* (Armenian History), G. Tēr-Mkrtch'ean and S. Malkhasean, eds. (Tiflis: Martiroseants', 1904; repr. Delmar, NY: Caravan Books, 1986). Cf. Thomson's partial translation in the "Appendix" to his *Ełishē: History of Vardan and the Armenian War*, Harvard Armenian Texts and Studies 5 (Cambridge, MA: Harvard University Press, 1982), pp. 251–327, especially p. 283.

[44]See the following pages in the 1904 Tiflis edition (bold pagination in Thomson's translation): 39, 42, 50–51, 55, 62, 70–71, 90, 92, 94, 119, 122, 139, 141, 170, 176, 192. The discovery of fragments older than the surviving manuscripts of Ghazar's *History* show that the Armenian text as it has come down to us is a medieval redaction of a much older text, represented by the discovered fragments (C. Sanspeur, "Le fragment de l'histoire de Lazare de P'arpi retrouvé dans le Ms. 1 de Jérusalem," *Revue des études arméniennes*, n.s. 10 [1973] 83–109; C. J. F. Dowsett, "The Newly Discovered Fragment of Lazar of P'arp's *History*," *Le Muséon* 89 [1976] 97–122). The fragments, however, cover none of the passages that mention St. Gregory. Thus, there is no valid reason to relegate the laudations of the Saint in those passages to a later redaction.

[45]According to the Karshuni version of Agat'angeghos (*Vk* 293–299), rendered from an Armenian vorlage in about 600 (text, [based on Jerusalem, St. Mark manuscript no. 38] with French trans. and commentary, in M. van Esbroeck, "Un nouveau témoin du livre d'Agathange," *Revue des études arméniennes*, n.s. 8 [1971] 13–167, especially pp. 93–94); cf. Khorenats'i, *History of the Armenians*, 2.91 (detailing how shepherds found and buried the Saint's body without knowing who he was, and how after some time his relics were revealed to a certain ascetic named Garnik (Amra in the Karshuni version) "who took them and buried them in the village of T'ordan"). On Garnik's story, see also the anonymous "Patmut'iwn yaghags giwti nshkharats' Srboyn Grigori Hayots' Metsats' Lusaworch'i" (History of the Discovery of the Relics of St. Gregory the Illuminator of Greater Armenia), *Ararat* 35 (1902) 1178–1183. For later versions of what became of St. Gregory's relics, see the *Panegyric* on him by Vardan Arewelts'i, *Sop'erk'*, 5:73–76 (trans., Selection IX), and Kirakos Gandzakets'i, *History of the Armenians*, 1 (ed. Melik'-Ohanjanyan, *Patmut'iwn*, pp. 10–14; trans. Bedrosian, *Kirakos Gandzakets'i's History of the Armenians*, pp. 8–11; trans. here, Selection X). In his commentary on the Karshuni version (p. 162) Esbroeck argues that the story about St. Gregory's relics and the invention of his cult does not predate the sixth century (so also *idem*, "Témoignages littéraires sur les sépultures de S. Grégoire l'Illuminateur," *Analecta Bollandiana* 89 (1971) 387–418. The cultic use of the Saint's relics in the second half of the fifth century, as attested by Ghazar, cannot be dismissed easily (see the preceding note and Thomson, *The History of Łazar P'arpec'i*, pp. 95 n. 2 and 238 n. 2), even though—one may add—Eghishē is altogether silent about St. Gregory in the *History of Vardan and the Armenian War* and in the earliest hymn to St. Gregory, by Movsēs Bishop of Siwnik' (trans., Selection I), the Illuminator is never called an apostle.

[46]See Thomson, *Ełishē*, p. 11.

[47]As in Gk. *marturia;* q.v. in G. W. H. Lampe, *A Patristic Greek Lexicon* (Oxford: Clarendon Press, 1961), pp. 828–829.

[48]A notable work in Armenian translation is St. Gregory Nazianzenus' *Homily on the Maccabees,* among several others by this much loved Cappadocian father; see M. van Esbroeck and U.

Zanetti, "Le manuscrit Érévan 993. Inventaire des pièces," *Revue des études arméniennes*, n.s. 12 (1977) 123–167, especially p. 156.

⁴⁹Thomson invites attention to the similarities in the speech of the dying Mattathias in 1 Macc. 2 (*Ełishē*, p. 158 n. 3). Eghishē's ideology of martyrdom has much in common also with the speeches of Eleazar to the Sicarii during the siege of Masada (Josephus, *The Wars of the Jews*, 7.8).

⁵⁰Thomson, *Ełishē*, p. 9. He wrote at the request of the priest Dawitʻ Mamikonean, to glorify the hero of the patron's clan.

⁵¹I have slightly modified Thomson's translation (p. 246); Arm. text, *Eghishēi vasn Vardanay ew Hayotsʻ Paterazmin* (Concerning Vardan and the Armenian War), E. Tēr-Minasyan, ed. (Erevan: Arm. Academy of Sciences, 1957), pp. 201–202.

⁵²Thomson invites attention to parallels in 2 Macc. 5:27 (p. 246 n. 12).

⁵³L. Khachʻikyan, ed., *Eghishei Araratsotsʻ Meknutʻiunē* (Eghishē's Commentary on Genesis) (Erevan: Zvartʻnotsʻ, 1992), p. 15. This description of languages, with minor variations, appears in the writings of several medieval authors, e.g., Stepʻanos Siwnetsʻi, Vardan Arewseltsʻi, Mkhitʻar Ayrivanetsʻi, Yovhannēs Erznkatsʻi, et al.

⁵⁴Khorenatsʻi synchronizes Aram and Ara with Ninus and Semiramis as well, the legendary founders of the Assyrian empire.

⁵⁵As Thomson and others observe (*Khorenatsʻi*, pp. 350–351 and notes), there is much reliance here on St. Gregory Nazianzenus' panegyric on St. Athanasius who is similarly likened to Moses: *In laudem magni Athanasi* (ed. Migne, *Patrologia Graeca* 35:1082–1128) and on St. Gregory of Nyssa, *Oratio funebris in magnum Meletium* (ed. Migne, *Patrologia Graeca* 46:852–892). The latter was attributed to St. Gregory Nazianzenus in Armenian literary tradition.

⁵⁶*Patmutʻiwn*, p. 143; Avdoyan, *Pseudo-Yovhannēs*, p. 102.

⁵⁷In the "Supplement" to Book IV concerning "the pious prince Abdlmseh and his sons," whose virtues are said to exceed many of those of the biblical worthies (in V. Vardanyan, ed., *Tʻovma Artsruni ev Ananun, Patmutʻyun Artsrunyatsʻ Tan* (Erevan: Arm. Academy of Sciences, 1978), pp. 305–326; Eng. trans., R. W. Thomson, *Thomas Artsruni, History of the House of the Artsrunikʻ* (Detroit: Wayne State University Press, 1985), pp. 368–387; see especially p. 310 (Eng. trans., p. 373). See also (Ps.) Yovhannēs Mamikonean, *Patmutʻiwn Tarōnoy*, where St. Gregory is said to be superior to Moses (p. 40) and is called "Sun of righteousness" (p. 123), an epithet used earlier in the *Patmutʻiwn* for Christ, in keeping with the Jewish apocalyptic writings of the Intertestamental period (p. 41; Avdoyan, *Pseudo-Yovhannēs*, pp. 58–59, 94). For a similar use of the epithet "Sun of righteousness" for St. Gregory, see the panegyric on the Saint attributed to St. John Chrysostom (*Sopʻerkʻ*, 4:31).

⁵⁸The *Prayerbook* is also known as *Matean Oghbergutʻean* (Book of Lamentations), P. M. Khachʻatryan and A. A. Ghazinyan, eds. (Erevan: Arm. Academy of Sciences, 1985); Eng. trans., T. J. Samuelian, *Speaking with God from the Depths of the Heart*, 2nd ed. (Erevan: Vem Press, 2002).

⁵⁹In *Bankʻ Chʻapʻaw*, p. 588.

⁶⁰From Erevan manuscript no. 848 (dated 14th–16th cent.), fols. 78–82, summarized by L. G. Khachʻeryan, *Gladzori Hamalsaranē Hay Mankavarzhakan Mtkʻi mej, XIII–XIV dd.* (The University of Glajor in Armenian Pedagogical Thought) (Erevan: Arm. Academy of Sciences, 1973), pp. 66–67, 141–147; cited by A. K. Sanjian, "Esayi Nchʻecʻi and Biblical Exegesis," in C. Burchard, ed., *Armenia and the Bible*, Univ. of Penn. Arm. Texts and Studies 12 (Atlanta: Scholars Press, 1993), p. 187.

⁶¹This short work, also known as *"Ban Hawatali"* (A Believable Word), became part of the *Girkʻ Tʻghtʻotsʻ* (Book of Letters), Y. Izmireantsʻ, ed., Sahak Mesropean Matenadaran 5 (Tiflis: Ṙotineantsʻ and Sharadzē, 1901), pp. 533–535. Since it is not a letter, it was not included by N. Pogharean in his rev. ed. of the *Girkʻ Tʻghtʻotsʻ* (Jerusalem: St. James Press, 1994).

⁶²These works have been collected in the small yet celebrated *Sopʻerkʻ Haykakankʻ* (Armenian Books) series; vol. 4: *Yovhannu Oskeberani ew Grigori Sarkawagapeti Nerbogheankʻ i S. Grigor Lusaworichʻ* (Panegyrics on St. Gregory the Illuminator by John Chrysostom, [His Disciple

Theophilos], and Gregory Sarkawagapet); and vol. 5: *Yovhannu Sarkawagay, Vardanay Bardzrberdts'woy, Yovhannu Erznkats'woy Nerbogheank' i S. Grigor Lusaworich'* (Panegyrics on St. Gregory the Illuminator by Yovhannēs Sarkawag, Vardan Bardzrberdts'i [read Arewelts'i], and Yovhannēs Erznkats'i) (Venice: S. Ghazar, 1853).

[63]See, e.g., the panegyrics of St. Gregory Nazianzenus (ed. Migne, *Patrologia Graeca* 35) and those of St. Gregory of Nyssa (collected in Migne, *Patrologia Graeca* 46). Cf. St. Athanasius' *Vita et conversatio S. Antonii* (ed. Migne, *Patrologia Graeca* 26:836–976).

[64]Text in *Sop'erk'*, 4:5–86 (colophon, pp. 86–87) and among the *Erkbayakan Chaŕk'* (Allegorical Homilies) in *Yovhannu Oskeberani Kostandnupolsi Episkopasapeti Meknut'iwn T'ght'ots'n Pawghosi* (John Chrysostom, Archbishop of Constantinople: Commentary on the Epistles of Paul), 2 vols. (Venice: S. Ghazar, 1862) 2:792–826 (colophon, p. 826). The colophon appears also in G. Yovsep'ean, *Yishatakarank' Dzeŕagrats'* (Colophons of Manuscripts) (Antelias: Armenian Catholicosate of Cilicia, 1951), no. 168, cols. 353–354, and elsewhere (see Yovsep'ean for references). The full title of the panegyric has this addition ". . . i Kokison Hayots' minch' yak'sorans ēr, i khndroy Hayazin orumn episkoposi ew vardapeti hamazgwoy norin Deoskoros anun koch'ets'eloy . . ." (. . . at Cucusa [Koukousos] in Armenia, while he was in exile, upon the request of a certain bishop and vardapet, his Armenian-born compatriot named Dioscoros . . .), suggesting that it was written between 404 and 407, the year of Chrysostom's deportation to Pityus or Colchis on the Black Sea (he died en route at Comana in Pontus). The popularity of Chrysostom as preacher and writer gave rise to several spurious works in Greek. The colophon by St. Nersēs the Gracious emphasizes the antiquity of the work, translated "from old and faded copies" (*i hin ew yeghts orinakats'*).

[65]Text in *Sop'erk'*, 4:89–125 and in *Yovhannu Oskeberani . . . Meknut'iwn T'ght'ots'n Pawghosi*, 2:826–841.

[66]Yovsep'ean, *Yishatakarank' Dzeŕagrats'*, no. 133, cols. 277–280, and elsewhere (references in *ibid.*).

[67]Alluding to Matt. 5:15 and parallels and to what follows in the colophon, that the translation was temporarily obscured, until the scribe Paul made a copy of it at the place where it was found.

[68]The monastery of "Royal Oaks," on which see H. Oskean, *Kilikiayi Vank'erē* (The Monasteries of Cilicia), Azgayin Matenadaran 183 (Vienna: Mkhit'arean Tparan, 1957), pp. 118–132.

[69]The cathedral of the famed monastery of Akner, known also as Surb Astuatsatsin (Holy Bearer of God), on which see Oskean, *Kilikiayi Vank'erē*, pp. 93–95.

[70]G. Zarbhanalean, *Haykakan hin dprut'ean patmut'iwn (IV–XII dar)* (History of Ancient Armenian Literature [4th–13th Centuries]), 2nd ed. (Venice: Mkhit'arean Tparan, 1897), pp. 599–605; N. Tsovakan (Pogharean), *Vanatur: Banasirakan yoduatsneru zhoghovatsoy* (Monastical: A Collection of Philological Essays) (Jerusalem: St. James Press, 1993), pp. 176–181. The *Commentary on Acts* is somewhat eclectic, incorporating segments from St. Ephrem's *Commentary on Acts* among others, and the *Commentary on the Gospel of John* is incomplete.

[71]Yovsep'ean, *Yishatakarank' Dzeŕagrats'*, no. 138, cols. 283–286; cf. cols. 279–280). The title of the latter work may wrongly suggest that the translation was done by Vkayasēr himself, his involvement notwithstanding: *Patmut'iwn Varuts' . . . Surb Yovhannēs Oskeberan Hayrapetin Kostandnupolsoy: T'argm. i Yunakanē i Hays, i Grigorē Kat'ughikosē Vkayasēr Koch'ets'eloy* (History of the life . . . of St. John Chrysostom, Patriarch of Constantinople, translated from Greek into Armenian by [order of] Kat'oghikos Grigor, called Martyrophile) (Venice: S. Ghazar, 1751).

[72]On the Pahlawunis' kinship to St. Gregory, see the eleventh letter in *Grigor Magistrosi T'ght'erē*, especially p. 40; Nersēs Shnorhali, *Vipasanut'iwn Haykazants'*, in *Bank' Ch'ap'aw*, pp. 539–608 (especially pp. 587–588). On the succession of the Pahlawuni Catholicoi, see 44–46.

[73]K. [H.] Maksoudian, *Chosen of God: The Election of the Catholicos of All Armenians from the Fourth Century to the Present* (New York: St. Vartan Press, 1995), p. 45.

[74]For the division of the world by lot among the Apostles, see *The Teaching of St. Gregory*,

685; cf. Thomson, *Teaching*, p. 172 n. 3, who invites attention to the apocryphal Acts (see The Acts of Thomas 1; cf. Eusebius, *Historia Ecclesiastica*, 3.1).

[75]Cf. the similar narrative in the *Buzandaran*, with reference to the consecration of St. Nersēs the Great (4.4).

[76]«Եւ ընծայել քեզ տեառն Աստուծոյ ժողովուրդ սեպական» (*Ew ĕntsayel k'ez tearn Astutsoy zhoghovurd sep'akan:* "And to present to you, Lord God, a special people"). Cf. p. 68, where this is realized upon the baptism of the people. Earlier, p. 40, the Saint acts upon the king's request to prepare the people for baptism: «Պատրաստեա զդոսա ժողովուրդ տեառն» (*Patrastea zdosa zhoghovurd tearn:* "Prepare them [to become] the Lord's people"). This seems to echo the new identity declared at the end of Agat'angeghos' *History* (900); cf. this line from the "Anaphora" of the Divine Liturgy, echoing Deut. 7:6; 14:2, 26:18: «...որ ժողովուրդ ինքեան առեալ զեկեղեցի, սեպհականեաց զհաւատացեալս ի քեզ...» (*. . . or zhoghowurd ink'ean areal zekeghets'i, sephakaneats' zhawatats'eals i k'ez*): ". . . who [i.e., the Word] having taken the Church to be a people to himself, made his own those who believe in you [i.e., the Father]"; Eng. trans. by D. Findikyan, ed., *The Divine Liturgy of the Armenian Church* (New York: St. Vartan Press, 1999), p. 29.

[77]David is cited as one who exemplifies patience in St. John Chrysostom, *De David et Saul*, 2.1 (ed. Migne, *Patrologia Graeca* 54:678); cf. *idem, Specimen expositionis in Job* (ed. Migne, *Patrologia Graeca* 64:504–656).

[78]Cf. the short, anonymous panegyric on the Illuminator's descent into the dungeon, in the *Yaysmawurk'* (Menology): *Liakatar Vark' ew Vkayabanut'iwn Srbots'* (The Complete Lives and Testimony of the Saints), M. Awgerean, ed. (Venice: S. Ghazar, 1810), pp. 213–216, where the Saint is said to have "altogether surpassed both Abraham and Isaac, for he was sacrificing and offering his body through diverse tortures" (p. 213).

[79]The biblical phraseology is evident: Chief Shepherd (Heb. 13:20); children of light (John 12:36).

[80]Cf. Eustratius of Constantinople, *De statu animorum post mortem*, 5 (ed. Allatius, p. 349), on St. Paul as "new Moses" or "second Moses"; John Monachus, *Hymnus in Basilium*, 3 (ed. Migne, *Patrologia Graeca* 96:1372), on St. Basil of Caesarea as such. See "Mōusēs" in Lampe, *A Patristic Greek Lexicon*, p. 896.

[81]In a similar vein of thought, the beginning of an anonymous panegyric on the Saint's release from the dungeon compares his fourteen years there with the four days of Lazarus' lying dead in the grave, with the thought that fourteen-year endurance in the pit is a much more dreadful existence than being dead for four days; moreover, the Saint brings up with his release those who are spiritually dead (in *Liakatar Vark' ew Vkayabanut'iwn Srbots'*, pp. 237–239). For a modern and abridged Armenian translation of this panegyric, see *Surberu Keank'ě* (The Lives of the Saints) (Beirut: Fraternité ecclésiastique arménienne, 1970), pp. 299–301.

[82]For other comparisons between St. Gregory and Daniel, see *Sop'erk'*, 4:95, 99, 108–111, 116 (where the period in the dungeon is fifteen years; for more on the number of years in the dungeon, see below, n. 143). The connection between the Saint's experience and that of Daniel is made explicit in Agat'angeghos, *History*, 179, and more so in the Karshuni version (*Vk* 53–71; Esbroeck, "Un nouveau témoin du livre d'Agathange," especially pp. 34–39).

[83]All three are published in *Sop'erk'*, 5 (pp. 5–36, 39–82, 85–164, respectively; that of Vardan Arewelts'i being wrongly attributed to Vardan Bardzrberdts'i).

[84]*Sop'erk'*, 4:129–157; under the title *Grigor Sarkawagapeti ew Chgnawori Khōsk' i S. Grigor Lusaworich', asats'eal i S. K'aghak'n yErusaghēm* (Discourse on St. Gregory the Illuminator by the Head-Deacon and Hermit Grigor, Recited in Jerusalem).

[85]Cf. the short, anonymous panegyric on the Illuminator's descent into the dungeon, in *Liakatar Vark' ew Vkayabanut'iwn Srbots'*, p. 214, where *The Teaching of St. Gregory* is compared with the burning bush, "ablaze with the love of God."

[86]Alluding to the tradition that at His baptism Jesus crushed the head of Satan, who was

lurking as a serpent in the Jordan, and thus fulfilled the prediction in Gen. 3:15 literally. For this recurring theme in early Christian writings on Adam and Eve, including patristic homilies on Gen. 3, see the sources in M. E. Stone, *A History of the Literature of Adam and Eve*, SBL Early Judaism and Its Literature 3 (Atlanta: Scholars Press, 1992), pp. 84–116. This traditional belief is at times depicted in medieval iconography of the baptism of Christ. Pharaoh as the personification of evil is common in the allegorical writings of Philo of Alexandria, which had an overwhelming influence on patristic exegesis.

[87]Cf. the opening words of the anonymous panegyric on the Illuminator's descent into the dungeon, in *Liakatar Vark' ew Vkayabanut'iwn Srbots'*, p. 213, where the Saint is addressed as "New Abraham, the progenitor of faith"; and again: "I speak of our glorious father, the God-approaching patriarch of the house of Israel" (p. 214).

[88]Following the Armenian Bible, in keeping with the Septuagint; the Hebrew has "a rod of an almond tree."

[89]For the details of the vision, see Agat'angeghos, *History*, 731–756.

[90]Cf. the anonymous panegyric on the Illuminator's descent into the dungeon, in *Liakatar Vark' ew Vkayabanut'iwn Srbots'*, pp. 213–214, where God is said to have gone down with the Saint as He did with Joseph when the latter was thrown in a pit (Gen. 37:12–36); however, the Saint is said to have surpassed Joseph when the latter was released, since the Saint came to save people not from the famine of the land but from the famine of hearing the Word of God (Am. 8:11).

[91]Cf. Koriwn, *Life of Mashtots'*, 25 (90.2–11), on the sorrow of the ever-active St. Mashtots' over the death of his associate St. Sahak, compared with the sadness, loneliness, and relative inactivity of the Apostle Paul because of the temporary absence of his associate Timothy (see above, n. 21).

[92]Similar comparisons abound in the other panegyrics by Arewelts'i: on St. Grigor Vkayasēr and his successors to the Catholicosate; on Sts. Sahak and Mesrop (Mashtots') and their pupils, the holy translators; on Sts. Aristakēs and Vrt'anēs and their descendant successors to the Catholicosate; and on St. Yovhan Odznets'i (works listed chronologically); see N. Pogh11arean, *Hay Groghner* (Armenian Writers) (Jerusalem: St. James Press, 1971), pp. 295–297. See also P'. Ant'abyan, "Vardan Arewelts'u Nerboghĕ Nvirvats Hayots' Greri Gyutin" (The Panegyric by Vardan Arewelts'i on the Discovery of the Armenian Letters), *Banber Matenadarani* 7 (1964) 365–397, especially p. 366.

[93]In addition to the text in *Sop'erk'*, 5:85–164, see the more recent edition by A. Erznkats'i Srapyan, *Hovhannes Erznkats'i, Bank' Ch'ap'av* (H. E.: Words in Verse), Hay K'narergut'yun Matenashar (Erevan: Sovetakan Grogh, 1986), pp. 136–199; and A. Ghazinyan, "Nerboghĕ hay hin grakanut'yan mej" (The Panegyric in Ancient Armenian Literature), in V. S. Nersisyan and H. G. Bakhch'inyan, eds., *Hay Mijnadaryan Grakanut'yan Zhanrer* (Genres of Medieval Armenian Literature) (Erevan: Arm. Academy of Sciences, 1984), pp. 127–178, especially pp. 150–152.

[94]Cf. the hymn by Erznkats'i, *"Aysōr zuarchats'eal ts'entsay ekeghets'i . . ."* (Reveling today the Church rejoices . . .), where St. Gregory is likened to Moses, Elijah, and John the Baptist (*Sharakan*, p. 273; trans., Selection XI).

[95]So also in the author's hymn likewise dedicated to St. Gregory, *"Lerink' amenayn . . ."* (All you mountains . . .) (*Sharakan*, p. 280; trans., Selection XII). For more on the Caves of Manē, see further below on Mount Sepuh, in the third part of the Introduction.

[96]In her survey of classical Armenian literature, S. [P.] Hairapetian (Hayrapetean) observes that nationalism and piety converge in Armenian hymns, more so from the eleventh century; *A History of Armenian Literature from Ancient Times to the Nineteenth Century* (Delmar, NY: Caravan Books, 1995), pp. 197, 265 (= *eadem, Hay hin ew mijnadarean grakanut'ean patmut'iwn* [Los Angeles: privately published, 1986], pp. 249, 340). Such convergence is discernible in Armenian literature from its inception in the fifth century.

[97]*Patmut'iwn Lusaworch'in ew Trdatay T'agaworin* (History of the Illuminator and of King Trdat), in Jerusalem manuscript no. 1647, pp. 206–281.

[98]Text in Ē. Khondkaryan, ed., *Mkrtich'Naghash* (Erevan: Arm. Academy of Sciences, 1965), pp. 105–106; Eng. trans., S. P. Cowe, "An Allegorical Poem by Mkrtich' Naghash and Its Models," *Journal of the Society for Armenian Studies* 4 (1988–1989) 143–144.

[99]Among short introductions to our author, see A. Srapyan (Erznkats'i Srapyan, Srapean), "Hovhannes Erznkats'i," in Ē. B. Aghayan et al., eds., *Hay Mshakuyt'i Nshanavor Gortsich'nerĕ* (The Prominent Shapers of Armenian Culture) (Erevan: State University of Erevan, 1976), pp. 343–352; *eadem et al.*, "Hovhannes Erznkats'i," in V. H. Hambardzumyan et al., eds., *Haykakan Sovetakan Hanragitaran* (Soviet Armenian Encyclopedia), 12 vols. (Erevan: Arm. Academy of Sciences, 1974–1986) 6:559–560; *eadem, Yovhannēs Erznkats'i-Pluz, Keank'ĕ ew Gortsĕ* (Y. E.-P: His Life and Works) (Erevan: Zvart'nots', 1993); *eadem*, "Yovhannēs Erznkats'i-Pluz," *"Gandzasar" Theological Review* 6 (1996) 421–425; *eadem*, "Yovhannēs Erznkats'i-Pluz," in H. Ayvazyan et al., eds., *K'ristonya Hayastan, Hanragitaran* (Christian Armenia: Encyclopedia) (Erevan: Haykakan Hanragitarani Glkhavor Khmbagrut'yun, 2002), pp. 619–624; cf. H. T'amrazyan, *Hay K'nnadatut'yun, V–XV Dar* (Armenian [Literary] Criticism: V–XV Centuries), 2 vols. (Erevan: Sovetakan Grogh, 1983–1985) 2:389–456; Pogharean, *Hay Groghner,* pp. 320–323; Hayrapetean, *Hay hin ew mijnadarean grakanut'ean patmut'iwn,* pp. 462–469.

[100]For centuries there was considerable confusion between the works of our author and those of a late contemporary named Yovhannēs (Erznkats'i) Tsortsorets'i (1283–1340), who abridged our author's grammatical *Compilation* and long outlived him. For more on the latter author, see L. G. Khach'erean, ed., *Yovhannēs Tsortsorets'i (1288–1340 t't'), Hamaṙawt Tesut'iwn K'erakani* (Y. TS. [1283–1340]: An Abridged Treatment of [the] *Grammar*) (Los Angeles and Glendale: Alco Printing, 1984). Following L. Khach'ikyan's colophonic elucidations (*ZhD-dari Hayeren Dzeṙagreri Hishatakaranner* [Colophons of 14th-Century Armenian Manuscripts] [Erevan: Arm. Academy of Sciences, 1950], pp. 111, 125, 146, 173, and 649—unaccounted for by A. K. Sanjian, *Colophons of Armenian Manuscripts, 1301–1480* [Cambridge, MA: Harvard University Press, 1969]), Srapyan sorts out the confusion and provides the texts of seventeen of our author's metrical compositions along with a list of sixty-one works in prose: *Hovhannes Erznkats'i, Usumnasirut'yun ev Bnagrer* (H. E.: A Study and Texts) (Erevan: Haypethrat, 1958); see especially pp. 25–38. See also *eadem, Hovhannes Erznkats'i, Bank' Ch'ap'av* (above, n. 93). For other samples of his poetry, see the anthology of *hayrenner* (widespread compositions of quatrains in couplets or *kafa,* each line in pentedecasyllabic meter of 2+3+2 // 3+2+3 syllables), prepared by A. Sh. Mnats'akanyan, *Hayrenner* (Erevan: Matenadaran, 1995), pp. 386–439. For a partial list of Erznkats'i's published works, see R. W. Thomson, *A Bibliography of Classical Armenian Literature to 1500 AD,* Corpus Christianorum (Turnhout: Brepols, 1995), pp. 221–222. See also Y. K'iwrtean, "Yovhannēs Erznkats'i," *Bazmavep* 80 (1929) 166–171; *idem*, "Yovhannēs Erznkats'i-Tsortsorets'i," *Bazmavep* 112 (1954) 242–245; *idem*, "Yovhannēs Erznkats'i Pluz ew Yovhannēs Erznkats'i Tsortsorets'i," *Bazmavep* 116 (1958) 186–196, *idem, Eriza ew Ekegheats' Gawaṙ* (Eriza and the District of Ekegheats'), 2 vols. (Venice: Mkhit'arean Tparan, 1953) 1:168–188, 204–224. Earlier studies tend to perpetuate the confusion between our author and Yovhannēs Erznkats'i surnamed Tsortsorets'i (and vice versa); cf. Gh. M. Alishan, "Erznka ew Yovhannēs Erznkats'i," in *idem, Yushikk'Hayreneats'Hayots'* (Memoirs from the Armenian Fatherland), 2 vols., 2nd ed. (Venice: S. Ghazar, 1920) 1:401–432; so also M. Abeghyan, *Hayots' Hin Grakanut'yan Patmut'yun* (History of Early Armenian Literature], 2 vols. [Erevan: Arm. Academy of Sciences, 1944–1946] 2:299–308). On the whole, the rhetorical and poetic skill of our voluminous author is more amply attested and documented than that of any of his contemporaries.

[101]See the colophon in A. S. Mat'evosyan, ed., *Hayeren Dzeṙagreri Hishatakaranner, ZhG Dar* (Colophons of Armenian Manuscripts, 13th Century) (Erevan: Arm. Academy of Sciences, 1984), pp. 339–340 (no. 279 = Erevan manuscript no. 823). Cf. Jerusalem manuscript no. 3392, pp. 493–496, colophon of the year 1280 by the scribe Yovhannēs at work in the same church, naming its builders: Bishop Sargis and his son Baron Yovhannēs; see also K'iwrtean, *Eriza ew Ekegheats' Gawaṙ,* 1:174–175.

[102]This he states in a few lines in the lengthy poem "Yaghags Erknayin Zarduts'" (On the Heavenly Adornments), in Srapyan, *Hovhannes Erznkats'i, Bank' Ch'ap'av*, pp. 258–259. He was probably related to the magistrates of the city, the Archbishop Sargis and his son Baron Yovhannēs who, as allies with the Mongols, were killed by the Turks in 1276. They were succeeded by the sons of Yovhannēs: Nersēs becoming archbishop and Gregoris, Baron. In a letter of condolences and restrained congratulations, Erznkats'i refers to himself as a relative; "T'ught' ař Ishkhans Ekegheats' Gawaři" (A Letter to the Rulers of the Province of Ekegheats') in Ē. M. Baghdasaryan, ed., *Hovhannes Erznkats'in ev Nra Khratakan Ardzakē* (Hovhannes Erznkats'i and His Hortatory Prose) (Erevan: Arm. Academy of Sciences, 1977), pp. 204–219.

[103]See Grigor Daranaghts'i, *Zhamanakagrut'iwn* (Chronography) (Jerusalem: St. James Press, 1915), p. 33. On the significance of the title, see R. W. Thomson, "*Vardapet* in the Early Armenian Church," Le Muséon 75 (1962) 367–384.

[104]*Sharakan*, pp. 565–571.

[105]Text in Srapyan, *Hovhannes Erznkats'i, Bank' Ch'ap'av*, pp. 200–233.

[106]For the text of these hymns see *Sharakan*, pp. 264–278 (trans., Selection XI), 568–570; cf. Srapyan, *Hovhannes Erznkats'i, Bank' Ch'ap'av*, pp. 123–132.

[107]The last compilation of the *Sharaknots'* was by St. Gregory of Tat'ew (d. 1409), the last of the great *vardapets* whose teachings are influential in the Armenian Church and the last of her revered saints.

[108]The contents seem to derive some of their inspiration from the panegyric attributed to St. John Chrysostom (*Sop'erk'*, 4:70–72).

[109]The latter was composed in 618/619 on the occasion of the transfer of the relics to the church built for St. Hřip'simē near Ējmiatsin (*Sharakan*, pp. 573–582).

[110]Text in *Sharakan*, pp. 278–281, and Srapyan, *Hovhannes Erznkats'i, Bank' Ch'ap'av*, pp. 130–132.

[111]Text in Srapyan, *Hovhannes Erznkats'i, Bank' Ch'ap'av*, pp. 115–116 (trans., Selection XIII).

[112]Cited by S. Vryonis, Jr., *The Decline of Medieval Hellenism in Asia Minor and the Process of Islamization from the Eleventh through the Fifteenth Century* (Berkeley, Los Angeles, London: University of California Press, 1971), p. 29 n. 151 (ed. van den Wyngaert, p. 327). For more on the earthquakes affecting Erznka, see further below. Vryonis also cites Qazwini (ed. Le Strange, pp. 95–98), who tells that the Seljuk 'Ala' al-Din rebuilt Erznka, Amasya, and parts of Konya (p. 221 n. 471) in the thirteenth century—presumably following an earthquake.

[113]For a comparative table of town populations, see Vryonis, *The Decline of Medieval Hellenism in Asia Minor*, p. 29 and n. 150.

[114]Alishan, *Yushikk' Hayreneats' Hayots'*, 1:405–408.

[115]Vryonis, *The Decline of Medieval Hellenism in Asia Minor*, p. 53.

[116]L. Khach'ikyan, "Erznka k'aghak'i 'Eghbarts' miabanut'ean' kanonagrut'yunĕ" (The By-laws of the "Community of Brothers" in the City of Erznka), *Banber Matenadarani* 6 (1962) 365–377; the lead manuscript of the text was penned before the author's death in 1293 (Erevan manuscript no. 2329, dated 1291; text, pp. 371–376).

[117]For more on these organizations, among which the Dervishes were prominent, see Khach'ikyan's introduction to the text of the "By-Laws," especially pp. 366–368, and Vryonis, *The Decline of Medieval Hellenism in Asia Minor*, pp. 396–402; note especially the references to Ibn Battuta's travels of 1331–1333 (ed. Gibb) in both sources.

[118]*K'iwrtean, Eriza ew Ekegheats' Gawař*, pp. 179–180.

[119]Vryonis, *The Decline of Medieval Hellenism in Asia Minor*, p. 238 n. 572, citing the thirteenth-century *Chronicon syriacum* of Bar Hebraeus, a.k.a. Gregory Abu'l-Faraj (ed. Budge, 1:408).

[120]Vryonis, *The Decline of Medieval Hellenism in Asia Minor*, p. 239 and n. 574, citing Ibn Battuta (ed. Gibb, 2:437).

[121]For the rest of the record in subsequent centuries and the later history of the city, see the

entry in H. S. Ēp'rikean, *Patkerazard Bnashkharhik Baṙaran* (Pictorial Topographical Dictionary), 2 vols., 2nd ed. (Venice: S. Ghazar, 1903–1905) 1:654–664.

[122]Probably after another sack of the city by the Tatars; see Kirakos Gandzakets'i, *History of the Armenians*, 59 (ed. Melik'-Ohanjanyan, *Patmut'iwn*, p. 375; trans. Bedrosian, *Kirakos Gandzakets'i's History of the Armenians*, p. 312).

[123]N. Bogharian (Pogharean), *Grand Catalogue of St. James Manuscripts*, 11 vols. (Jerusalem: St. James Press, 1966–1991) 4:552–555; cf. N. Adonts' [Adontz], *Aruest Dioniseay K'erakani* (Dionysius' *Ars Grammatica*) (St. Petersburg: Kayserakan Tparan, 1915), pp. lxxxii–xci, and Mat'evosyan, *Hayeren Dzeṙagreri Hishatakaranner, ZhG Dar*, pp. 706–713 (no. 574; both based on Erevan manuscript no. 2266, dated 17th century). For a study on the preface, see A. Terian, "A History of Armenian Grammatical Activity: An Account by Hovhannes Yerznkats'i," in J. A. C. Greppin, ed., *Proceedings of the Fourth International Conference on Armenian Linguistics, Anatolian and Caucasian Studies* (Delmar, NY: Caravan Books, 1992), pp. 213–219. For the full text of the work, see the edition by L. G. Khach'erean, *Yovhannēs Erznkats'i (1230–1293 t't'), Hawak'umn Meknut'ean K'erakani* (Y. E. [1230–1293]: Compilation of Commentary on Grammar) (Los Angeles and Glendale: Alco Printing, 1983), and R. R. Ervine, *Yovhannēs Erznkac'i Pluz's 'Compilation of Commentary on Grammar',* 3 vols. Columbia University Dissertation, 1988.

[124]«Նախադրութիւն բանի, Հաւարման մեկնութեան քերականի, եւ աղերս խնդրոյ աշխատաւորին Յովհաննիսի, առ սպասաւորդ բանի» Minor variants are discernible in Jerusalem manuscript no. 2392, where the title of the preface reads: «Նախադրութիւն բանի ի գրցցս պատճառի, Հաւարման մեկնութեան քերականին, եւ աղերս խնդրոյ աշխատաւորիս Յովհաննիսի, առ սպասաւորդ բանի» "A foreword to show the reason for the *Compilation of Commentary on Grammar*, and an address by Hovhannēs, who has labored on this subject, to you stewards of the word."

[125]M. Aghawnuni, "Yovhannēs Vardapet Erznkats'i (Ukhtawor Erusaghēmi—1281)" (Y. V. E.: [Jerusalem Pilgrim—1281]), *Sion* 12 (1938) 213–219.

[126]Gh. M. Alishan, *Sisuan ew Levon Metsagorts* (Venice: S. Ghazar, 1885), p. 224.

[127]The *Compilation* could have been completed a year earlier. Its dedication to the "king" in 1293 poses no problem since the monastically minded Het'um II is consistantly referred to as king even between his reigns (1289–1293, 1295–1296, 1299–1301, 1301–1306) and after his final abdication; see Mat'evosyan, *Hayeren Dzeṙagreri Hishatakaranner, ZhG Dar*, pp. 706–713; cf. Ervine, *Compilation of Commentary on Grammar,*' p. 125 n. 167. For the text and trans. of the dedication, see Ervine's comprehensive work, pp. 433–440, 727–735 (cf. Khach'eryan, *Compilation of Commentary on Grammar*, pp. 299–303).

[128]The critical texts of several of his hortatory writings are provided by Baghdasaryan, *Hovhannēs Erznkats'i and His Hortatory Prose;* among them note especially "Khrat Hasarakats' K'ristonēits'" (Exhortation to All Christians), pp. 143–203, which is an abridged and simplified version of Canon Law for the most part and exists in more than a hundred manuscripts, including one penned during the author's lifetime (Erevan no. 2329, dated 1291), available in Western Arm. trans. by A. Daniēlean, *Khrat Bolor K'ristoneanerun* (Exhortation to All Christians) (Antelias: Armenian Catholicosate of Cilicia, 1984). Note also his *Yaghags Miabanut'ean Eghbarts'* (Concerning the Community of Brothers) in Ē. Baghdasaryan, ed., "Yovhannēs Pluz-Erznkats'u 'Yaghags Miabanut'ean Eghbarts'' Khratakan T'ught'ē" (The Exhortatory Epistle of Y. P.-E.: "Concerning the Community of Brothers"), *"Gandzasar" Theological Review* 6 (1996) 454–472 (especially pp. 459–472), a work that exists in a single manuscript known to us (Erevan manuscript no. 728, penned in Gandzak in 1621—not to be confused with the bylaws for the brotherhood in Erznka).

[129]Srapyan, *Hovhannes Erznkats'i, Bank' Ch'ap'av*, p. 13.

[130]On the year of his death, see Mat'evosyan, *Hayeren Dzeṙagreri Hishatakaranner, ZhG Dar*, pp. 714–715.

[131]The Armenian version of Agat'angeghos makes no mention of St. Gregory's burial(s)

after recounting his death on Mount Sepuh (891). For the legends surrounding the Saint's death, burial(s), and the discovery of his remains, see Khorenats'i, *History of the Armenians*, 2.91, relying on a tradition attested in the Karshuni version of Agat'angeghos (*Vk* 293–299; Esbroeck, "Un nouveau témoin du livre d'Agathange," pp. 93–94). For the subsequent discovery and veneration of his relics, see above, n. 45. The *Buzandaran* places the burial of St. Gregory "in the district of Daranaghik', in the village of T'ordan," and that of his younger son and successor Aristakēs, who apparently preceded his father in death, "in the district of Ekegheats', in the town of T'il" (3.2). As for Vrt'anēs, the elder son and second successor of St. Gregory, his body was brought "to the village of T'ordan in the district of Daranaghik'. *And there they laid his holy bones to rest next to the great patriarch Grigor*" (3.11; trans. Garsoïan, p. 82; *italics* mine). The years of St. Vrt'anēs's pontificate are generally accepted to be 333–341, though 327–342 are more likely (following the chronology of Ananean [Ananian]).

[132]Gandzakets'i, *History of the Armenians*, 1 (ed. Melik'-Ohanjanyan, *Patmut'iwn*, p. 14; trans. Bedrosian, *Kirakos Gandzakets'i's History of the Armenians*, p. 11; trans. here, Selection X).

[133]Prior to the reforms of Catholicos Yovhan(nēs) Mandakuni (in office 484–490), this single feast of St. Gregory was celebrated on March 9, as a fixed day. Mandakuni's reforms made it moveable, to the fifth Saturday of the Lenten period, thus falling between March 1 and April 10 (with Easter falling between March 22 and April 25, a 35-day variable). The other feast days of St. Gregory were introduced at a later time. Eventually, the fifth/sixth Saturday of the Lenten period was relegated to commemorating the saint's confinement in the pit, and the old feast was moved to its present place in the liturgical calendar. For the early history of the Gregorid feasts, see R. V. Vardanyan, Hayots' Tonats'uyts'ē (4–18rd darer) (The Church Calendar of the Armenians: 4th–18th Centuries) (Erevan: Arm. Academy of Sciences, 1999), pp. 589–612.

[134]M. Ormanean, *Azgapatum* (National History), 3 vols. (Constantinople: Tēr-Nersēsean and Jerusalem: St. James Press, 1912–1927; repr. Beirut: Sevan, 1959–1961) 2:3065–66, 3101–09 (§§2101, 2124–28). Sundays in the Armenian Church are considered perpetual Easter and are reserved for celebrating events in the life of Christ (Tērunakan tōnk'). As for "great" saints, they are commemorated on Saturdays; others on Mondays, Tuesdays and Thursdays (Wednesdays and Fridays are for fasting).

[135]The Armenian version of Agat'angeghos leaves no doubt about the fact that the first Armenian churches built by St. Gregory were at Ashtishat, an early center of Syriac Christianity in Western Armenia and the patriarchal see until the late fourth century; *History*, 809–816, 836 (cf. *Buzandaran*, 3.3, 14, 19). The politically motivated move to Vagharshapat is legitimized through the Saint's vision, the descent of the heavenly "man, tall and fearful" and the subsequent vision regarding Shoghakat' (Agat'angeghos, *History*, 731–756, and Thomson's notes to sections 735–736 especially, pp. 478–479). Given the Syriac roots of Armenian Christianity and the established tradition at Ashtishat, it is not surprising that the Karshuni version (*Vk*) and one of the Greek texts (*Vo*) omit the vision in its entirety; whereas the other Greek text (*Vg*) and one of the Arabic texts (*Va*) place the vision at Artashat, the site of Gregory's confinement, "which somewhat spoils the purpose of the vision" (Thomson, *Agathangelos*, p. lvi). On the prior name of the cathedral at Vagharshapat (called Ējmiatsin in later centuries), based upon the subsequent identification of the heavenly "Man, tall and fearful" [Agat'angeghos, *History*, 735] with the Only-begotten), see Ormanean, *Azgapatum*, 1:97–98 (§66); A. Khachatrian, *L'architecture arménienne du IVe au VIe siècle*, Bibliothèque des Cahiers Archéologiques 7 (Paris: Klincksiek, 1971), p. 85. On the memorials built at Vagharshapat by St. Gregory and the elemental basis of his mystic vision, see *idem*, "Données historiques sur la fondation d'Edjmiatsin à la lumière des feuilles récentes," *Handes Amsorya* 76 (1962) 100–106, 227–250, 425–452. For the significance of the feast of Shoghakat', see the panegyric by the eleventh-century *vardapet* Anania Sanahnets'i (wrongly attributed either to Anania Shirakats'i or to Anania Narekats'i), "Eranelwoy hōr Ananiayi hogevarzh p'ilisop'ayi Nerboghean asats'eal i surb Kat'oghikē Ekeghets'i, or ē i Nor K'aghak', or ayzhm koch'i Vagharshapat . . ." (Panegyric by the Blessed Father Anania, the

Spiritual Philosopher, on the Holy Cathedral in Nor K'aghak', Nowadays Called Vagharshapat
. . .), in *Girk' or koch'i Zhoghovatsu* (Book Called Miscellanea) (Constantinople: Astuatsatur
Kostandnupolsets'i, 1747), pp. 441–483 (repr. 1793, pp. 403–442; and A. Ayvazean, ed., *Chrak'agh* 1
[1859] 265–272, 291–298, 323–332, 359–366, 399–406).

[136]See the preceding note. The year 484 is a crucial time in the history of Ējmiatsin. The year
that saw the transfer of the see to Dwin by Catholicos Yovhan(nēs) Mandakuni (in office
484–490) was also the year when the *marzpan* Vahan Mamikonean completely rebuilt the cathedral (Ghazar, *History,* p. 157; Thomson, *Łazar,* p. 217; cf. Khachatrian, *L'architecture arménienne,*
p. 87; *idem,* "Données historiques sur la fondation d'Edjmiatsin," col. 107). On the history of the
times, see K. Maksoudian, *Chosen of God,* pp. 44–50.

[137]The enshrining was at Ashtishat in Tarōn and Bagawan in Bagrewand, according to
Agat'angeghos, *History,* 810–816, 836. Following local tradition, Erznkats'i claims that the
enshrining of the relics of St. John the Baptist was on Mount Sepuh (§38). Similar claims were
made at other medieval monasteries in Armenia.

[138]See above, nn. 45, 131.

[139]See the last of Erznkats'i's colophons to the *Compilation of Commentary on Grammar,* in
Mat'evosyan, *Hayeren Dzeřagreri Hishatakaranner, ZhG Dar,* pp. 709–713.

[140]See, e.g., the account by Kirakos Gandzakets'i, *History of the Armenians,* 20–35, 59 (ed.
Melik'-Ohanjanyan, *Patmut'iwn,* pp. 231–284, 372–377; trans. Bedrosian, *Kirakos Gandzakets'i's
History of the Armenians,* pp. 193–246, 309–313), and Vardan Arewelts'i, *Historical Compilation*
(Arm. text in *Vardan Vardapet Metsn: Hawak'umn Patmut'ean Vardanay Vardapeti, lusabaneal* (Var-
dan Vardapet the Great: The Collected History of Vardan Vardapet, Annotated [by Gh. Alishan,
the unnamed editor]) (Venice: Mekhitarists, 1862), especially pp. 155–159, on his meeting with
Hulagu Khan (Eng. trans., R. W. Thomson, "The Historical Compilation of Vardan Arewelc'i,"
Dumbarton Oaks Papers 43 [1989] 125–226); see also Grigor Vardapet Aknerts'i, *Patmut'iwn
T'at'arats'* (History of the Tatars), N. Pogharean, ed. (Jerusalem: St. James Press, 1974); also
known as *Patmut'iwn vasn Azgin Netoghats',* R. P. Blake and R. N. Frye, eds. and trans., *Gregory
of Agner: History of the Nation of Archers* (Cambridge, MA: Harvard University Press, 1954), unfor-
tunately translated from a poorer edition; see also the near-contemporeneous account by Het'um
Kořikosts'i (Anton), written originally in French *(La Flor des estoires de la Terre d'Orient [Liber
Historiarum Partium Orientis]),* in 1307, trans. from Latin into Arm. by M. Awgerean, *Het'um
Patmich' T'at'arats'* (Het'um the Historian of the Tatars) (Venice: S. Ghazar, 1842). A primary
source for all the cited works is the now lost history by Vanakan Vardapet, the teacher of Gandzakets'i, Arewelts'i, and Aknerts'i—among others (Arewelts'i, in turn, was the teacher of
Erznkats'i). For an excellent assessment of the medieval Armenian sources, see R. Bedrosian,
"Armenia during the Seljuk and Mongol Periods," in R. G. Hovannisian, ed., *The Armenian People from Ancient to Modern Times. Vol. I: The Dynastic Periods: From Antiquity to the Fourteenth Century* (New York: St. Martin's Press, 1997), pp. 241–271.

[141]For comparable accounts especially in eastern Anatolia, see Vryonis, *The Decline of
Medieval Hellenism in Asia Minor,* pp. 80–85, 155–160 (cf. 175 n. 245), 244–249, 418–421.

[142]Vryonis, *The Decline of Medieval Hellenism in Asia Minor,* p. 226 n. 493 (citing O. Turan,
"Les souverains seljoukides et leurs sujet non-musulmans," *Studia Islamica* 1 [1953] 94).

[143]Vryonis, *The Decline of Medieval Hellenism in Asia Minor,* p. 271 n. 761 (citing the Vilayet-
name, ed. Gross, pp. 71–73); cf. pp. 281 n. 791 and 374.

[144]Alishan, *Sisuan ew Levon Metsagorts,* p. 164.

[145]For the various versions and the two recensions, see Thomson, *The Teaching of St. Gregory*
(rev. ed.), pp. 3–5; cf. Winkler, "Our Present Knowledge of the History of Agat'angełos," pp.
125–141.

[146]See above, n. 135.

[147]Khosrov's regnal years were hitherto problematic; for a consensus in scholarship, see
above, n. 26 (the work of Toumanoff especially).

[148]On the much debated beginning of Trdat's reign, which is invariably linked to that of the Christianization of Armenia, see the sources cited above, n. 26.

[149]The number of years is given variously in Agat'angeghos: thirteen (122, 124, 132), fifteen (215, 233), "many years" (217). So also in the various versions.

[150]The earlier religious center was at Ashtishat, in Western Armenia (see Agat'angeghos, *History*, 814; *Buzandaran*, 3.14), as were also the Gregorid domains, in westernmost Armenia. For more on the move to Vagharshapat, see above, nn. 135–136.

[151]Cf. Khorenats'i, *History of the Armenians*, 2.90–91. Both Agat'angeghos and Khorenats'i refer to the place as "the mountain called the Caves of Manē."

[152]Cf. *Buzandaran*, 3.6 (applied to Grigoris, the martyred grandson of St. Gregory) and Koriwn, *Life of Mashtots'*, 25 (90.11–16, applied to the founder of the Armenian letters). St. Gregory died in 328; see Anancan's (Ananian's) studies, cited above, n. 26.

[153]*Buzandaran*, 3.11–12; 4.14. These domains were passed on to the Mamikoneans following the death of the last patriarch of the Gregorid house, St. Sahak the Great (*ca.* 387–439). His daughter, Sahakanush, was married to Hamazasp Mamikonean.

[154]Khorenats'i, *History of the Armenians*, 2.91; for later embellishments, see M. Awgerean, ed., *Liakatar Vark' ew Vkayabanut'iwn Srbots'* (The Complete Lives and Testimony of the Saints), 12 vols. (Venice: 1810–1815) 3:130–138, and the study by B. Outtier, "Movsēs après Movsēs," in D. Kouymjian, ed., *Movsēs Xorenac'i et l'historiographie arménienne des origines*, Catholicossat arménien de Cilicie, 1700ème centenaire de la proclamation du Christianisme en Arménie 7 (Antélias: Catholicossat arménien de Cilicie, 2000), pp. 99–112. The Karshuni version of Agat'angeghos (*Vk* 291) is the only other ancient source that refers to Manē in association with the martyred nuns, alleging that she escaped at the time of their martyrdom. Her name appears to be somewhat related to Nanē, a goddess closely associated with Anahit and whose temple stood in nearby T'il in the province of Ekegheats', one of the Gregorid burial grounds in the fourth century (see Russell, *Zoroastrianism in Armenia*, p. 339).

[155]See above, n. 131.

[156]Cf. his "Preface" to the *Compilation of Commentary on Grammar*, where he refers to the monasteries around Mount Sepuh in plural: "hasoyts' i learn hangstean surb Lusaworch'in meroy srboyn Grigori yanapatsn" ([the grace of God's mercy] brought [us] to the monasteries at the mountain of the rest of our holy Illuminator, St. Gregory); text in Khach'erean, *Hawak'umn Meknut'ean K'erakani*, p. 83; see also Gh. M. Alishan, *Hayapatum* (Armenian History), 2 vols. (Venice: S. Ghazar, 1901) 2:510 (cited by Khach'erean, p. 317 n. 7).

[157]J.-M. Thierry, "Le Mont Sepuh: Étude archéologique," *Revue des études arméniennes*, n.s. 21 (1988–1989) 385–449.

[158]«Արժանապատիւ քահանայապետն Գրիգորիոս իւրովք ձեռոք յօրինեաց զփայտակերպ խորանն սուրբ յանուն Արեգականն Արդարութեան Արուսեկին եւ Կարապետին Յովհաննու» (*Arzhanapatiw k'ahanayapetn Grigorios iwrovk' dzerōk' yōrineats' zp'aytakerp khorann surb yanun Aregakann Ardarut'ean Arusekin ew Karapetin Yovhannu*). "The high priest worthy of honor, Gregory, built with his own hands the holy shrine resembling the Wood, in the name of the Sun of Righteousness, the Morning Star, and [in the name] of John the Forerunner."

[159]On the remains of this church, see Thierry, "Le Mont Sepuh: Étude archéologique," pp. 400–401.

[160]*Ibid.*, pp. 416–417 (a possible confusion may be detected at the bottom of p. 401, where the colophon in question leaves little doubt about the chapel being at *Awagavank'*); see Mat'evosyan, *Hayeren Dzeřagreri Hishatakaranner*, JhG Dar, pp. 14–17 (no. 2, colophon of the year 1201 by Yovhannēs Daranaghts'i, in Jerusalem manuscript no. 3274); cf. Bogharian (Pogharean), *Grand Catalogue*, 10:73.

[161]Agat'angeghos, *History*, 810–816, 836.

162 *"Lerink' amenayn . . ."* (All you mountains . . .) (*Sharakan*, p. 280; trans., Selection XII); cf. Agat'angeghos, *History*, 813.

163 *Sop'erk',* 5:73; more in Selection IX. See Thierry, "Le Mont Sepuh," pp. 407–409 and 438–439, figs. 17–19.

164 A unique story is preserved in Jerusalem manuscript no. 1650 (published by Bogharian [Poghorean], *Grand Catalogue*, 5:475), according to which "the emperor of the Greeks" sent princes to look for the remains of St. Gregory. As their search proved to be disappointing, one of them asked a Kurdish shepherd, who was blind in both eyes, about the place. He responded: "Take me to Mount Sepuh, for at night there burns a light like the sun, at a famous spot where there is a small fountain." When taken there, he washes his eyes and begins to see and goes on to point out a place nearby. The princes marvel at the Saint's ability to perform miracles even in death.

165 See, e.g., the ancient source on Greater Armenia utilized in the *Ashkharhats'oyts'* of Anania Shirakats'i: A. Abrahamyan, ed., *Anania Shirakats'u Matenagrut'yunĕ* (The Writings of A. Sh.) (Erevan: Matenadaran, 1944), p. 349; cf. the annotated trans. by A. G. Abrahamyan and G. B. Petrosyan, *Anania Shirakats'i, Matenagrut'yun* (A. Sh.: Writings) (Erevan: Sovetakan Grogh, 1979), pp. 291–292; Eng. trans., R. H. Hewsen, *The Geography of Ananias of Širak (Ašxarhac'oyc'): The Long and the Short Recensions*, Beihefte zum Tübinger Atlas des vorderen Orients, Reihe B (Geisteswissenschaften) 77 (Wiesbaden: Reichert, 1992), pp. 59–60.

166 Cf. Isocrates *Panegyricus* 13; *Panathenaicus* 36; Pseudo-Cicero *Ad Herennium* 3.6.11; Philo of Alexandria *De Vita Mosis* 2.1.

167 For the Classical tradition, see, e.g., Anaximenes *Rhetorica ad Alexandrum* 1440b5–1441b29; Aristotle *Rhetoric* 1366a23–1368a37; Cicero *De Oratore* 2.84.340–86.350; *Partitiones Oratoriae* 21.71–23.82; Pseudo-Cicero *Ad Herennium* 3.6.10–8.15; and Quintilian *Institutio Oratoria* 3.7.1–28 and 8.4.1–29.

168 *Sharakan*, pp. 554–560; trans., Selection I. For more on Movsēs Siwnets'i and his hymns, see Poghorean, *Hay Groghner*, pp. 109–110.

169 The later, Karshuni version of Agat'angeghos (*Vk* 8) claims that St. Gregory was conceived at the hill where St. Thaddaeus was martyred; Esbroeck, "Un nouveau témoin du livre d'Agathange," p. 24. So also in Khorenats'i, *History of the Armenians*, 2.74: "And there [by the grave of the holy apostle in the plain of Artaz] they say the mother of our holy and great Illuminator conceived. Therefore he received the grace of that same apostle, and having been begotten beside his grave he completed what was lacking in his spiritual labors" (trans. Thomson). This providential birth of St. Gregory, to which several subsequent writers allude, such as in the panegyric on the Saint by Vardan Vardapet Arewelts'i (*Sop'erk',* 5:46, 49), is contemplated also in this panegyric (§§5, 21–22, 24).

170 Precious little of the twelve tortures of St. Gregory is contemplated in the author's speech to King Trdat in an imagined presence, chastizing him for having excessively mistreated the heavenly emissary (§27). Far less is mentioned near the end: a fleeting allusion to the eleventh torture, that of molten lead being poured over him; and the twelfth, the commitment to the pit (§55).

171 *Sop'erk',* 5:85–164.

172 Srapyan, *Hovhannes Erznkats'i, Bank' Ch'ap'av*, pp. 136–199.

173 Cf. Poghorean's reasons for favoring prose over verse in editions of Narekats'i's *Soliloquies*, in Tsovakan (Poghorean), *Vanatur*, pp. 159–168. Free verse as a literary development is rather late.

Panegyric
Recited in Praise of Saint Gregory
the Illuminator of the Armenians
by Yovhannēs Vardapet Erznkatsʻi

[Proemial adulation]

I Ց[^1]

Rejoice, holy Church, reveling profusely in endless joy,[^2] wondrously new

§1

[^1]: The initial letters of the first seven strophes or sections in this proemial adulation of St. Gregory yield an onomastic acrostic, spelling out the author's name, ՅՈՀԱՆԷՍ (Yohanēs). This is his signature to the composition as a whole.

[^2]: The opening words of the panegyric are reminiscent of a hymn in alphabetical acrostic by Erznkatsʻi, found in the Armenian hymnal (*Sharakan Hogewor Ergotsʻ Surb ew Ughghapʻaṙ Ekeghetsʻwoys Hayastaneaytsʻ* [Hymnal of Spiritual Songs of the Holy Orthodox Armenian Church] [Jerusalem: St. James Press, 1936; reprinted New York: St. Vartan Press, 1986], pp. 264–274). The hymn, *"Aysōr zuarchatsʻeal tsʻntsay ekeghetsʻi* . . ." (Reveling today the Church rejoices . . .), is likewise dedicated to St. Gregory and used for the feast commemorating his placement in the dungeon (trans., Selection XI; for a comparable acrostic composition by the author, see below, §18). The opening words of the panegyric, like the hymn, seem to have been inspired by Ps. 132:9 (131:9 LXX), one of the Lectionary readings for the feast of the discovery of the Saint's remains (*Giwt Nshkharatsʻ*), on which see the third part of the Introduction. Other hymns by our author also bear close resemblance to certain parts of the panegyric, e.g., *"Or zloys anchaṙ shnorhatsʻ* . . ." (Who [caused] the light of indescribable graces . . .), dedicated to the great-great-grandson of St. Gregory, St. Nersēs the Great (Catholicos, *ca.* 353–373); text in *Sharakan*, pp. 565–571; cf. the versification by A. Erznkatsʻi Srapyan, *Hovhannes Erznkatsʻi, Bankʻ Chʻapʻav* (H. E.: Words in Verse) (Erevan: Sovetakan Grogh, 1986), pp. 123–130; 134–135. Note also pp. 115–116, where she provides the text of a long-lost composition by our author on the suffering of St. Gregory: *"Tagh Srboyn Grigori Lusaworchʻin Hayotsʻ"* (Ode to St. Gregory the Illuminator of the Armenians), in onomastic acrostic, yielding the name *"Grigorios Lusaworichʻ Hayotsʻ"* (Gregorios the Illuminator of the Armenians; trans., Selection XIII). Erznkatsʻi has yet another hymn, also dedicated to St. Gregory and focused on Mount Sepuh (*Sharakan*, pp. 130–132; trans., Selection XII), in keeping with §29 in this panegyric.

and bright heaven,[3] adorned with luminaries fashioned by God.[4] For the intelligible Sun risen in you[5]—the delightful moon a nocturnal com-

---

[3]The notion that the Church is a symbolic representation of heaven is commonplace in early Christian theology; see *"Ouranos"* (Heaven) 10.g. in G. W. H. Lampe, ed., *A Patristic Greek Lexicon* (Oxford: Clarendon, 1961), p. 979. The symbolism recurs in several of the author's hymns; see the preceding comment.

[4]That is, the saints, including St. Gregory. Much of what follows is based on the traditional belief that the souls of the righteous dead shine like stars in heaven, a belief derived from Dan. 12:3; cf. "saints who have become as stars in the new heaven" (§11), and King Trdat becoming a star (§27). Erznkats'i, however, is quite knowledgeable about astronomy, as his lengthy poem *"Yaghags Erknayin Zarduts'"* (On the Heavenly Adornments) or *"Yaghags Erkni"* (On Heaven) indicates (in Srapyan, *Hovhannes Erznkats'i*, pp. 234–269).

[5]As in §11, the designation is evidently short for "the Sun of Righteousness" (§38), a common epithet applied to Christ since the rise of Jewish Messianism, owing to Mal. 4:2 (as in *The Teaching of Saint Gregory*, 566, 684; for more on the latter work, to which there are several references and possible allusions in the panegyric, see the second comment at §6, where these references begin, and R. W. Thomson, *The Teaching of St. Gregory*, rev. ed., AVANT: Treasures of the Armenian Christian Tradition 1 [New Rochelle: St. Nersess Armenian Seminary, 2001], especially pp. 56–61). Some further biblical imagery of the sun and the moon seems to be contemplated here, as in *The Teaching of Saint Gregory*, 676–678; i.e., Joel 2:31, "The sun will be turned to darknness and the moon to blood," applied to the scene of the crucifixion of Christ (Matt. 27:45 and parallels), the time when the Law was "nailed" to the cross (Col. 2:14), as "the shadowy Law" in the rest of the sentence seems to indicate. St. Gregory is but a brilliant star (or a lesser sun) reflecting "the intelligible Sun" in this newly fashioned heaven—the Church (§§13, 18, 20, 22–24); and his teaching and preaching, like the moon and the stars, reflect the light of that "Sun" (§11; cf. "the righteous Sun" in the hymn to St. Gregory by Erznkats'i, *'Aysōr zuarchats'eal ts'ntsay ekeghets'i . . ."* [Reveling today the Church rejoices . . .] [*Sharakan*, p. 274]; trans., Selection XI). In the *Panegyric* attributed to St. John Chrysostom, St. Gregory is said to have been given this appellation, "Sun of Righteousness," by the Lord himself; for unlike the Twelve Apostles who divided the world for evangelism among themselves, the Armenian Saint alone was privileged to preach universally (*Sop'erk'*, 4:31; trans., Selection II); however, later in the same work the Saint is said to be "the brightest light that arose after the Sun of Righteousness" (p. 79) and enlightened the world from East to West (pp. 80–81; cf. the *Panegyric* by Yovhannēs Sarkawag Vardapet, *Sop'erk'*, 5:9, where the Saint is a spiritual beam of the intelligible Sun; and the *Panegyric* by Vardan Vardapet Arewelts'i, where at one time Christ is referred to as "Sun" and at another time the same word, *aregak*, is used for the Saint, *Sop'erk'*, 5:42, 81). In (Ps.) Yovhannēs Mamikonean, *Patmut'iwn Tarōnoy* (History of Tarōn), "Sun of righteousness" is an epithet of Christ (p. 41) as well as of St. Gregory (p. 123; Arm. text, ed. A. Abrahamyan [Erevan: Haypethrat, 1941]; Eng. trans.: L. Avdoyan, *Pseudo-Yovhannēs Mamikonean: The History of Tarōn*, Occasional Papers and Proceedings: Columbia University Program in Armenian Studies 6 [Atlanta: Scholars

forter—fulfilled the shadowy Law completely.[6] And the sum of constellations of fiery and amazing stars He assembled within your lofty and domed tabernacle in living succession: the Patriarchs one and all, the files of Prophets, the ranks of Apostles, the assemblies of martyrs, the countless fathers, the bands of ascetics, and the shining lights of all those adorned by God. Among them we, upward gazing rational beings, behold in the uppermost lodges—even among the countless ranks of those with fiery appearances inundated with variegated light—the altogether wondrous and great martyr from the East,[7] the bright and delightful star that gives light to the world, Gregory, shining with superior glory, eternally, beyond all, in whose congenial light we are enfolded on the Saint's memorial day.[8]

Press, 1993], pp. 59, 94). For more on the significance of the epithet to Armenians, see the third comment at §38.

[6] Echoing Heb. 8:5; 10:1—if not also Col. 2:14 (see the preceding comment).

[7] Although St. Gregory did not die a martyr's death, his manifold suffering was considered sufficient for this, often repeated epithet (*nahatak*, §§5, 8, 9, 16, 18, 32, 44, 51, 55, and 57) by which he is revered even among non-Armenians (see, e.g., L. V. Ayvazyan, *"Grigor Lusavorch'i pashtamunk'ē Byuzandakan kaysrut'yunum"* (The Veneration of Gregory the Illuminator in the Byzantine Empire) *Ējmiatsin* 41 [1984/6] 40–47). The author calls him: "Martyr, since he was sacrificed while alive in the body" (§16), and states that he shed his blood in the course of suffering for the sake of Christ (§44). In one of Erznkats'i's hymns dedicated to St. Gregory, *"Aysōr zuarchats'eal ts'ntsay ekeghets'i . . ."* (Reveling today the Church rejoices . . .), he is called "a living martyr" (*kendani vkay*) (*Sharakan*, p. 274; trans., Selection XI). In the *Panegyric* attributed to St. John Chrysostom, St. Gregory is likewise presented in a heavenly setting, among the angels, the Prophets and the Apostles, and is called a martyr since no other earthly being endured so much suffering—whether before or after the time of Christ (*Sop'erk'*, 4:6–7); he is *mets khostovanogh* (great confessor) (p. 11); although Isaiah the prophet was sawed asunder, St. John the Baptist beheaded, St. Stephen stoned, St. Peter crucified, and St. Paul beheaded, the martyr St. Gregory appropriated the suffering of them all in his endurance (p. 15). For more on the meanings of the word *nahatak* (e.g., "champion" and "hero"), see Agat'angeghos, *History*, 16 (Arm. text, G. Tēr-Mkrtch'ean and S. Kanayeants', eds., *Agat'angeghay Patmut'iwn Hayots'* [Agat'angeghos' History of the Armenians] [Tiflis: Martiroseants', 1909]; Eng. trans., R. W. Thomson, *Agathangelos: History of the Armenians* [Albany: State University of New York Press, 1976]; unless otherwise indicated, all subsequent references to Agat'angeghos are to the Armenian version [*Aa*] and to this edition). Note also Thomson's comment on the use of the word in Eghishē's "Preface" (Arm. text, E. Tēr-Minasyan, ed., *Eghishēi vasn Vardanay ew Hayots' Paterazmin* [Concerning Vardan and the Armenian War] [Erevan: Arm. Academy of Sciences, 1957], p. 5; Eng. trans., R. W. Thomson, *Eḷishē: History of Vardan and the Armenian War*, Harvard Armenian Texts and Studies 5 [Cambridge, Mass.: Harvard University Press, 1982], p. 58 n. 2).

[8] Each of the first three sections ends with an emphasis on the festal occasion. Taken

2 *Ո*

Rejoice, paradise planted by God,[1] thick with desirable plants and blooming with blossoms that wither not, a land of light and a place for delight,
where the streams of Eden flow ever wide. In you is planted the Tree of Life
that bears the Immortal Fruit,[2] and in you the True Vine grows with many

together, these and other references to the feast (§§9, 11, 15) leave no doubt that this was
the foremost of the three annual feasts of St. Gregory in the Armenian Church: that
commemorating his death and the discovery of his remains (*Giwt nshkharats'*). In the
thirteenth century this feast was celebrated on the sixth Saturdaiy of the Lenten period,
nowadays on the third Saturday after Pentecost (see the discussion on the various feast
days of St. Gregory in the third part of the Introduction). The panegyric, composed
either at the traditional site of the Saint's primary burial on Mount Sepuh or at the
nearby monastery of St. Minas where the author was ordained to the priesthood and
where he retired later in life, was to commemorate this feast of great local importance.
Within the Great Monastery of the Holy Illuminator (*Mets Surb Lusaworch'i Vank'*) was
the most venerable site for pilgrims: the Church of the Illuminator's Resting Place
(*Hangist Lusaworch'i*), on the remains of which and on other venerated sites in the area,
see J.-M. Thierry, "Le Mont Sepuh: Étude archéologique," *Revue des études arméniennes,*
n.s. 21 (1988–1989) 385–449, especially pp. 390–402.

§2

[1]The paradisiac imagery of the Church is commonplace in early Christian literature, including Armenian. In Jewish allegory, Paradise symbolizes the tabernacle with
its holy and most holy compartments, and these in turn symbolize heavenly realities.
The same interpretation appears in Christian allegory on the Church. For more on this
imagery in patristic writings, see *"Paradeisos"* (Paradise) E.4. in Lampe, *Lexicon,* p. 1012.
For a ninth-century list of earlier Greek-speaking Church Fathers who allegorized
Paradise in terms of the Church, see Anastasius Incertus, *In hexaemeron,* 7 (ed. Migne,
Patrologia Graeca 89:961–962). In patristic writings, as in Jewish apocalyptic literature,
Paradise is far above the earth, some specific place in heaven, with or without limits or
borders; see W. K. Bietz, *Paradiesesvorstellungen bei Ambrosius und seinen Vorgängern*
(diss. Giessen, 1973). The Edenic description here, as in several Armenian hymns, owes
to the early Syriac Fathers; see, e.g., Aphrahat, *Demonstrations,* 8 and 23; Ephrem, *De
Paradiso, passim.* For a comprehensive survey see R. Murray, *Symbols of Church and
Kingdom: A Study in Early Syriac Tradition* (Cambridge: Cambridge University Press,
1975), pp. 95–130. Garden imageries and other such floral depictions—as in the
sequel—are commonplace in medieval Armenian lyric poetry, due to Persian influence.
[2]Referring to the centrality of the Christ-bearing Cross; cf. §§14 (where the Cross
is referred to as "the Immortal Wood") and 38 (where it is simply "the Wood"). On the
earliest sources on this symbolic theme, the Christ-bearing Cross as the Tree of life,
owing to Rom. 11:23, see Murray, *Symbols of Church and Kingdom,* pp. 320–324. In
medieval typology, however, the Blessed Virgin Mary becomes the Tree of Life that
bears the Immortal Fruit: Jesus (see below, on "the burning bush" at §29).

branches ever bearing, revealing its attractive and pleasant cluster, the one who imparts the cup that gives joy.[3] For when we look at the fragrant garden of your beneficence[4] we see the distinct, altogether bright blossom ever fair,[5] the fruitful plant with many leaves,[6] the bubbling brook from the Fountain of Life, the sweet cluster of the True Vine, Gregory, the Illuminator of the Armenians,[7] the author of our spirituality, in whose remembrance elated we rejoice with spiritual rejoicing.

[3]Throughout, Christ is the True Vine (John 15) and St. Gregory the special cluster or branch. The imagery here implies apostolic ranking for St. Gregory, a consistent theme in the panegyric. The popularity of the imagery of the vine in Eastern Christianity owes to the early Syriac Fathers, in whose writings Israel is the cluster containing the grape which is Christ; see Aphrahat, *Demonstrations*, 23 ("On the Grape," a lengthy meditation on Isa. 65:8); so also in St. Ephrem, the grape and the vine cluster are constant types of Christ: *Hymns on the Nativity*, 1, 3, 6, 11, 13. A slight shift in the use of the imagery is to be noticed here, in that St. Gregory is identified with the pleasant cluster or grape. He is also "the one who imparts the cup that gives joy," alluding, as in §13, to the eucharistic chalice, often distinguished from "the cup of bitterness" or "the cup of God's fury," reserved for the wicked on the day of judgment; cf. *The Teaching of St. Gregory*, 507, 514, where the Apostles are presented as bearers of the sacred cup.
　　[4]Speaking about the Church to the Church.
　　[5]St. Gregory as a new blossom burgeoning after the others, Christ and the Prophets before Him, is highlighted in the "Ode Representing the Prophets and Christ and the Illuminator" by Mkrtich' Naghash, the fifteenth-century archbishop of Amid; text in Ē. Khondkaryan, ed., *Mkrtich' Naghash* (Erevan: Arm. Academy of Sciences, 1965), pp. 105–106; trans. by S. P. Cowe, "An Allegorical Poem by Mkrtich' Naghash and Its Models," *Journal of the Society for Armenian Studies* 4 (1988–1989) 143–154, especially pp. 143–144. The apostolic ranking of St. Gregory is implied here.
　　[6]St. Gregory as a desirable plant in the paradisiac garden, the Church, is a recurring theme in the panegyric (§§13, 18, 21). In a hymn by Erznkats'i, *'Aysōr zuarchats'eal ts'ntsay ekeghets'i . . ."* (Reveling today the Church rejoices . . .), likewise dedicated to St. Gregory, he is called "a plant of immortality, a fruitful branch of the True Vine" (*tunk anmahut'ean . . .*) (*Sharakan*, p. 264; trans., Selection XI).
　　[7]A distinctive epithet given to St. Gregory the Parthian in the Armenian Church, whereby he is distinguished from other saints by the same name. The attribution is first attested in Movsēs Khorenats'i, *History of the Armenians*, 2.80 (text in M. Abeghean and S. Yarut'iwnean, eds., *Patmut'iwn Hayots'* [History of the Armenians] [Tiflis: Martiroseants', 1913]; Eng. trans., R. W. Thomson, *Moses Khorenats'i: History of the Armenians*, Harvard Armenian Texts and Studies 4 [Cambridge, MA: Harvard University Press, 1978]). Cf. the usage of the word *lusaworich'* in the earliest hymn to the Illuminator, ascribed to Movsēs Bishop of Siwnik' (*ca.* 670–731); *Sharakan*, p. 558 (trans., Selection I, pt. V). Baptism was referred to as "illumination" in the early church, hence the epithet is invariably an allusion to St. Gregory as catechist and to his *Teaching* as catechism, preparing the catechumen for the foremost sacraments of baptism and the Eucharist—to which those newly-baptized drew near being robed in white and hold-

3 ὰ

Great assembly of children of the common faith, freeborn of the free mother, of Zion above,[1] beloved progeny born of the pure, spiritual womb,[2] noble and chosen people with pre-ordained calling [to Christianity], heirs of the greatest Name:[3] Play on the instruments a new praise to Him who restores you,[4] to Him who bestows blessings ever new. For today your mother, the Church,[5] built by the Father's wisdom and erected by the genius of the Spirit, opens up her storehouses full of [divine] mystery and shows off to her pious children the spiritual goods of her treasures. For when you see the beauty of the treasures that cannot be looted, there shall also your hearts be set inseparably[6]—where we see the glittering and pure gold: the Orthodox faith; the choice and tested silver: the delightful sayings of the Lord; the pellucid and bright gems: the individual saints shining in sanctity and adorned with virtue; the pearl born of the sea—with all the magnifi-

ing a lit, palm-size lamp in the hand (see E. L. Nitowski, *Luchnia, Inscribed Lamps of the Byzantine Period*, Occasional Papers of the Horn Archaeological Museum 4 [Berrien Springs, MI: Andrews University Press, 1986]). In the Ethiopian Church the same attribution, *käsáth-berhan* ("Illuminator" in Ge'ez), is used for St. Frumentius, the evangelist from Tyre who brought Christianity to the Kingdom of Aksun early in the fourth century—not long after St. Gregory's mission to Armenia.

§3

[1]Allusion to Gal. 4:26; cf. §§8, 11, 33.

[2]Allusion to the baptismal font (cf. §46), and possibly to John 3:5.

[3]Allusion to Rom. 8:15–17; cf. Acts 15:17; James 2:7. St. Gregory is later described as the begetter of the Armenian people through his suffering and pain (§§33, 52, 55; as well as through his teaching, §§16, 50), giving them birth through the baptismal font and presenting them to God as His "peculiar people." In the *Panegyric* attributed to St. John Chrysostom, the presentation of the Armenian people to God takes place through the conversion of the king, who asks St. Gregory to prepare the people for baptism (*Sop'erk'*, 4:34, 40, 68); this is in fulfillment of the promise made by God to St. Gregory, as to Abraham of old, that He will multiply his descendants "as the stars of heaven and as the sand of the sea" (pp. 29–30; cf. Gen. 22:17–18).

[4]Echoing Ps. 96:1 (95:1 LXX); 149:1.

[5]The metaphor of the Church as the mother of Christian believers is common-place in patristic writings, especially in the works of Cyprian (e.g., *Epistulae* 74.5; cf. the often quoted sentence from his *De unitate ecclesiae*: "*habere non potest Deum patrem qui ecclesiam non habet matrem*" [6]). Among the Greek Fathers, see Clement of Alexandria, *Paidagogos*, 1.5, 21; Cyril of Jerusalem, *Catecheses*, 18.26. The metaphor recurs in this panegyric: §§8, 11, 14, and 50.

[6]Allusion to Matt. 6:21; cf. Luke 12:34.

cence of its beauty—in which we see the all-encompassing treasure-house:[7] his very person shining like gold, the one resplendent in faith; the hallowed and pure silver: the true preacher of the intelligible Word; the variegated gem: the one made beautiful by superior virtue, Gregory, the father of our faith, the fitting crown of the holy Armenian Church, in whose celebration his spiritual children have adorned themselves, those who have their various needs supplied from the paternal treasuries.

4   Ա

Open anew the treasuries of your minds so as to receive of the divine treasures.[1] Cleanse the tablets of your hearts so as to have engraved in you the live imprint of the venerable image,[2] to have drawn on your souls the handsome, praiseworthy figure, that of the author of our faith, the one constant and steadfast in the knowledge of hope, the saintly and faithful steward of love,[3] the toiler for total goodness, the steady guide to the true worship of God, the example of goodly obedience, the epitome of valiant endurance, the proof of wholesome thought and modesty, the performer of wondrous

---

[7]Echoing the twin parables of "The Hidden Treasure" and "The Precious Pearl" in Matt. 13:44–46 (contemplated also in §42).

§4

[1]These words echo a feature of Christian mysticism, namely, that the divine mystery is attained through the portals of the mind. Note especially the following proclamation that precede the Eucharistic Prayer in the Divine Liturgy of the Armenian Church: "The doors, the doors! With all wisdom and good heed lift up your minds in the fear of God," to which the clerks respond: "We have them lifted up to you, O Lord almighty." The church doors were shut to those uninitiated into the divine mysteries through baptism, thus keeping them away from the Eucharistic liturgy. By way of contrast, those initiated are directed to the portals of the mind, in view of the realization of the "Responsary of the Great Entrance" (Ps. 24:7–10 [23:7–10 LXX]): "Lift up your gates, O princes; let the everlasting doors be lifted up, and the king of glory shall come in" (Eng. trans. by D. Findikyan, ed., *The Divine Liturgy of the Armenian Church* [New York: St. Vartan Press, 1999], pp. 25, 29). The mystical awareness of the author is seen also at §35, where, commenting on St. Gregory's offering the Eucharist, he remarks that by raising the gifts (the eucharistic bread and wine) the Saint was seeking "to apprehend the higher wisdom of Him who is true and perfect."

[2]Cf. §42 below, where the appeal to cleanse oneself is repeated. A call to cleanse oneself in preparation for celebrating the Saint's memorial day is likewise made at the beginning of the *Panegyric* attributed to St. John Chrysostom (*Sopʻerkʻ*, 4:5).

[3]Echoing 1 Cor. 13:13.

and amazing miracles,[4] the brave and renowned captain,[5] the courageous and advancing soldier, this Gregory, the possessor of every virtue, the one nurtured in holiness, the virtuous in conduct, the one shining in righteousness, in whose memory we delight ourselves today as we proceed through the arena of his martyrdom[6] and thrive in his paternal beneficence. And to that sweet and pleasant name we address this stream of words, saying:

5   Է

Gregory, good martyr:[1] Together we strive to attain to your remarkable perseverance, to walk in the fragrant garden of your rational and expressive blossoms, your variegated and praiseworthy life; to enter the vineyard of your manifold and ever delightful clusters, to head for the orchards of your pleasant and abundant fruit.[2] Which fresh blossom shall I pick to hide it in the bosom of my words, or which gladdening cluster shall I squeeze to thrill so many souls? By which fruit shall the flow of my words be made lofty, or what shall it focus on from that unattainable height?[3] Which of the beautiful, praiseworthy things concerning you shall I tell? The most marvelously accomplished conception,[4] or the grace bestowed at birth?

[4]Agat'angeghos cites a few such miracles, e.g., the survival of the Saint, the healing of the king, and the destruction of the pagan temples with the sign of the Lord's cross (813 especially). In later times the Saint is said to perform miracles in death (§39).

[5]Cf. §45, St. Gregory as a mighty captain; so also in the *Panegyric* attributed to St. John Chrysostom (*Sop'erk'*, 4:83).

[6]The sentence implies participation in the experiences of St. Gregory, as one contemplates them while celebrating the feast.

§5

[1]On St. Gregory as martyr, see the seventh comment at §1.

[2]The appeal is here made to those who have come to Mount Sepuh, the site of St. Gregory's seclusion and death, to also consider entering the spiritual quarters of the Saint's life. The words seem appropriate for a processional.

[3]A likely reference to a plant substance with narcotic effects.

[4]The later, Karshuni version of Agat'angeghos (*Vk*), rendered from an Armenian vorlage in about 600, claims that St. Gregory was conceived at the hill where St. Thaddaeus was martyred (text and commentary in M. van Esbroeck, "Un nouveau témoin du livre d'Agathange," *Revue des études arméniennes*, n.s. 8 [1971] 13–167; especially §8, p. 24). So also in Khorenats'i, *History of the Armenians*, 2.74: "And there [by the grave of the holy apostle in the plain of Artaz] they say the mother of our holy and great Illuminator conceived. Therefore he received the grace of that same apostle, and having been begotten beside his grave he completed what was lacking in his spiritual labors."

The nurturing in absolute piety, or the graceful tuning of your mind to learning? Your course of heavenly virtues, or your following after the One crucified for our sake? The spectacle of your unbearable tortures, or your incomprehensible endurance in the depth of the pit? Your release under divine protection, or the bewildering details of your awesome vision?[5]

6 *Ḷ*

Gregory, overseer of the Essential Goodness, of His manifold beneficence handed down to us through you: How great are these gifts![1] To which magnificent and incomparable thing shall we devote ourselves, we who are enlightened by your copious teaching,[2] who are the devotees of your high-priestly entreaties, who are shepherded by your dauntless watchfulness, who are protected by your ceaseless prayers, who are comforted by your

---

This providential birth of St. Gregory, mentioned by several subsequent writers (e.g., in the *Panegyric* on the Saint by Vardan Vardapet Arewelts'i, *Sop'erk'*, 5:46, 49), is contemplated again in this panegyric (§§21–22, 24) as well as in one of the author's hymns dedicated to St. Gregory, *"Aysōr zuarchats'eal ts'ntsay ekeghets'i . . ."* (Reveling today the Church rejoices . . .) (*Sharakan*, p. 266; trans., Selection XI). On the later versions of Agat'angeghos, see G. Winkler, "Our Present Knowledge of the History of Agat'angełos and its Oriental Versions," *Revue des études arméniennes*, n.s. 14 (1980) 125–141; on the recensions among the various versions, see Thomson, *The Teaching of St. Gregory* (rev. ed.), pp. 3–5. In the region of Artaz is the famous monastery of St. T'atē, the traditional site of the Apostle's martyrdom, on which see H. Oskian, *Vaspurakan—Vani Vank'erē*, 2 parts; Azgayin Matenadaran 149, 151 (Vienna: Mkhit'arist Press, 1940, 1942) 2.455–500.

[5]The preceding lines scan the Saint's life, including his grand vision of Shoghakat' as recorded by Agat'angeghos, *History*, 69–122, 211–225, 731–756 (Thomson, *Agathangelos*, pp. 79–135, 217–227, 273–297).

§6

[1]Lit., "What sort of gifts!"

[2]An allusion perhaps to the catechism preserved in the middle of the Armenian version (*Aa*) of Agat'angeghos' *History* (259–715) and ascribed, albeit questionably, to our Saint; Eng. trans., Thomson, *The Teaching of Saint Gregory* (rev. ed). For a summary of scholarship favoring the ascription of this catechism to St. Mashtots' or, more likely, to a period following his death, see *ibid.*, pp. 56–61, and L. Ter Petrosyan, *Daser Hay Ekeghets'akan Matenagrut'yunits' (E Dar)* (Lessons from Armenian Ecclesiastical Bibliography [5th Century]) (Soch'i: Armenian Diocese of Nor Nakhijevan and Russia, 1993), pp. 7–24. Whether directly or indirectly, *The Teaching of Saint Gregory (Vardapetut'iwn)* is referred to several times in this panegyric (§§11, 13, 14, 27, 35, 37, 44, and 45; the same adjective, *bazmaban*, with reference to *The Teaching*, is used in §37.

resting place and venerable grave?[3] Even now, with burdened souls we flock to you, comforting father, including myself, a debtor for the immeasurable gifts from you, a recipient of the beneficence distributed without par, attempting with mere words to make a payment against the register of my dear debts. According to my parents' hope, you mediated my coming into being from nothing and became the cause for this useless fruit to exist blessedly, [giving] opportunity to my rational part[4] to be active and prompting it to remain constant in the same. Accept now this obligation in words, [written] with your help.[5]

7 *U*

Sketcher I would be of an honorable portrait of your most holy person; sculptor in words of your sublimity's most special deeds; stamper in letters of your extreme beauty, your superior glory; a soaring, spirited minstrel of your blessed acts; of your atoning sermons,[1] a recounter in amiable words

---

[3]A repetitious designation of the same place. On the Illuminator's Resting Place (*Hangist Lusaworchʻi*), see the archaeological survey and report by Thierry, "Le Mont Sepuh," pp. 390–402.

[4]That is, of the soul, the human mind, or the faculty of reason that distinguishes humans from other earthly creatures. Ever since Classical times it was believed (especially in Stoicism) that this inherent rationality was transmitted at the time of insemination. The author attributes his rationality to the intercession of St. Gregory, the Saint's goodness to the author's parents. St. Gregory thus continues to be the source of inspiration for our author (cf. §60). At this juncture Erznkatsʻi is fulfilling another panegyrical requirement: self-effacement or minimizing one's own role so as to underscore the greatness of the one praised (cf. Isocrates *Panegyricus* 13; *Panathenaicus* 36; Pseudo-Cicero *Ad Herennium* 3.6.11; Philo of Alexandria *De Vita Mosis* 2.1).

[5]A thought repeated in the concluding section, with reference to the panegyric as a whole.

§7

[1]An allusion to the collection of twenty-three homilies known as the *Yachakhapatum* which, like *The Teaching*, is traditionally attributed to St. Gregory. Arm. text: *Srboy Horn meroy eranelwoyn Grigori Lusaworchʻi Yachakhapatum chaṙkʻ lusaworkʻ* (Often-repeated and Enlightened Sermons of Our Blessed Father St. Gregory the Illuminator), ed. A. Tēr Mikʻelean (Ējmiatsin: Mother See Press, 1894). Armenian scholarship, relying on Agatʻangeghos, *History*, 886, tends to attribute the primary authorship of the collection to St. Gregory and its translation and expansion to St. Mashtotsʻ and his School. According to H. Achaṙyan, *Hayotsʻ Grerĕ* (The Armenian Letters) (Erevan: Haypethrat, 1968), pp. 335–346, the homilies belong to the latter part of the fifth cen-

to your spiritual children. But with what colors could I present your glorious, lordly stature? What words would suffice to accomplish a fair account of your special deeds, your superlative life, your wondrous acts, your awe inspiring and seraphic purity by which my feeble words are overwhelmed but to which my lowly soul aspires? The overwhelming [reality] leads to hopelessness, but aspiration does very daring things. Hopelessness would show it impossible to put the joints and the members to good use, but daring longs for wisdom especially [when it comes to] skillful weaving in ordinary words. I long to have a pure mind and a diction flowing and swift, like the swallows' capability. I lay my incapable hand to work on this subject broad as the waters, to present a gracious picture of the marvelous work of our holy Illuminator to the souls and minds of a multitude of believers.

[II. Invocations]

8 [*Prayer to Father, Son, and Spirit*]

And now,[1] since my heart fully desires, with much longing, to draw a portrait, beautiful as the sun, of our divinely adorned father, Saint Gregory the Illuminator, on the live tables of the hearts of his children, his people, not in shiny, material colors, but immaterial, encompassing martyrdom and dreadful suffering by which the royal image of his most pure soul was made

---

tury. For a summary of contents and scholarship, see Ter Petrosyan, *Daser Hay Ekeghets'akan Matenagrut'yunits'*, pp. 25–41.

§8

[1]This is the first of three consecutive sections beginning with "And now . . ." (*Ew ard . . .* §§8–10 [11–14]), a recurring phrase found at the start of several other sections (§§21, 26, 28, and 47); cf. the final appeal in three consecutive sections beginning with "Now . . ." (*Ard . . .* §§55–57). These two tri-partite sets with nearly identical opening words, one near the beginning and the other near the end of the panegyric, seem to function as a *chiasm* or framing. More importantly, in the invocations of §§8–10 [11–14], we discern the author's three-part declaration of intent: first in his three-part prayer to Father, Son, and Spirit (§8); second in his call to celebration (§9); and third in his outline of four subjects of immediate concern (§10), spelled out in what follows (§§11–14) and elaborated in the sequel. Moreover, this three-part prayer to the Trinity, which fulfils a panegyrical requirement of entreating for guidance from God or from a muse, diety, etc., at the beginning of an epic composition, corresponds with the three-part

beautiful,[2] O Heavenly Father, with intelligible pigments from the source of your bountiful mercies grant color to what is meant, to make fittingly beautiful the composition of this desirable portrait, delightfully charming in beauty.

And since I am inclined to weave a glorious wreath to our mother, the holy Church,[3] neither of material gems nor of sea-born pearls, but of most excellent virtues and the incorporeal life of Christ's martyr, Saint Gregory,[4] O Head of the Church, Son and Word of God,[5] Jesus, grant me artistic skill and the insight of a contemplative mind, that my hand may move successfully in laying out the tapestry of his life, [arranged like] brilliant gems, pearls that could speak, an adornment for the Head of the Holy Church.

And since we have come to build a desirable sanctuary, not with sawn wood and hewn stones but with living plants to be grown by the water of the holy font and to be nurtured with the Orthodox confession of our father full of grace and divine mercy, Saint Gregory, and with rational stones with which—like living rocks—we are built into a spiritual sanctuary founded on the Chief Cornerstone[6] and still are being raised[7] in purity to welcome our high priest,[8] more so the Holy Spirit for whom he became

prayer addressed to St. Gregory at the conclusion of the panegyric (§§58–60), thus strengthening the structural frame of the composition.

[2]The teleological benefit of suffering owes to Heb. 5:8; a notion derived from Stoicism. Cf. the author's long-lost composition on the suffering of St. Gregory: *"Tagh Srboyn Grigori Lusavorch'in Hayots'"* (An Ode to St. Gregory the Illuminator of the Armenians), in Srapyan, *Hovhannes Erznkats'i*, pp. 115–116, translated in the Appendices at the end of this book. On the twelve tortures of the Saint, culminating with his being thrown into the pit or dungeon of Khor Virap, see Agat'angeghos, *History*, 69–122 (cf. the "Ode to the Holy Illuminator" by St. Nersēs Shnorhali [trans., Selection VIII]).

[3]On the motherhood of the Church, see above, §3; the metaphor recurs in §§11, 14, and 50.

[4]On St. Gregory as martyr, see the seventh comment at §1.

[5]Common Christological titles, as of the New Testament (Eph. 5:23; Col. 1:18; John 1:1, 14; etc.).

[6]Allusion to Eph. 2:20.

[7]The verbs *shineal ēk'* and *shinik'* are second person plural ("you are built" and "you are being built/raised"), here rendered as third person plural for consistency.

[8]Throughout the panegyric "high priest" is a designation for St. Gregory (§§33, 38, 41, 44, 48, 56, 58); so also in the "Chrysostomian" panegyrics (*Sop'erk'*, 4:46, 91). The Christian appropriation of the title goes back to the Epistle to the Hebrews, where Christ is the High Priest of the New Covenant (especially chs. 5 and 7).

a pleasing sanctuary, O ingenious Architect of Wisdom,[9] Holy Spirit of God, grace this edifice for the newborn children of Zion[10] to whom you gave birth through the holy font, restoring them constantly from the corruption of sin so as to remain unshaken, strong, and to become a sanctuary to welcome you and to rejoice on this joyous feast day of the father adorned by you.

9 [*Call to celebration*]

And now, since the reality we face is sublime, we ought to gaze with the soul's eyes at the heavenly hope, with love of Christ's holy martyr;[1] to cleanse the physical eyes with clear insights and in tears to prompt the motion of the hands unto prayer and the ears unto listening; and to ask for wisdom of discernment from the Holy Spirit, to be able to take part in the service with fear and trembling on this memorial day of the confessor of Christ, Saint Gregory, and to have inscribed on the hearts of this grand assembly a memorial to his incorporeal life.

And you, prepare yourselves at this time to commune in purity with that heavenly life, on this feast day when grace is imparted.[2]

---

[9]As in Judaism, so also in early Christianity, the Holy Spirit was identified with the artificer Wisdom of God at work in the creation of the world, animating the life of the church and of individual believers (Prov. 8:22–31; Wis. 7:22; cf. Justin Martyr, *Dialogus cum Tryphone*, 61.3; 126.1; 129.3; Clement of Alexandria, *Stromata*, 5.89.4; 6.138.4; 7.7.4; Irenaeus, *Adversus haereses*, 4.20.1–4; 5.17.1; Theophilus of Antioch, *Ad Autolycum*, 1.7; 2.10; etc.).

[10]Allusion to Gal. 4:26. On the self-definition of the Armenians vis-à-vis the people of God, see the first part of the Introduction and §§3, 11, 33.

§9

[1]On St. Gregory's "martyrdom," see the seventh comment at §1.

[2]That the author was addressing an audience of pilgrims at the monastery on Mount Sepuh is sufficiently clear in these lines. His audience seems to have consisted mostly of clergy about to conduct the special services for the day (cf. the direct talk to the hierarchs in the last third of the panegyric, §§46, 51–53, 55–57). The occasion must have been the foremost of the three annual feasts of St. Gregory in the Armenian Church: that commemorating his death and the discovery of his remains (*Giwt nshkharats'*), on which see the third part of the Introduction.

10 [*Introduction of four subjects of concern*]

And now, let us consider these four topics[1] worth being marveled at and remembered:

[A]   This time and day of joyous festivity.
[B]   The resting place of Saint Gregory.[2]
[C]   His most praiseworthy and laudable image.
[D]   Roles assumed at this time and place.

11 (A)

At this time we, the children of Zion, are gathered at the gates of our mother, the Church.[1] We the offspring of the Word preached by Saint Gregory[2] [have come] to our spiritual father. In this spiritual spring-season, in accordance with the joy of springtime,[3] this heavenly tabernacle

§10

[1]Erznkats'i introduces four subjects of immediate concern, which he treats summarily (§§11–14). Other occasional introductions of distinct units are found in the panegyric: of a poem in alphabetical acrostic dedicated to St. Gregory (§17); of an encomium on St. Gregory (§19); of an oracle to King Trdat in an imagined presence (§26); of an encomium on Mount Sepuh (§28); of a lament over the land, the people, and the Church of Armenia (§47); and of an appeal to the hierarchs (54).

[2]The word *teghis* (from *teghik*) may also be construed as plural. In which case, it suggests the place where the Saint died and the adjacent place where he was buried by the shepherds who found his unrecognized remains. For details on the Gregorid burial places, see the third part of the Introduction; for the sites on Mount Sepuh, see the report by Thierry, "Le Mont Sepuh," pp. 385–449, and the comments below at §§33 and 43.

§11

[1]The Church as a mother begetting children of God, who constitute New Zion, is a recurring metaphor in this panegyric; see especially §§3, 8, 14, 50. There also seems to be an echo here of Heb. 12:22 along with Gal. 4:26.

[2]An allusion to the Gospel as preached by St. Gregory and possibly also to the writings traditionally attributed to him: the catechism or *The Teaching* and, especially, the twenty-three homilies known as the *Yachakhapatum*. On these, see the pertinent comments at §§6–7.

[3]As indicated in the third part of the Introduction and elsewhere in the Commentary (see the proper comments at §§1, 9, 15), the feast of the discovery of St. Gregory's remains was the occasion for this panegyric. This was celebrated early in the Spring, on the sixth Saturday of the Lenten period. The other feast days, of slightly later der-

glitters; and the intelligible Sun causes His rays of delicate light to beam there, making the enlightening injunctions preached by him to shine reflectively like the moon. And the circles of saints who have become as stars[4] in the new heaven rise in purity, [as] the springs of his teaching gush forth most clearly and flow like a river, figuratively, for all to hear.[5]

12 (B)

This place of our assembly, this mountain where God dwells, where our holy Illuminator was laid to rest,[1] is made bright by the resplendent rays of his prayers and lies beneath the canopy of his spiritual grace. And now, by the power of his love, the mountain is beautifully adorned with rational plants, shooting forth their leaves toward the light and spreading diverse flowers of virtue and the perfect fruit of the good gifts bestowed by God.[2] And these [plants], through the mediation of our holy Illuminator, through his petitioning, are brought together in this multitude [of worshipers]. And, as in the very nature of flowers, they glow side by side and turn one and all in the direction of the sun.[3]

ivation, commemorate his placement in the dungeon (mid-March) and his release from the dungeon (mid-June).

[4]On the resemblance of the souls of the righteous dead to stars, see the opening lines of the panegyric and the fourth comment at §1. Cf. §18, where St. Gregory is said to be "a sun-lit torch," etc. Contextually, the setting is not in heaven itself but in the Church, the "new heaven."

[5]Another allusion perhaps to *The Teaching of Saint Gregory*, referred to earlier (§6) and elsewhere in the panegyric, here contemplated alongside the *Yachakhapatum* collection of homilies. It is possible that on the Saint's feast day some of his writing was read publicly. The light of his preaching and the flow of his teaching "like a river" in the "heavenly tabernacle" carry reminiscences from Ezek. 47:1–2.

§12

[1]On the Illuminator's Resting Place (*Hangist Lusaworch'i*), see the archaeological survey and report by Thierry, "Le Mont Sepuh," pp. 390–402. Erznkats'i is claiming for Mount Sepuh what the Scriptures hold for Mount Zion as "this mountain where God dwells"; for more on this motif, see §§29, 34, 36.

[2]Allusion to the gifts and fruits of the Spirit (Eph. 5:22–23).

[3]Allusion to the easterly orientation in worship, the direction of the altar in Armenian and other churches.

13 (C)

Yet the most praiseworthy and laudable image is that of Gregory, the renowned and bright sun of the Armenians,[1] who dissipated the darkness of idolatry[2] and those frozen in sin he made fruitful by the warm rays of his prayers. This well-bearing branch of the True Vine, who delighted us with the gladdening cup;[3] this beautiful and joyous spring-season of the soul, who through his abundant teaching declared unto us the grace of the Spirit;[4] this shading garden in hot and scorching season; this renowned star, who in his bright appearance guided us who were lost at life's sea; this choice figure with a luminous image, resembling Moses in glory;[5] this

§13

[1]In the *Panegyric on St. Gregory* attributed to Theophilos, a disciple of St. John Chrysostom, St. Gregory is repeatedly referred to as the sun rising from the East (*Sop'erk'*, 4:91), whose radiance cannot be prevented (p. 96), even while he was in the pit (pp. 99–100), which was transformed into a garden, a temple of light, a heavenly sanctuary (p. 108), since the Saint is the sun that shines over Armenia (p. 109); he is even brighter than the sun, having come to remove the darkness from the land (pp. 119–120). Cf. the "Ode to St. Gregory" by Catholicos Grigor III Pahlawuni (in office 1113–1166), where the imagery of the sun is likewise applied to our Saint (trans., Selection VII).

[2]The etymology of *krapashtut'iwn* is from *kurk'* ("idol[s]") and not *krak* ("fire"). In either case, it is taken as a reference to the pre-Christian Armenian religion, including Zoroastrianism; cf. §§27, 30, 33. See J. R. Russell, *Zoroastrianism in Armenia*, Harvard Iranian Series 5 (Cambridge, MA: Harvard Univ. Press, 1987).

[3]On St. Gregory's relation to Jesus as that of a branch to the Vine, and on his apostolic role as "cupbearer," see the third comment at §2.

[4]Cf. the following sentence in Erznkats'i's hymn to St. Gregory, *"Aysōr zuarchats'eal ts'ntsay ekeghets'i . . ."* (Reveling today the Church rejoices . . .): «Յորդառատ բանիւ հոգեւոր ծննդեամբ լուսաւորեցեր զՀայաստան աշխարհս» ("With abundant wisdom and spiritual birth you enlightened the land of Armenia") (*Sharakan*, p. 273; trans., Selection XI), alluding to catechism and its culmination with baptism. The "teaching" here, as elsewhere, refers to the catechesis attributed to our Saint, *The Teaching of Saint Gregory;* see the second comment at §6.

[5]Alluding to Ex. 34:29–35; cf. Agat'angeghos, *History*, 854, 891 (owing to Koriwn's description of the joyous Mashtots' on his way to Greater Armenia with the newly finalized Armenian alphabet, likened to Moses on his way down from Mount Sinai with the newly received Decalogue, *Life of Mashtots'*, 52:1–8; for the text, see M. Abeghyan, ed., *Vark' Mashtots'i* [Erevan: Haypethrat, 1941]; Eng. trans., B. Norehad, *Koriwn: The Life of Mashtots* [New York: AGBU, 1965]). In this panegyric St. Gregory is compared repeatedly with Moses (§§22, 29, 33, 39, 44, 48, 58); similarly, in the "Chrysostomian" panegyrics, St. Gregory is said to be a second Moses (*Sop'erk'*, 4:12,

[man of] praiseworthy stature, in height nine times a palm's span, was pleasing to those of the nine heavenly ranks;[6] this path of variegated light, by whom the way to the True Light became known,[7] a living beam of light descending on us from on high; this sweet and healing medicine, who healed the pain inflicted by the venomous bites of the dragon; this awe-inspiring and desirable vision, who also became a seer of the seraphic glory;[8] this red and fragrant rose, who blossomed from a thorny stem[9] and filled the land of Armenia with fragrant perfume; this desirable plant in the garden of the Church,[10] who delighted us with his sweet and delicious fruit; this refreshing dew, who descended with the grace of the Spirit and refreshed with goodness the spoiled and withering plants. This is the image of the one of whom words are insufficient to speak worthily.

14 (D)

Now to roles assumed at the present time: The shepherds of the rational flock of Christ, folding you within the comfortable confines of your mother the Church,[1] lead you to the place of green pastures and nurture you by the

---

42, 77, 122; the latter page trans., Selection III); so also in the *Panegyric* by Yovhannēs Sarkawag Vardapet (*Sopʻerkʻ*, 5:28–34; trans., Selection VI) and in that by Vardan Vardapet Areweltsʻi (*ibid.*, pp. 53–54, 74–75; trans., Selection IX).

[6]On the nine celestial ranks or orders, see the *Heavenly Hierarchy* (6.2) in the mystical theology of Pseudo-Dionysius the Areopagite, translated into Armenian in the eighth century by Stepʻanos Siwnetsʻi; critical text and Eng. trans. by R. W. Thomson, *The Armenian Version of the Works Attributed to Dionysius the Areopagite*, Corpus Scriptorum Christianorum Orientalium 488–489 (=Scriptores Armeniaci 17–18) (Louvain: Peeters, 1987).

[7]The "light" terminology here is reminiscent of the mystical use of the term; the True Light, of course, is Jesus (owing to John 8–12); cf. §21.

[8]Cf. Agatʻangeghos, *History*, 731–756.

[9]Lit., "thorn-bearing root." In a hymn by Erznkatsʻi, *"Aysōr zuarchatsʻeal tsʻntsay ekeghetsʻi . . ."* (Reveling today the Church rejoices . . .), likewise dedicated to St. Gregory, he is said to be a rose grown from a thorny bush (*Sharakan*, p. 267; trans., Selection XI). On how the author resolves the stigma of St. Gregory's ancestry, especially of his father Anak, the murderer of the Armenian King Khosrov I (279/280–287; known also as Trdat II), see §§20–21 and the proper comments.

[10]On the metaphor of the plant with reference to the Saint, see the sixth comment at §2 (cf. §§18, 21).

§14

[1]The motherhood of the Church is a recurring metaphor; see §§3, 8, 11, and 50.

comforting water of vital teaching.[2] The tillers of the soil, like lowly and docile oxen, bring you under the easy yoke of Christ[3] and plow through the rational fields of your souls and minds, sowing in you the Word of life; then they wait with hope and joy for the good fruit.[4] The spiritual fishermen[5] catch you with the bait of the Word from this transient life for the one eternal and from murk-loving existence to heavenly deportment. The keepers of the garden of life show you the divine plantation[6]—the lives of divine men—and offer you the fragrance of the knowledge of the immortal Tree.[7]

And you, being invigorated, like bees gathering from the divine [plants], store it in the cells of your minds.

[III. Prelude to an encomium on St. Gregory]

15 [The place of St. Gregory in history]

And what an occasion for a large assembly,[1] the joy and the love for this feast which is a celebration in memory of the one named "wakeful" and "watchful"![2] For it is the feast of our patriarch, Saint Gregory, our Illumi-

---

[2]As elsewhere, this is a possible reference to *The Teaching of Saint Gregory;* see the second comment at §6. The preceding part of the sentence echoes Ps. 23:2 (22:2 LXX).

[3]Allusion to Matt. 11:29–30.

[4]Lit., "the fruit of goodness."

[5]Allusion to Matt. 4:19; cf. Mark 1:17.

[6]Reflecting the allegory of Philo of Alexandria, according to whom, the garden which God planted in Eden is the garden of virtues; see *Legum Allegoriae* 1.45–46, 53–55, 64, 89; *De Plantatione* 37; *De Confusione* 61; *De Migratione* 37. Dependence on Philo's allegory is commonplace in the writings of the Fathers.

[7]That is, the Cross; cf. §38. The Cross is referred to as "the Tree of Life" in §2.

§15

[1]The author appears to be building anticipation in §§15–18 for the encomium introduced at §19. There is a discernible three-part prelude to that encomium on St. Gregory (§§20–25): the place of St. Gregory in history (§15), the attributes of St. Gregory (§16), and the special poem in alphabetical acrostic (§§17–18).

[2]On this special feast, commemorating the discovery of the remains of the Saint, see the third part of the Introduction and also the pertinent comments at §§1, 9 and 11. In his use of the synonyms "wakeful" and "watchful," the author is employing the meaning of the Saint's Greek name (*Gregorios*). The first adjective in conjunction with the Saint's name appears also in the *Panegyric* by Yovhannēs Sarkawag Vardapet (*Sop'erk'*, 5:35) and in the "Ode to St. Gregory" by Catholicos Grigor III Pahlawuni, in

nator endowed with apostolic grace and prophetic honor.[3] Adorned by the Father, he was elevated to the prophetic honor; and being sent with filial love by the Son, he was filled with apostolic grace; and chosen by the Holy Spirit, he was elevated to the patriarchal throne. [The spiritual gifts of] the three periods, the early, the middle, and the late, these threefold gifts he encompassed in himself.[4] Wherefore in honor he is equal to the Prophets, in rank equal to the Apostles, and inspired by God like unto the holy fathers who have put on God.[5]

office 1113–1166 (trans., Selection VII). The second adjective, also in conjunction with the Saint's name, appears later in this panegyric (§32). Another synonymous adjective, *hskogh* ("watchful"), is found in §§24 and 33; also used by Sarkawag Vardapet with reference to the Saint (*ibid.*).

[3]Cf. the hymn by Erznkats'i, *"Aysōr zuarchats'eal ts'ntsay ekeghets'i . . ."* (Reveling today the Church rejoices . . .), where St. Gregory is likened to Moses, Elijah, and John the Baptist (*Sharakan*, p. 273; trans., Selection XI). In the *Panegyric* attributed to St. John Chrysostom, St. Gregory is said to have been called from his youth to become "a prophet of the Most High" (*Sop'erk'*, 4:44; cf. Luke 1:76, on the birth of St. John the Baptist). In the same work he is repeatedly compared with the Prophets and the Apostles of old and is said to have surpassed them in a variety of ways (see especially pp. 12–15, 28, 30–31 [trans., Selection II], 74–81). Similarly, in the *Panegyric* attributed to Theophilos, a disciple of St. John Chrysostom, St. Gregory is said to be an apostle like Peter and Paul, and a prophet like Moses, Elijah, and Daniel (pp. 92, 94, 104, 116, 122 [trans., Selection III]; cf. the *Discourse* by Grigor Sarkawagapet, *ibid.*, pp. 132–137 [trans., Selection V], 156–157, and the *Panegyric* by Vardan Vardapet Arewelts'i, *ibid.*, 5:44, 53–54, 73–75 [Moses and Elijah; trans., Selection IX], 62 [Daniel and Jonah]). In that by Yovhannēs Sarkawag Vardapet, the testimony of the Armenian martyrs, such as the Illuminator, is much more effective than the word of Elijah when he spoke against iniquity and consequently brought drought upon the land (1 Kgs. 17:1; 18:1; cf. Luke 4:25; James 5:17); their inspired messages that have been transmitted to the faithful are comparable to the sayings of the biblical worthies, those well known to God and familiar to us in the Old and New Testaments (*Sop'erk'*, 5:7). The notion of regarding St. Gregory as a prophet and as an apostle, however, goes back to Agat'angeghos, *History*, 854, 891 (owing to Koriwn's *Life of Mashtots'*, 9 [52.1–19]; 25 [90.2–11]).

[4]The point here is that St. Gregory encompasses in himself the prophetic, the apostolic, and the patristic gifts or graces; that he represents the three periods when these diverse gifts were operative in the divine economy of redemption. During the first period, the Father is deemed the prime actor; during the second, the Son; and during the third, the Spirit.

[5]So also at §59. Cf. Rom. 13:14: "put on the Lord Jesus Christ" (§44).

16 [*The attributes of St. Gregory*]

We call him father since he begot us through the Word of Truth and nurtured us with the abundance of his matchless mercy and reared us with the Orthodox confession of faith.[1] We call him teacher since he taught the fine points of the heavenly virtues; shepherd, since he gathered unto the flock of the True Shepherd[2] those who believe in the Holy Trinity; husbandman, since with much toil and sweat he tilled the fallow fields of our minds and sowed the seed of worshiping God; faithful warrior, since he fought against the visible and invisible enemy;[3] witness, since through much suffering he testified to the unity of the Trinity and the true Godhead; martyr, since he was sacrificed while alive in the body;[4] victor, since he did not yield under enormously ingenious tortures; ascetic, since on every occasion he took upon himself the austere life. Wherefore the Armenian nation is all the more exalted.[5] For just as we have one father who attained personally to every good thing, so also the Armenian nation is one and of the same faith and honored with every magnificent gift.

§16

[1] St. Gregory as one who begets and rears up children of God or of the Church through his enlightening catechism or *Teaching*, giving birth to them through the baptismal font, is a recurring theme; see below, §50 (elsewhere, he gives them birth through his suffering, §§33, 52, 55).

[2] Echoing John 10:1–18; so also at §24 and in a hymn by Erznkats'i, "*Aysōr zuarchats'eal ts'ntsay ekeghets'i* . . ." (Reveling today the Church rejoices . . .), likewise dedicated to St. Gregory (*Sharakan*, p. 266; trans., Selection XI). Cf. §18, where St. Gregory is said to be "a true shepherd." In the *Panegyric* attributed to St. John Chrysostom, St. Gregory is said to be an example for shepherds, unmoved, like David (*Sop'erk'*, 4:12).

[3] Erznkats'i draws the word *marteaw* ("he fought") from *martiros* (lit., "martyr," as in Greek), thus drawing an Armenian etymology from a Greek word, compelling us to translate *martiros* as "warrior," a secondary meaning of the word. The singular "enemy" is Satan.

[4] As noted earlier (§1), although St. Gregory did not die a martyr's death, his manifold suffering was considered sufficient for this epithet.

[5] Lit., "exalted higher." Erznkats'i is pursuing an interesting line of reasoning embedded in the covenantal theology of the ancient Israelites (Deut. 28:1–14; 30:1–10; etc.): the Armenian people are great because of the greatness of St. Gregory, since he is our father and we his children spiritually.

17 [*Introduction of a special poem*]

Wherefore we, in honor of our father to whom we owe much, shall present the following panegyrical arrangement.[1]

18 [*A poem in alphabetical acrostic*]

Gregory —	beautiful as sunrise;[1] sun-lit torch,[2] full of unquenchable light.	Ա
Gregory —	goodly branch; flower-garden in bloom; golden censor with conciliatory incense.	Բ
Gregory —	springtime of blossoms; abundantly flowing river,[3] spreading out beautifully as it streams.	Գ
Gregory —	garden adorned by God; handy harp; preceptor and pedagogue.	Դ

§17

[1]Every so often Erznkats'i introduces the special units of his overall composition; see the first comment at §10 and the last part of the Introduction.

§18

[1]The form and the contents of the poem have much in common with the author's hymn in alphabetical acrostic, *"Aysōr zuarchats'eal ts'ntsay ekeghets'i . . ."* (Reveling today the Church rejoices . . .); trans., Selection XI. The contents seem to derive some of their inspiration from the *Panegyric* attributed to St. John Chrysostom (*Sop'erk'*, 4:70–72). As for the arrangement in alphabetical acrostic, like several such compositions in the hymnal of the Armenian Church, it is inspired by the famous hymn for St. Hrip'simē and her companions by Catholicos Komitas I (in office 615–628): *"Andzink' nuirealk' siroyn K'ristosi . . ."* (Devoted Persons, given to the love of Christ). The latter was composed in 618/619 on the occasion of the transfer of their relics to the church built for St. Hrip'simē near Ējmiatsin (*Sharakan*, pp. 573–582).

[2]On the Apostles as torches, see *The Teaching of St. Gregory*, 683.

[3]Cf. §§20 and 43, where St. Gregory is likened to the river flowing from Eden. In the *Panegyric* attributed to Theophilos, a disciple of St. John Chrysostom, the people address St. Gregory upon his release from the dungeon: "Come, O divine river . . ." (*Sop'erk'*, 4:121).

Gregory —   citizen of heaven;   * բ*
             notable star,
             shedding light along its path through the sky.

Gregory —   by the power of the Self-Existent   *Ձ*
             you have adorned yourself
             with various pretty flowers.

Gregory —   ideal image   *է*
             of the ideal good,
             enriched by the grace of the truly Self-Existent.

Gregory —   soaring to heaven   *Ը*
             in an eminent way,
             prominent among many others.

Gregory —   fertile field;   *թ*
             crowned with glory,
             winged away to the higher, ethereal sanctuary.[4]

Gregory —   fresh flower;   *ժ*
             vigorous tiller of the soil;[5]
             hoard of goodness for many.

Gregory —   truly overflowing   *ի*
             with wisdom from above;
             peaceful harbor to those afloat at sea.

Gregory —   path with variegated lights;   *լ*
             altogether accomplished;
             Illuminator of the Armenian nation.

Gregory —   thoughtful genius,   *խ*
             purified in thoughts;
             confidant of the higher Intelligence.

Gregory —   sea of laughter;   *ծ*
             impediment to the traitorous;
             stout and fruitful tree.

Gregory —   author of a good testament;   *կ*
             glorious image
             of the One living eternally, forever.

---

[4]That is the "heavenly sanctuary," described in Heb. 8:1–6.
[5]Cf. §42; so also in the *Panegyric* attributed to St. John Chrysostom (*Sop'erk'*, 4:82).

Gregory —	good author;	Ձ
	denouncer of the passions;	
	empowered by the genius of the Spirit.[6]	
Gregory —	forewarning voice	Ձ
	crying from on high;	
	man of praiseworthy stature.	
Gregory —	a lit lamp;[7]	Ի
	sailor through the sea of life	
	with the rudder of faith.	
Gregory —	true shepherd;	Ձ
	bright beam of glory,	
	pathway to eternal life.	
Gregory —	mother of the church,	Ս
	pure in sanctity;	
	in thought soaring to the ranks of the seraphim.	
Gregory —	manifold gifts	Յ
	to us, earthborn species,	
	from the Light bright as the sun.[8]	
Gregory —	dedicated to the Most High	Ի
	with ever-new, joyous glory;	
	much tortured martyr.[9]	
Gregory —	living beam of light;	Շ
	golden chain strung with pearls;	
	graceful wreath for the holy Church.[10]	
Gregory —	glittering spring, like gold,	Ո
	streaming beautifully;	
	guide to straight paths.	
Gregory —	celestial pride;	Ձ
	tormentor of the evil one	
	through your physical tortures.	

[6]Echoing Acts 1:8.

[7]So also in the *Panegyric* attributed to Theophilos (*Sop'erk'*, 4:101); a likely allusion to Matt. 5:14–16.

[8]A reference to God; possible allusion to 1 John 1:5.

[9]On St. Gregory as martyr, see the seventh comment at §1.

[10]In a hymn by Erznkats'i, *"Aysōr zuarchats'eal ts'ntsay ekeghets'i . . ."* (Reveling today the Church rejoices . . .), likewise dedicated to St. Gregory, he is referred to as "a graceful wreath woven for the holy Church" (*Sharakan*, p. 266; trans., Selection XI).

Gregory —   fruitful land,   *η*
              with plants bearing abundantly;
              honored with the gifts of the Spirit.

Gregory —   through your fervent prayers,   *Ձ*
              through the living and God-receiving water,[11]
              you have wiped away sins.

Gregory —   delightful balm;   *Ռ*
              highway of light,
              leading high, to eternal life above.

Gregory —   awe-inspiring vision;   *Ս*
              soaring in seraphic glory
              from earthly places to heaven.

Gregory —   reddish rose;   *Վ*
              fervent in faith;
              in conviction steadfast like a rock.

Gregory —   desirable plant   *Տ*
              of the Lord's garden,[12]
              beloved of the superior ones above.

Gregory —   good teacher,[13]   *Ր*
              the pride of teachers,
              rejoicing in divine light.

Gregory —   hedge of the faith,   *Յ*
              joy to the nations,
              refreshing dew to the rational plants.

Gregory —   to the emaciated in spirit,   *հ*
              to the weaver of this oration,
              healing balm for pains.

Gregory —   lustrous flower,   *φ*
              bouquet of violets;
              very ornate lantern, receptacle of light.

---

[11]Lit., "God-containing water," an allusion to the sanctified and sanctifying baptismal water where the Spirit descends as the oil of confirmation (*miwṙon*) is poured. The belief that baptism wipes away all previous sins is common in early Christian writings.

[12]On the metaphor of the plant with reference to the Saint, see the sixth comment at §2 (cf. §§13, 21).

[13]So also in the *Panegyric* attributed to Theophilos (*Sopʿerkʿ*, 4:103).

Gregory —   unblemished priest;   *ℓ*
                true preacher;
                sweet-sounding harp, talking to God.

[IV. Encomium on St. Gregory]

19 [*Introduction*]

Gregory, the much beatified witness, the one out of this world among visible creatures, the native of the heavenly Jerusalem, is kin to the incorporeal ranks in purity.[1] Now, should it [still] seem desirable to anyone that his lineage and provenience be recounted according to the panegyrical principles,[2] then it is proper for us to demonstrate it—we ought to, from the topmost point.[3]

20 [*Birth and upbringing: ancestral*]

From Abraham the great and the beloved of God he descends. From the ancient patriarch a new patriarch is bequeathed; from the father of the righteous a parent of righteousness is proclaimed.[1] He shines in absolute

§19

[1]The opening remarks here serve both as a summary of the preceding poem and as an introduction to the following encomium, which necessarily begins with his birth and upbringing. After affirming the heavenly origin of our Saint, the author is in effect asking: "What more could one say about his birth?"—a thorny subject for the Armenian fathers. The author's point is repeated at the beginning of §22.

[2]The author is cognizant of the panegyrical or encomiastic tradition, the principles of which were determined ever since classical times; e.g., Anaximenes *Rhetorica ad Alexandrum* 1440b5–1441b29; Aristotle *Rhetoric* 1366a23–1368a37; Cicero *De Oratore* 2.84.340–86.350; *Partitiones Oratoriae* 21.71–23.82; Pseudo-Cicero *Ad Herennium* 3.6.10–8.15; and Quintilian *Institutio Oratoria* 3.7.1–28 and 8.4.1–29. Koriwn's *Life of Mashtots'* is the foremost example of Armenian encomia, a source with which our author must have been well acquainted.

[3]Another of the author's seven introductions of specific units within his overall composition. Others are found at §§10, 17, 26, 28, 47, and 54.

§20

[1]Erznkats'i begins and ends with the Saint's purported relation to Abraham, from one father of righteousness (Rom. 4; cf. Gen. 15:6) to another; however, there is more

wisdom from the mind of the "elect [father] of sound."[2] He is the fragrance of incense concealed behind the descendants of Keturah,[3] to whom he

than a spiritual emphasis here because of the shortcomings of St. Gregory's father, who was a murderer. See the remaining comments on this section. In the dedicatory preface to the *Panegyric* by Vardan Vardapet Arewelts'i, addressed to his patron Tēr Hamazasp, Bishop of Haghbat (1243–1261), he refers to the Saint as "your Abraham" (*Sop'erk'*, 5:40).

[2]This is the etymology of "Abraham" according to Erznkats'i in his *Commentary on Grammar*, ch. 15 (see R. Ervine [to whom I am indebted for this observation], *Yovhannēs Erznkac'i Pluz's 'Compilation of Commentary on Grammar',*" 3 vols. Columbia University Dissertation, 1988, 1:362–363; cf. L. G. Khach'erean, *Yovhannēs Erznkats'i (1230–1293 t't'), Hawak'umn Meknut'ean K'erakani* [Y. E. (1230–1293): Compilation of Commentary on Grammar] [Los Angeles and Glendale: Alco Printing, 1983], p. 246). The same etymology appears in various Patristic *Onomastica Sacra* that draw upon the allegory of Philo of Alexandria. Among Philo's works, the etymology is found in *Quaestiones in Genesim* 3.43 and elsewhere (R. Marcus, ed., *Philo Supplement I: Questions and Answers on Genesis,* The Loeb Classical Library [Cambridge, MA: Harvard Univ. Press, 1953], p. 236 n. *f*). Moreover, Abraham symbolizes the wise and virtuous man (*ibid., passim*) and knowledge acquired through teaching (*ibid.,* 4.144; see also L. L. Grabbe, *Etymology in Early Jewish Interpretation: The Hebrew Names in Philo,* Brown Judaic Studies 115 [Atlanta: Scholars Press, 1988], pp. 126–128). This fragmentary work of Philo is extant only in an old Armenian translation and, like other works by the Alexandrian Jewish exegete and philosopher of the first century, was well known among learned Armenians (as further suggested by the nearly thirty extant Armenian manuscripts containing several of Philo's works—a few of which survive only in Armenian—and the more than fifty manuscripts containing commentaries on them).

[3]Keturah was Abraham's wife after Sarah's death. By her he had six sons who became the ancestors of several Arabian tribes inhabiting lands known for their incense (Gen. 25:1–4). As a righteous person, St. Gregory is invariably related to Abraham, who exemplifies righteousness and is deemed the progenitor of the righteous ones who believe in God (Rom. 4). As for our author, however, he is contemplating more than the allegorical relationship between Abraham and St. Gregory. He has in mind the elaborate genealogy of St. Gregory as found in the *Panegyric* by Vardan Vardapet Arewelts'i, where the Saint's clan of the Pahlawunis, like that of their cousins the Arsacids, is said to have come from Bahl (Bactria), a city built by [Z]imran and his brothers, the children of Abraham and Keturah (*Sop'erk'*, 5:45). This theory, in turn, depends on a tradition found in Khorenats'i, where the origin of these Parthian clans is traced to Bahl and the "seed of Abraham out of the descendants of Keturah" (*History of the Armenians,* 2.1–2, 68). Erznkats'i seems to dwell further on the tradition found in Khorenats'i, especially the conflated promise to Abraham in Gen. 17:6 and 16: "Kings of nations will come forth from you" (*ibid.*). In a note to this passage Thomson invites attention to the *Yachakhapatum* (p. 228 of the 1954 Venice edition), according to which the Arsacids are descended from Abraham like all kings of the earth—as the patriarch was promised (*Moses Khorenats'i,* p. 130 n. 7). Thus, the "Eastern and Northern nations" of the next sentence seem to be the Iranians and the Armenians ruled by

joined the children born of the baptismal font as an adornment in shining gold, to the six sons of Keturah. The heavenly promise to the Eastern and Northern nations was fulfilled;[4] spiritual light shone from the easterly part of the world. For the grace of the blessings bestowed upon the children of light[5] by the father who birthed the stars, came concealed with them.[6]

And as the Euphrates gushes forth from Eden, from the recesses of the bosom of the earth and through the crevices of the deep, and down the borders of Armenia it streams, so also our Illuminator.[7]

He was born of the courageous and mighty Parthian race, the Pahlawuni chiefs who were summoned with their splendor from the royal country of the Shahs by the crown-adorned Arshakunis and were sur-

the two branches of the Arsacid Dynasty: to the East and North of the Taurus. The North, as further below in this panegyric (§§24, 37) and elsewhere, refers to Armenia; see the author's hymn *"Aysōr zuarchats'eal ts'ntsay ekeghets'i . . ."* (Reveling today the Church rejoices . . .) dedicated to St. Gregory (*Sharakan*, p. 265; trans., Selection XI); cf. Koriwn, *Life of Mashtots'*, 16 (64.21); Agat'angeghos, *History*, 175, 741–742; and Khorenats'i, *History of the Armenians*, 1.10, 17; 3.68. Moreover, by referring to Keturah's descendants Erznkats'i seems to be connecting our Parthian Saint with the incense-bearing "wise men" (the Magi, three by tradition, who paid homage to the infant Jesus, Matt. 2:1–12) who, according to the apocryphal *Gospel of the Infancy* (ch. 11), are somehow related to Abraham—presumably descendants of Keturah's sons to whom "Abraham gave gifts . . . and sent away to the Land of the East" (Gen. 25:6). For the various Armenian versions of the *Gospel of the Infancy*, some fragmentary, see *Ankanon Girk' Hin ew Nor Ktakaranats'* (Non-canonical Books of the Old and New Testaments), T'angaran Haykakan Hin ew Nor Dprut'eants' 2 (Venice: S. Ghazar, 1898). Erznkats'i has yet another layer of thought in these lines, in the words *khunk'* ("incense"), *oski* ("gold"), and *kenturah* (cf. *kntruk*, "myrrh"; note the connection with the name Keturah), which show a reflection on the three gifts presented by the Magi (cf. Matt. 2:11 and the *Gospel of the Infancy* 11:2).

[4]That is, the Iranians and the Armenians primarily (see the preceding comment).

[5]This Johannine designation for Christian believers (12:36, borrowed from Jewish apocalyptic literature and frequently attested in the Dead Sea Scrolls) is here appropriated for the Armenian faithful, as also in §23. Elsewhere, the Armenian people are referred to as "children of the common faith" (§3), "children of Zion" (§§8, 11), "children of the covenant" (§51) and, in the concluding prayer, "children of your [i.e., St. Gregory's] Church" (§60).

[6]That is, Abraham (cf. Gen. 15:5; 22:17; 26:4). St. Gregory is part of both the descendants of Abraham and the blessings passed on by him. The pronoun *"them"* refers to the descendants of Keturah, including the incense-bearing Magi and, by extension, St. Gregory (see the third comment above) who is vicariously represented by them as they presented their gifts to the newborn King.

[7]The Edenic imagery of the Euphrates is from Gen. 2:10–14; cf. §§18 and 43, where St. Gregory is similarly likened to the Euphrates.

named Arshakuni.[8] He came to us like dew of gladness from dark clouds, from the Surēnian line, and shone with a luminous birth. Stemming from Anak his father, like a rose with flaming petals from a thorny bush,[9] he bloomed with fragrance for us. He appeared to us like an antidote derived from the venomous fangs of serpents, [like] the shimmering purple dye from unseemly snails yet given to adorn imperial clothing; so was he given as a life-giving gift for our souls, from traitorous ancestors, murderers of their masters. [He is like] a delicious date palm[10] with fruit of righteousness and beautiful leafage,[11] grown in a thorny vale; a pearl taken from a fetid and smelly sea yet given to be used for royal crowns; from rough stones, the hardness of rocks, a discovered topaz, beautiful in its vivid color.

And how and to what end are such things done? [They are done] by the most inventive Artisan, the Worker of miracles, the Creator and Transformer of nature, who raises up children to Abraham from stones,[12] who

---

[8]A nobleman of Parthian descent, St. Gregory was of the house of Surēn-Pahlaw, one of the seven branches of the ruling Arshakuni (Arsacid) Dynasty. The Sasanians, who rose to power early in the third century by putting an end to the Arshakuni Dynasty in Persia (226), were determined to wipe out the ruling Arshakunis in Armenia, legitimate claimants to the Persian throne and potential antagonists of the usurping Sasanians. At the instigation of the Sasanians, St. Gregory's father, Anak, murdered the Armenian King Khosrov I (279/280–287; known also as Trdat II). The much weakened Arshakuni Dynasty in Armenia came to an end shortly after the Edict of Theodosius in 387, when Armenia (the Arshakuni Kingdom and the largely autonomous Satrapies) was divided into vassal states subject to either Byzantine or Sasanian rule. On the origin of the Parthian aristocracy and the high lineage of the Surēneans, see S. K. Eddy, *The King is Dead: Studies in the Near Eastern Resistance to Hellenism 334–31 B.C.* (Lincoln: University of Nebraska Press, 1961), pp. 81–92. On the Pahlawuni family, see *Vipasanut'iwn Haykazants'* (Epic History of the Descendants of Hayk) by St. Nersēs Shnorhali, in which he, as a member of the Pahlawuni family, traces his lineage to St. Gregory; text in *Tn. Nersesi Shnorhalwoy Hayots' Kat'oghikosi Bank' Ch'ap'aw* (Words in Verse by Lord Nerses Shnorhali, Catholicos of the Armenians [1166–1173]) 2nd ed. (Venice: S. Ghazar, 1928), pp. 539–608.

[9]Erznkats'i has thus resolved the stigma of St. Gregory's father Anak, the murderer of the Armenian King Khosrov I (see the preceding comment). Anak is the thorny bush that bears the beautiful rose, the venom that provides medicine, the unseemly shell that produces the purple dye, etc.

[10]St. Gregory is likened to a palm tree also in the author's hymn *"Aysōr zuarchats'eal ts'ntsay ekeghets'i . . ."* (Reveling today the Church rejoices . . .) (*Sharakan*, p. 267; trans., Selection XI); so also in the *Panegyric* attributed to Theophilos, a disciple of St. John Chrysostom (*Sop'erk'*, 4:106).

[11]Lit., "beautiful hair."

[12]Alluding to Matt. 3:9; cf. Luke 3:8.

turns old age to youth and barrenness to giving birth,[13] who hangs a live ram as fruit from lifeless plants, providing it for the needed sacrifice.[14] His wisdom is boundless and power unlimited; His will is an accomplished act, as the creation of the world in His thought.[15] Moreover, at times He performs His wondrous acts like skilled workers, as when tillers work the soil, those who cultivate with care, who wish to transform the sour and bitter pomegranate trees to sweet ones. They graft the wood of the pine tree,[16] as they report, into the roots of the sour pomegranate, thus changing the fruit of bitterness to one of sweetness by the power of the substance in that wood; and the essence of bitterness dissolves and melts away and the sour taste becomes sweet, delicious and savory.

21 [*Birth and upbringing: physical*]

And now, since these are done in the natural realm, why wouldn't such an amazing, wonderful miracle be wrought afresh by the Husbandman of the well-bearing branches of the True Vine?[1]

When this heaven-reaching plant[2] from the sour-bearing parent tree with bitter roots was to be planted—having been anticipated from distant centuries and early times down to the appointed hour, a proper place for the bearing of this plant was prepared beside the tombstone covering the

[13]Alluding to the birth of Isaac through the aged Sarah (Gen. 18:9–15; 21:1–8).

[14]Alluding to Gen. 22:13, as also in §§29 and 31.

[15]The medieval belief that the creation of the world—whether *ex nihilo* or from primordial matter—began in the thought of God, could be traced to Philo of Alexandria (see especially *De opificio mundi 7–28* and *De Providentia* 1.6–8; the latter work survives only in Armenian and was well known to medieval Armenian scholiasts) and, ultimately, to Plato's notion of the "ideas" and the creation myth in his *Timaeus*.

[16]The tree name is a *hapax legomenon*, a word that occurs but once in extant Classical Armenian texts—in this panegyric (q.v. 'P;u;ski' [*Peweski*], in G. Awetik'ean et al., eds., *Nor Baŕgirk' Haykazean Lezui* [New Dictionary of the Armenian Language], 2 vols. [Venice: S. Ghazar, 1836] 2:647). Its exact meaning is uncertain. Bedrossian's dictionary, however, gives "pine; lighted pine-branch, fire-stick, fire-brand"; q.v. «Պեւեսկի» (*Peweski*), in M. Bedrossian (Petrosean), *New Dictionary: Armenian–English* (Venice: St. Lazarus, 1879), p. 613.

§21

[1]Alluding to John 15:1–6.

[2]On the metaphor of the plant with reference to the Saint, see the sixth comment at §2 (cf. §§13, 18).

grave of the [first] illuminator of our land and nation, which happened to
be near the [parents'] lodge. By virtue of this [site] the mortal and bitter
plant was able to yield delicious fruit of immortality.[3]

From a family that betrayed its lord, an heir to the Lord's throne was
raised.[4] From a belligerent nation,[5] a savior of the world was affirmed.
From the apostolic remains, an apostle of Christ was chosen. From the
God-lit light, a light-giving lamp was fashioned for this great world,[6] eternal, so that the world may be enlightened through his learned word and his
virtuous, remarkable life; that those held in the darkness of indifference and
ignorance may be enlightened by the light of wisdom and knowledge. He
was sent by the Savior and the Benefactor and the Father of Wisdom[7] to

[3]The author here applies his agricultural illustration of deriving sweet fruit from a
bitter plant (§20) to the birth of St. Gregory, who was conceived—according to later
tradition—near the grave of St. Thaddaeus, the Apostle who traditionally was first to
evangelize Armenia. St. Gregory thus becomes the spiritual progeny of St. Thaddaeus,
whose remains were believed to have affected the conception and subsequent birth.
The author pursues this theme in §§22 and 24. On the early sources of the tradition
about the miraculous birth of St. Gregory, see the fourth comment at §5.

[4]There is a play on the words *tiraneng* (a family *that betrayed its lord*) and *tirakan*
(an heir to *the Lord's* throne) in this comparison between father (Anak) and son (St.
Gregory). The betrayal refers to Anak's crime of murdering King Khosrov I in 287.

[5]Describing the Parthians as "belligerent" is rare in Armenian sources, where they
are usually called "a sinful nation" primarily for Anak's crime (see the preceding comment). At the time when Armenians embraced Christianity, the Parthian Empire of
the Arsacids was history, being overthrown by the Sassanids in 226/7. The old and long
struggle between the Romans and the Parthians over Armenia, however, continued.
This state of affairs at the "Roman frontier" did not end with the short-lived peace
agreement of 280 between Probus and Narses, son of Shapur I (240–271), who was left
as King of Eastern Armenia (Armenshah; later, in 293, Great King of Persia; badly
defeated in Armenia by Caesar Galerius in 297), while Western Armenia remained
under Roman authority. A more lasting settlement came with the Edict of Theodosius
in 387, whereby Armenia (the Arsacid Kingdom and the autonomous Satrapies) was
divided into vassal states subject to either Byzantine or Sassanid rule.

[6]That is, St. Gregory's mission transcends national boundaries; cf. §22. He is
vaguely credited for evangelizing neighboring regions; Agat'angeghos, *History*,
842–845. The author probably had Matt. 5:14–16 in mind; see above, the seventh comment at §18, and also below, several of the comments at §24. The universal role of St.
Gregory is a recurring theme in the panegyrics.

[7]Obviously a Trinitarian formula. The designation of the Spirit as the "Benefactor" is rare, and it seems to derive from the biblical doctrine of "Spiritual Gifts" of 1
Cor. 12–14 (in patristic writings the term is usually used for the Father and the Son, but
not for the Spirit; q.v. "Euergetēs" [Benefactor] in Lampe, *Lexicon*, p. 564).

invite to the heavenly banquet, to the table made ready and to the bowl of those who drink the wine of gladness,[8] to summon the people of Armenia.

This thorny plant guarding this delicious fruit—like the brittle stem bearing the full ear of wheat—yielded to the Planter to reap this joyous fruit.[9] Just as when the grains of wheat are ripe, harvested with the sickle of the Word, heaped for the righteous judgment, and the dust-like chaff is blown away by the wind,[10] so were his kinsmen and people wiped out with the sword and only our Illuminator was left, sheltered in the bosom of God's care, then given as a gladdening cluster for the winepresses of the Church. This bread, stabilizing the hearts of the hungry, was then kept in the storehouse—under protection from on high—by his nurses who brought him to the great capital, Caesarea in Cappadocia. The dew of the garden of the Church was lifted up to the cloud of God's care, saved from the bloody massacre of his kinsmen,[11] like the Lord Jesus who from the sword of Herod was smuggled away by a light cloud to Egypt.[12]

[8]Eucharistic/liturgical echoing of Luke 22:30.

[9]The fruit and the grain contemplated here remind of the Eucharistic wine and bread (see further below). In this ongoing apology for the ancestry of St. Gregory, there is an echo of John 12:24 (cf. Matt. 25:26, on Christ as Sower and Reaper). Similes of agriculture abound not only in the Scriptures but also in *The Teaching of St. Gregory*, 517–531, 617, 641–654.

[10]Alluding to Matt. 3:12; cf. Luke 3:17. With such agricultural imageries Erznkats'i continues his apologetics for the stigma attached to St. Gregory's father, the murderous Anak; cf. §§13 and 20.

[11]Another survey of St. Gregory's early life, as found in Agat'angeghos, *History*, 18–36. However, our author presents St. Gregory's custody as that of the preparation of the Eucharistic gifts: "a gladdening cluster for the winepresses of the Church" and as "bread . . . kept in the storehouse" (cf. §58, where St. Gregory is said to offer his virtue as sacrifice).

[12]Referring to Matt. 2:13–15. The imagined role of the cloud may have been derived from one of the several late versions of the apocryphal "infancy gospels," owing to the *Protoevangelium of James* (see 19:2 in the latter work, on the mysterious cloud over the cave in Bethlehem; in M. R. James, ed., *The Apocryphal New Testament* [Oxford: Clarendon, 1924]; cf. F. C. Conybeare, "*Protoevangelium Jacobi* [From an Armenian Manuscript in the Library of the Mechitarists in Venice]," *American Journal of Theology* 1 [1897] 424–442; also, *Girk' Tghayut'ean K'ristosi* [Book of the Infancy of Christ], ch. 15, on the flight and sojourn in Egypt, in S. Yovsēp'eants' et al., eds., *Ankanon Girk'* [Non-canonical Books], 3 vols. [Venice: S. Ghazar, 1896–1904] 2:60–70).

22 [*Birth and upbringing: spiritual*]

Now, what a marvelous birth! Why should we speak of his genealogy according to the flesh since it has been shown that he is ranked above bodily nature, [having] the most excellent of earthly lives, the loudest praise ever in the district?

He, the crown of pride of the Arshakuni kings,[1] the bestowed child of the Apostle Thaddaeus,[2] a progeny blessed by his living remains, the chosen overseer appointed to his realm, of eastern origin, whose rising is bright like the sun, was nurtured in holiness in the land of the Gamri[3] and tutored in the wisdom of the Christian faith.

Having reached a mature age with love for the wisdom of worshiping God, his undying deeds in life became a spiritual law for the world: not of the letter engraved on boards, like the stone slabs of Moses,[4] nor written admonishments as commands inscribed on paper with ink, but a man of

§22

[1]On St. Gregory's relation to the Arshakunis (Arsacids), see above, §20.

[2]Once more the author alludes to the providential conception of St. Gregory near the grave of St. Thaddaeus (see §§5, 21, and 24). St. Thaddaeus (with St. Bartholomew) is the first of the two Apostles traditionally named as having evangelized the land of Armenia, where also they are said to have been martyred. St. Gregory, as the later evangelist of Armenia, is perceived as the spiritual descendant and successor of St. Thaddaeus (there is no mention of St. Bartholomew in the early tradition[s] surrounding St. Gregory). Unlike the Karshuni version of Agat'angeghos (*Vk*), the extant Armenian version (*Aa*) is silent about this story of a miraculous birth, even about St. Thaddaeus, perhaps to obliterate the earlier Syriac strain of Armenian Christianity as the pro-Byzantine Orthodoxy gained grounds within the nascent Armenian Church. Moreover, the extant Armenian version seeks to heighten the achievement of the St. Gregory. In his *Panegyric* Vardan Vardapet Arewelts'i provides a fair assessment of the relationship between the earlier Apostles and St. Gregory: the former sowed the seed and the latter reaped the harvest (*Sop'erk'*, 5:50).

[3]Armenian form for Cappadocia (Greek), also known as Gamirk', derived from the name of the Gimirri or Kimmerians, a province west of Armenia Minor. It was at its metropolitan See of Caesarea where St. Gregory and several of his descendant successors were consecrated as chief bishops of Armenia.

[4]Allusion to the Decalogue inscribed on the two tablets given to Moses on Mount Sinai (Ex. 31:18; 32:15–19; 34:1, 28). Erznkats'i draws on the spiritualization of the Law in the Prophets (Isa. 51:7; Jer. 31:33 [38:33 LXX]; Ezek. 11:19) and in the New Testament (Gal. 5:16–18; 6:1–2; cf. Rom. 2:14–15; 3:21, 28; 6:14; 8:1–4; 10:4; 13:8–10; 1 Cor. 9:21; etc.). For comparisons with Moses elsewhere in this document, see §§13, 29, 33, 39, 44, 48, 58.

angelic piety, in pure body, set for the entire creation,[5] to teach the whole earthborn, human race.[6]

23 [*Accomplishments in virtue: marriage*]

And as in everything, so also regarding the God-written law of marriage, from which he did not turn away as from a detestable and disdainful thing; nor did he succumb to it as to a mandatory and irrevocable bond, but enough to demonstrate the reason for and the fulfillment of His law.[1] The reason: for the sake of begetting children and to fulfil God's blessed command.[2] Was it not fitting that heaven should pride itself with perceptible luminaries, by displaying these elegant bodies? So it was with our father, shining like the Sun, overseeing his progeny of light. Would he not beam over them within the arches of the new heaven, I mean the Church, this bearer of spiritual torches?[3] And after his marriage, having fulfilled his obligation and the extent of his duty, he gave himself to the piety of celibacy, attaining resplendent purity. Hence the ordinance of marriage was not slighted by him, nor left without a wholesome example, nor has the

---

[5]Lit., "created nature."

[6]The universality of St. Gregory's role is contemplated also in the preceding section.

§23

[1]As in most versions of the Agat'angeghos cycle, the author has very little to say about St. Gregory's married life. His wife remains anonymous in the earliest sources, except in one of the three Greek versions (*Vg*), where her name is Julitta (see Thomson, *Agathangelos*, p. lx). In the *Panegyric* by Vardan Vardapet Arewelts'i, her name is Mariam (*Sop'erk'*, 5:47).

[2]The begetting of children as the only reason for marriage is a classical notion and part of the larger concept of the law of nature (e.g., Musonius Rufus *Fragment 12: On Sexual Indulgence*), popularized in the patristic tradition through the widespread use of the works of Philo of Alexandria, especially by Clement of Alexandria (in Philo, see, e.g., *Quaestiones in Genesim* 4.86; *Quaestiones in Exodum* 2.19; *De Abrahamo* 248–249; *De Specialibus Legibus* 2.23; etc.; and in Clement, see, e.g., *Paedagogus* 2.10.83.1–2; *Stromateis* 2.11.71.4; 3.15.96.2; cf. 2.23.142; 3.45–72).

[3]The logic of the argument is faint, yet simple: since heaven rejoices over its luminaries, then St. Gregory, who reflects the Sun's light in the Church, the new heaven, likewise rejoices over his progeny—both physical and spiritual. They—and more so his descendants and successors to the Patriarchal See—are the "torches" he brings to adorn this new sanctuary. On the Apostles as torches, see *The Teaching of St. Gregory,* 683; on St. Gregory as a torch, see above, §18.

honor of perfect celibacy been ignored or disregarded by those in married lives and ranks.

24 [*Accomplishments in virtue: mission*]

After having left these examples he hastened to become the father of righteous deeds, and became an example of righteousness. Never was he found beholden to anyone, according to the apostolic admonition.[1] Because of this, filled with spiritual radiance, as from the fullness of the Sun's light, he reached from east to west, even as the sun traverses at noontime, moving in the direction of Arcturus.[2] So also he moved in the direction of the northern nations and tribes[3] in order to melt down—as by the sun—the ice of barrenness, to dissipate the mass of darkness, to plant the particles of light and day.

To this end he came to Trdat, the great king of the Armenians, to serve him sincerely and thus settle the betrayal debt incurred through his father's cunning deceitfulness;[4] to inherit the apostolic allotment, his ancestral land and people,[5] won through suffering and blood, that which was handed

§24

[1]Alluding to St. Paul's admonition in 2 Thess. 3:6–15.

[2]The brightest star in Boötes, a northern constellation. In the *Panegyric* by Vardan Vardapet Arewelts'i, the radiance of St. Gregory reaching from east to west is applied to his alleged travel to Rome with King Trdat (*Sop'erk'*, 5:65–66; cf. Agat'angeghos, *History*, 873–880, an account repeated also by Kirakos Gandzakets'i, *History of the Armenians*, 1 (Arm. text: K. A. Melik'-Ohanjanyan, ed., *Kirakos Gandzakets'i: Patmut'iwn Hayots'* [Erevan: Arm. Academy of Sciences, 1961], pp. 10–14; Eng. trans., R. Bedrosian, *Kirakos Gandzakets'i's History of the Armenians* [New York: Sources of the Armenian Tradition, 1986], pp. 8–11; trans. here, Selection X).

[3]An allusion to Armenia and the surrounding regions (cf. §§20 [and the third comment in particular] and 37).

[4]The crime committed against the royal family by Anak, the father of St. Gregory, is contemplated earlier (§20). Erznkats'i is most likely original in his supplying a good reason for the Saint's entering the royal service; i.e., to compensate for the crime committed by his father.

[5]This satement seems to echo an apostolic tradition, based on the New Testament mission charges (Matt. 28:19–20; Luke 24:47–48; Acts 1:8; 10:42) and later apocryphal sources claiming that the world was parceled out by lot among the Twelve Apostles for evangelism (The Acts of Thomas 1; cf. Eusebius, *Historia Ecclesiastica*, 3.1; *The Teaching of St. Gregory*, 609, 688). St. Gregory, who for our author is no less than an apostle, was entrusted with the land of Armenia. In the *Panegyric* attributed to St. John Chrysostom, St. Gregory, unlike the Twelve Apostles who divided the world for evan-

down to him by the hand stretching from the grave;[6] and to bear in his own flesh, before the royal tribunal, what was lacking in the suffering of the Lord[7] for the sake of the body of Christ which is the Armenian Church.[8] It is therefore necessary to mention here the suffering of the Saint by which he was thoroughly purified like the luster of gold[9]—a purification through the furnace of trials—and to refer to the mysterious number of his tortures[10] which he bore in Christ-like compassion for our sake, so as to deliver us from afflicting burdens and to heal the scars of our sins through the suffering of his sacred body.

Like the Lord, this faithful, God-loving servant and watchful[11] and brave shepherd for Christ, the True Shepherd,[12] brought us together—separate and detached members that we are—that he may join us to our Head. And with his God-praising voice he declared:

"For I have other sheep which are not of this fold . . ."[13] He continues to mingle these with the divine flock.

gelism among themselves, was privileged by God to preach universally (*Sop'erk'*, 4:31 and 79–81).

[6]An allusion to the supposed contact with the remains of St. Thaddaeus at the time when St. Gregory was conceived, on which see §§5, 21–22 and the proper comments.

[7]Cf. Rom. 8:17; 2 Cor. 1:5; 4:10–11; Gal. 6:17; Phil. 3:10; 1 Pet. 4:13, on participation in Christ's suffering through persecution for His sake. The thought is repeated in a hymn by Erznkats'i, *"Aysōr zuarchats'eal ts'ntsay ekeghets'i . . ."* (Reveling today the Church rejoices . . .) (*Sharakan*, p. 267; trans., Selection XI) and in Narekats'i's "Ode to the Holy Illuminator" (*Tagher*, p. 176; trans., Selection IV).

[8]Cf. Rom. 12:4–5; 1 Cor. 12:27; Eph. 1:22–23; 4:12, 25; 5:23, on the Church being the body of Christ.

[9]Alluding to 1 Pet. 1:7.

[10]A reference to the twelve tortures of St. Gregory, as described by Agat'angeghos, *History*, 69–122. In Hellenistic Judaism as well as in Early Christianity much was made of the mystical power of numbers, especially in allegorical interpretations of the Bible.

[11]In the first of the two adjectives (*hskogh*), used also at §33 and modifying "shepherd," the author is making use of the meaning of the Greek name (*Gregorios*); this adjective is used in conjunction with the Saint's name by Yovhannēs Sarkawag Vardapet (*Sop'erk'*, 5:35). For the use of other synonymous adjectives in conjunction with the Saint's name and reflecting its meaning, see §15.

[12]Echoing John 10:1–18; so also at §16 and in a hymn by Erznkats'i, *"Aysōr zuarchats'eal ts'ntsay ekeghets'i . . ."* (Reveling today the Church rejoices . . .), likewise dedicated to St. Gregory (*Sharakan*, p. 266; trans., Selection XI). Cf. the *Panegyric* attributed to St. John Chrysostom, where St. Gregory is said to be an example for shepherds, unmoved, like David (*Sop'erk'*, 4:12).

[13]John 10:16. The quotation seems to be by way of recall, for it differs slightly from the text of the Armenian Bible, which at this point reads: «ԵՒ ԱՅԼ ԵՒՍ ՈՉԽԱՐՔ ԵՆ

Just as the city of the living God cannot be hidden, since it set on the mountain of faith, and the much enlightening lamp—lit by the breath of God—cannot be placed under a bowl,[14] so also the truth about his faith; it became known to the king. The man of solitude was soon brought to the judgment hall, questioned and tried by fearsome and terrifying characters. Overwhelming fear and serious threats, full of wrath, kept coming from the king.

25 [*Accomplishments in virtue: forbearance*]

Courageous withstanding and virtuous answers,[1] full of the Saint's wisdom and prudence, these I shall omit for brevity of words; and of the mysterious sum of his tortures and suffering,[2] only the good that was garnered for us I shall describe.[3] For the king, full of much wrath, commanded to bind his hands behind him, and to place a muzzle over his mouth, and to lower blocks of salt onto his back, and to put fetters upon his chest, and to tighten the ropes of the chest fetters, and to have him pulled up by machines and suspended from the highest part of the palace wall. And he remained thus for seven days.

իմ, որ ոչ են յայսմ զաւթէ» (I have other sheep also, which are not of this fold).

[14]Allusion to Matt. 5:14–16 (and parallels); cf. the above poem in alphabetical acrostic (§18), where St. Gregory is said to be a lit lamp, and the seventh comment referring to the *Panegyric* attributed to Theophilos, a disciple of St. John Chrysostom.

§25

[1]For the dialogue between St. Gregory and King Trdat, see Agat'angeghos, *History*, 48–68.

[2]See the preceding section, n. 8.

[3]Lit., "I shall tell in words." The details of the twelve tortures are given in Agat'angeghos, *History*, 69–122. Of these, Erznkats'i dwells on the initial tortures recorded in the first section of his source, following them almost verbatim (see the third part of the Introduction) and omitting the more repulsive ones; cf. the list of the Saint's suffering in §27 and in the author's hymn, *"Aysōr zuarchats'eal ts'ntsay ekeghets'i . . ."* (Reveling today the Church rejoices . . .) (*Sharakan*, pp. 268–271; trans., Selection XI). In his *Panegyric* Vardan Vardapet Arewelts'i gives a similar index of the Saint's suffering (*Sop'erk'*, 5:58–61).

[V. ORACLE TO KING TRDAT]

26 [*Introduction*]

And now, bearing in mind the perverted actions of the unjust council and of the foolish councilmen, I tremble with astonishment, and not without tears I offer this mournful composition.[1]

27 [*Oracle*]

O mighty king:[1] How in your lordship over numerous armies and lands and peoples did you behave so irrationally and insensibly, without having any of the princes or co-regents to bring you to your senses? And why so much hardness of heart—like stone—that under the gentle dew of his orally delivered teachings, descending as it were from the clouds, the hardness of your heart did not soften?

How, O king, did you weigh yourself down like sand, sinking deep, and resisted him who was to lift you up [to become] a heavenly star, soaring lightly high?[2] Instead, heinous tortures you inflicted upon the one who brought you goodness and consolation. The uplifted hands, reaching high, outstretched in prayer through the expanse of the ethereal sanctuary, dedicated to your conciliation, extending grace to you through the divinely wrought oil [of anointing], the right hand clothing your nakedness and the sanctifying fingers, how did you bind—holding them back with your hands and restraining their movement from good deeds?

---

§26

[1]Erznkats'i at times introduces certain of the units that comprise his overall composition (see the first comment at §10), such as the following imagined rebuke and challenge to the king, inspired by the preceding section on the Saint's suffering.

§27

[1]The king is addressed similarly in the "Chrysostomian" panegyrics (*Sop'erk'*, 4:25–26, 111–113).

[2]To become a heavenly star means to become a saint, based on the belief that the souls of the righteous dead shine like stars in heaven, a belief derived from Dan. 12:3; cf. "saints who have become as stars in the new heaven" (§11). King Trdat, like Constantine the Great and King Abgar of Edessa, is a prominent saint in the Armenian Church.

And how did you gag him even with a muzzle put on his chin, on [the lips that utter] the Word that flows into life and gushes like a fountain,[3] [restraining] the movement of those graceful lips that because of his eloquence resemble a harp painted in red, after [the likeness of] which you were to build a sanctuary to God, joining it together fittingly like a harp and painting and glazing it in beautiful red—symbolic of the blood of Christ?[4] [How did you gag him] who was composing with the love of Christ—as with a harp—and was beautifying with the reddish paint of faith, that is, with the honey and the milk dripping from the Word[5] that waters the mouth:[6] nourishing milk to those who are infants in Christ and delicious honey to those established in the faith?[7] Did you not feel remorse or dread for putting the muzzle on his chin, on the instrument for [proclaiming] the Word taught by God, which is to be desired more than gold, even more than many precious gems,[8] and which is like a pouch of aromatics, of fragrant incense—according to the praises by the man of wisdom,[9] [the Word proclaimed by] this teacher of right doctrine,[10] who was making you wise by the faithful Word—you who have infant-like mind and are unwise like children though advanced in years, who was lighting up with the light of the commandments the waning lamp of your mind, who through his lips was sowing from the heart the bright lily of wholesome thought[11] in your barren field and was pouring myrrh for the burial of your carnal and filthy deeds?

[3]Echoing John 7:38. The recurring references to the Word in this section stand for the Logos and/or the Scriptures, as proclaimed by St. Gregory.

[4]Cf. the vision of the red columns surmounted by crosses in Agat'angeghos, *History*, 747, where the red represents the blood of Christ and of the Christian martyrs. For similar description of red-painted pillars in another composition by our author, also dedicated to the Illuminator, see Selection XIII. In patristic writings the color red is often associated with the radiance of paradisial or heavenly phenomena and the splendor of churches.

[5]Echoing 1 Pet. 2:2.

[6]Lit., "that makes the tongue move."

[7]Echoing 1 Cor. 3:2; Heb. 5:12.

[8]Echoing Ps. 19:10 (18:11 LXX).

[9]Refering to King Solomon and his "Proverbs," with echoes of his "Song of Songs" (Cant. 1:13; 3:6; 4:6, 14).

[10]Alluding, it seems, to *The Teaching of Saint Gregory*, referred to repeatedly in the panegyric; see the second comment at §6.

[11]There seems to be a likely allusion here to Prov. 16:23.

Blocks of salt you laid heavily on the back of the bearer of the yoke of the divine Law, you who have not tasted the salt of worshiping God. And with fetters and ropes you contrived to squeeze his heart, the abode of the holy and sanctifying Spirit. You who are a crawler on earth and bestially minded, how did you [treat] the heavenly man who from his good heart had let goodness flow, who to the natural warmth of his heart had added the fire of the love of this earth's Planter and who was desiring to set your frozen heart aflame?

Now, the one who delivers you from that much wickedness and brings you countless blessings, in streams, you tortured so unsparingly, with many contrived ordeals. Did you not know what you were doing—as the Jewish mob did not when rushing to crucify God the Word and Lord Jesus Christ?[12] And like the Lord who was beseeching—as a son would a father: "Father, forgive them, for they do not know what they are doing,"[13] so also he was pleading with fatherly compassion for the sinful son and was seeking the heavenly good instead of evil. With his bound hands, accustomed to good deeds, he was pleading earnestly that the bound and restricted hands of the Armenian people might be set free, [that those hands] which fashioned idols and offered sacrifices to demons and incense to breathless images[14] might be taught to be raised to God.

The muzzle was put on his God-proclaiming mouth so that we who are bestial in nature and irrational in thought—like horses and mules whose jaws it is proper to restrain with bridles and muzzles—may turn our rebellious and unbridled nature to the Giver of Reason, the Creator. Thus he took upon himself to bear the suffering proper to us, the compassionate father of children who return evil [for good],[15] that he may bring us back from the irrational love of filth and the estrangement into bestiality to the heavenly wisdom, by way of obedience to the Father and Creator. His chest and heart were squeezed with fetters and ropes, the one who was clean in heart and worthy of divine contemplation, that he may cleanse our hearts from evil conscience and make them vessels for the heavenly treasures. He

---

[12]Alluding to the arrest and trial of Jesus, Matt. 26–27 and parallels.

[13]Luke 23:34. The quotation is in keeping with the text of the Armenian Bible, which has *dots'a* (them/those) instead of *sots'a* (them/these).

[14]Deriding the pre-Christian faith of the Armenians; cf. §§13, 30, 33.

[15]So also in the *Panegyric* attributed to Theophilos, a disciple of St. John Chrysostom, St. Gregory is referred to as a compassionate father (*Sop'erk'*, 4:102).

bore the heavy load of salt on his back, so dreadful and difficult to bear, he who was to become the seasoning salt of Armenia,[16] that through the flavorful salt of certainty and truth he may transform the tastelessness and the corruption of their deeds to sweet savor.

[VI. Encomium on Mount Sepuh]

28 [*Introduction*]

And now, all phases of his suffering were thus significant, redemptive, and liberating, and [giving] us opportunities for goodness. To mention them all would make this oration long, especially if the stories and the encomia recounted by the holy fathers were to be earnestly evoked. Ours is but an observation on this mountain of holiness, which became the place of the Saint's asceticism for thirty years[1] and of the grave where his holy body was laid to rest, to which very topic I now direct my words.[2]

---

[16]Echoing Matt. 5:13 (and parallels). This metaphor, common to the genre, is repeated near the end of §43.

§28

[1]This rounded figure is based on the traditional date (301) for the Christianization of Armenia by St. Gregory, following which he retired to "this mountain of holiness."

[2]An important introduction to the longest unit in the composition (§§28–42). This unit is as central as the encomium on St. Gregory (§§19–25). For other introductions of specific units, see the first comment at §10 and the last part of the Introduction. In his praise of Mount Sepuh from here on, through §42, the author adds to his ongoing comparison (seen before this point in his comparing St. Gregory with others of great fame, especially Moses). With this, he more than fulfills a basic requirement in encomiastic or panegyrical writing, namely, comparison with the intent of showing the greatness—if not superiority—of that which (or the one who) is magnified (Aristotle *Rhetoric* 1368a11–25; cf. Cicero *De Oratore* 2.85.348; Aphthonius in his *Progymnasmata* has this admonition: "add comparison, in order to infer a greater position for the one being praised," from R. Nadeau, "The Progymnasmata of Aphthonius in Translation," *Speech Monographs* 19 [1952] 273).

29 [*Prelude*]

Many mountains,[1] and with renowned names, are highly revered in the world for various reasons. First of all, after the universal flood, Mount Ararat was revered with its high summit Masis, the resting place of [Noah's] ark,[2] which signified the mystery of the Church and became the second bearer of humankind.[3] Abraham was about to sacrifice Isaac on the mountain of the Amorites.[4] Mount Horeb is revered for the marvelous vision which Moses had, symbolic of the Virgin: the bush which was burning without being consumed.[5] Mount Sinai is revered for the mani-

§29

[1]The opening words of this section are reminiscent of a hymn composed by Erznkats'i, *"Leřink' amenayn . . ."* (All [you] mountains . . .) and likewise dedicated to St. Gregory for the festival commemorating his entering the dungeon; text in *Sharakan*, pp. 278–281, and Srapyan, *Hovhannes Erznkats'i*, pp. 130–132; trans., Selection XII. For his other hymns, also dedicated to St. Gregory, see the second comment at §1. In what follows here, the author covers the renowned mountains of the Old Testament first, then those of the New Testament, and then others in the rest of the world—before stating his intent to dwell on the praise of Mount Sepuh.

[2]Earlier Armenian tradition, however, identifies Mount Ararat or the biblical mountains of Urartu (Gen. 8:4) with Mount Sararad in the district of Korduk' or Qardü in the Assyrian March of southern Armenia, south of Lake Van (*Buzandaran*, 3.10; T'ovmay Artsruni, *History of the House of the Artsrunik'*, 1.1 [p. 19], both following the tradition in Josephus, [*Antiquities*, 1.3.6] and Eusebius, [*Chronicle*, ed. Aucher 1:37]).

[3]In patristic writings, ever since Tertullian in the second century, Noah's ark typifies the Church; for this typology in the Greek Fathers, see *"Kibōtos"* (Ark) A.1.a. in Lampe, *Lexicon*, p. 753. The ark or the Church as the bearer of humankind is similarly contemplated in the notion of the Church as mother, a common metaphor in the Fathers (see the fifth comment at §3). As such, the Church, "the second bearer," enables people to be born again.

[4]Mount Moriah is meant (cf. Gen. 22:2); the substitution may be explained on the basis of the closeness of the names. The sacrifice of Isaac is a recurring subject in this panegyric (§§20 and 31).

[5]Referring to Ex. 3:2. On the burning bush typifying the Blessed Virgin Mary in patristic writings, see *"Batos"* (Bush) 1.f. in Lampe, *Lexicon*, p. 294. Such typology is rare in medieval Armenian theology, limited to discussions of the incorruptibility of the body of the incarnate Christ, the veracity of which was argued by pointing, *inter alia*, to the constant virginity of Mary—just like the unchanging nature of the burning bush where God was found (see, e.g., Step'anos Siwnets'i, *Vasn Anapakanut'ean Marmnoyn K'ristosi* [On the Incorruptibility of the Body of Christ], ed. by G. Tēr-Mkrtch'ean, *Ararat* 35 [1902] 368–400). A more common and related figure or type for the Blessed Virgin is that of the "Tree of Life." On the latter, see A. Mnats'akanyan, ed., *Haykakan mijnadaryan zhoghovrdakan erger* (Popular Medieval Armenian Songs) (Erevan:

festation of God, for there were given to Moses the tablets inscribed by God and [the pattern of] the ark in which the Law was kept, which was hid on the same mountain at the hand of Jeremiah the prophet, in the very cleft of the rock where God shut Moses with a dense cloud at noon and with light at night.[6] Mount Nebo in the Araboth of Moab, where Moses ascended, where God showed him the Promised Land, and where he died.[7] Mount Zion was revered, for God chose it to be the place in which to establish the reputation of His power.[8] David fortified the same mountain and Solomon built the Temple there, magnificent in structure.[9] Solomon, whom God made wise, sacrificed a thousand oxen to God on the mountain of the Gibeonites and asked for wisdom, which he received beyond measure.[10] Elijah prayed atop Mount Carmel and with consuming fire and water chastened the violators of God's Law.[11] On the same mountain Elisha prayed in the manner of his teacher, at which point the heavenly armies descended, and by the prayer of the prophet the eyes of the young man were opened and he saw the mountain full of chariots and riders.[12]

Haypethrat, 1956), p. 295; cf. *"Paradeisos"* (Paradise) E.2. in Lampe, *Lexicon*, p. 1012, referring to the Blessed Virgin metaphorically as Paradise. A popular hymn, *"Khnki tsaŕid nman es . . ."* (You are like an incense tree . . .), attributed to Grigor Vardapet Ostants'i and chanted at the five great Marian feasts, likens her to an incense tree—among other imageries from the Exodus experiences, including the golden jar filled with manna and the blossoming rod of Aaron, both of which were kept in the Ark of the Covenant (Ex. 16:33–34; Num. 17:8–10; cf. §32, where St. Gregory is likened to the golden jar filled with manna); for the text, see N. Bogharian, *Grand Catalogue of St. James Manuscripts*, 11 vols. (Jerusalem: St. James Press, 1966–1991) 1:377, 4:412. The biblical types from Exodus are common in Orthodox hymnody to stress the theme of the Blessed Virgin Mary as the Ark of the Covenant, the Menorah bearing Jesus—the light of the world, etc.; see also *"Luxnia"* (Lamp) 4. in Lampe, *Lexicon*, p. 817, referring to Zech. 4:2–3.

[6] As narrated in Ex. 19–25. The tradition that Jeremiah hid the Ark of the Covenant on Mount Nebo during the siege of Jerusalem under Nebuchadnezzar (587–586 BS) is prevalent (2 Macc. 2:2–8; cf. the pseudepigraphical 2 Baruch 6:7, which suggests that the Ark was concealed in Jerusalem). Not so prevalent is the tradition that Jeremiah hid it on Mount Sinai, where it was given.

[7] As narrated in Deut. 34:1–8. See below, §33, for further comparison between the death of Moses and that of St. Gregory.

[8] Alluding to the Theophany that led to the purchase of the threshing floor of Araunah the Jebusite by David (2 Sam. 24:18–25).

[9] Following 2 Sam. 5:6–16 and 2 Chr. 3–7; cf. §34 below.

[10] Actually a mound, a cultic "high place" according to 2 Chr. 1:3.

[11] Following the narrative in 1 Kgs. 18:16–46.

[12] According to 2 Kgs. 6:8–23, this was on the hill of Samaria and not on Mount Carmel.

And the Lord, sitting high on the mountain, taught His disciples the nine beatitudes.[13] Mount Tabor was revered, for there the Lord revealed the glory of His divinity and a taste of the life to come and the symbolism of the Church at such unequalled height.[14] Golgotha was honored with superior glory, for there the Lord was glorified through the Cross over the grave of the first-created man and liberated his descendants.[15] Mount Olivet was adorned with grace, for there the Lord gave the right of priesthood to His disciples.[16] From Senir and Hermon gush the springs of the Jordan, where the Lord was baptized, giving us the same [rite] for spiritual birth.[17]

[13]As found at the beginning of the Sermon on the Mount, Matt. 5:1–12; the unnamed Galilean mount has been variously identified in Christian tradition.

[14]Although Mount Tabor is not mentioned by name in the canonical Gospels, it was traditionally believed to be the site of the Transfiguration (Matt. 17:1–13). A seventh-century description of Mount Tabor by an anonymous Armenian pilgrim, found at the end of *"Haytnut'iwn Teaṙn i T'ap'ōr Leṙin"* (The Epiphany of the Lord on Mount Tabor), has been wrongly attributed to Eghishē in *Srboy hōrn meroy Eghishēi Vardapeti Matenagrut'iwnk'* (Writings of Our Holy Father Eghishē Vardapet); see R. W. Thomson, "A Seventh-Century Armenian Pilgrim on Mount Tabor," *Journal of Theological Studies* 18 (1967) 27–33, with translation of the text found in the 1859 Venice edition of the works attributed to Eghishē (by the given title), pp. 236–239. It is likely that such a description is in keeping with the requirements set in the *Progymnasmata*, the popular textbooks of rhetorical exercises in Late Antiquity, which included a section on descriptive writing. Like the Tabernacle of the Hebrews, the Church as a symbol of heaven is commonplace in patristic writings (see *"Skenē"* [Tabernacle] A.2.b. in Lampe, *Lexicon*, p. 1237; cf. Philo of Alexandria, *Quaestiones in Exodum*, 2.49–106; Heb. 8:2; 9:11, 23–24).

[15]The long-standing tradition that the Cross stood at the grave of Adam owes to St. Paul's comparison between the death of the First Adam and that of Christ, the Second Adam (Rom. 5:12–21; 1 Cor. 15:21–22). Contributing to this seminal tradition is the Hebrew or Aramaic etymology of Golgotha in the Gospels: "The Place of the Skull" (Matt. 27:33; Mark 15:22; John 19:17; cf. Luke 23:33), later believed to have been an allusion to the skull of Adam, supposed to have been unearthed when digging to erect the Cross of Christ. This becomes a recurring motif in the Christian extra-canonical "Adam literature," and in the iconography of the Crucifixion; see especially M. E. Stone, *A History of Literature of Adam and Eve*, SBL Early Judaism and Its Literature 3 (Atlanta: Scholars Press, 1992), p. 2 (cf. p. 91, referring to the burial of Adam on Golgotha, according to the *Cave of Treasures*, 23).

[16]The summit east of Old Jerusalem and the traditional site of the Ascension. The allusion is to the parting words of Jesus and to His final blessing of the disciples (Luke 24:50–53; Acts 1:1–11). This last act of Jesus was interpreted by the Fathers as the disciples' priestly ordination. The notion is repeated in §38.

[17]Senir (*Sanir*) is a biblical synonym for Hermon—if not also a name for the entire

And there are numerous others which bear famous names because of their natural majesty and physical properties: in Italy there is the mountain called Aureus,[18] two mountains in Sicily: Parthenos, from where two great rivers flow, and Vulcanus, the summit of which is always ablaze.[19] [Others are:] the Great Lebanon and Carmel in the land of the Arameans,[20] Didyma in Phrygia,[21] Taurus in Syria, Ante-Taurus in Cappadocia, Olympus in Cyprus.[22] So also in Greater Armenia, in our Land, is Argaeus,[23] lest we should be—in anything—inferior to any of the notable nations and lands.

But in these last days, in accordance with the prophetic voice,[24] is revealed Mount Sepuh, between the borders of two districts: Ekegheats' and Daranaghik',[25] with peculiar glory, alongside all significant and highly

Lebanon Range of which Hermon (Jabal ash-Shaykh) is the southern spur (Deut. 3:9; 1 Chr. 5:23; Cant. 4:8; Ezek. 27:5). According to the tenth-century Arab geographer, Ibn Hokal, Senir is the northern section of the Anti-Lebanon Range (Jabal ash-Sharqi). The sources of the Jordan around Mount Hermon are: the Bareighit ('Ayoun) and the Hasbani to the west, the Leddan to the south, and the Banias to the east. On the baptism of Jesus, see Matt. 3:13–17 and parallels.

[18]Lit., "Gold," Greek, *Chrysos.* One of the peaks in the Cispadane (Aemilia) region of the Apennines, the highest point of which is Monte Corno.

[19]Probably Mounts Enna and Etna are meant (the name Parthenos for the former is rather unusual). The first is in central Sicily, where also some of the tributaries of the two major rivers, Salso and Simeto, have their origin. The second is the highest volcano in Europe, which has never been completely dormant (see M. I. Finley, *A History of Sicily: Ancient Sicily to the Arab Conquest* [New York: Viking Press, 1968], pp. 14, 44).

[20]Lit., "Assyrians," i.e., the Syriac (Western Aramaic) speaking inhabitants of ancient Syria (Aram), called Assyrians by the Armenians who imagined them, together with the inhabitants of northern Mesopotamia (Edessa and Nisibis, as well as Mosul with its environs), to be related to the ancient Assyrians—an error perpetuated by the Crusaders and continued to this day even by the local inhabitants. Carmel is mentioned earlier in this section, in conjunction with the activities of the prophet Elijah.

[21]Mount Didyma is in the ancient province of Argolis, Greece, and not in Phrygia.

[22]Also known as Olimbos or Chionistra.

[23]Or, Argos; possibly the Greek form for Mount Aragats (Alagöz), and certainly not the mountain known by this name in Cappadocia, central Asia Minor.

[24]The author employs apocalyptic language here, with the attendant prophetic ambiguity; cf. Heb. 1:2; 9:26; 1 Pet. 1:20; etc.

[25]These adjacent districts in westernmost Greater Armenia have long been associated with the hereditary domain of the Gregorid house, with its ancestral village and necropolis at T'ordan in the district of Daranaghik' and another ancestral necropolis at T'il in the district of Ekegheats' (*Buzandaran Patmut'iwnk'*, 3.11–12; 4.14; for the text,

revered mountains. It is proper for us to compare it in [exalting] words, to praise it in our oration, and to show its familiar, genuine grandeur.

30 [*Part I*]

Rejoice, Mount Sepuh,[1] and revel in deeper mystery than that of Ararat with its high summit Masis. Though there rested the ark built of wood by Noah,[2] yet on you [rested] the living ark, Gregory,[3] fashioned compassionately through the will of the Father, formed with Christ-like virtue, made beautiful through the power of the Holy Spirit. The other ark made it possible for human beings and the species of animals to survive the catastrophe of water, but this living ark [made it possible to escape] the floods of sin and idolatry,[4] restored the rational soul to the people of Armenia, and became the kernel of Orthodoxy—which is true and unsullied life.[5] From that ark, as from a mother's womb, emerged the patriarch Noah to offer sacrifice when the waters dried out; but from this ark was reborn the Armenian nation through the tuneful proclamation of the bountiful Word,

see *P'awstosi Buzandats'woy Patmut'iwn Hayots' i ch'ors dprut'iwns* [P'awstos Buzandats'i's History of the Armenians in Four Registers] [4th ed., Venice: Mekhit'arean Tparan, 1933]; Eng. trans., N. G. Garsoïan, *The Epic Histories (Buzandaran Patmut'iwnk')* [Cambridge, Mass.: Harvard University Press, 1989]). Mount Sepuh, with its caves of Manē to which St. Gregory retired (Agat'angeghos, *History*, 861; cf. Khorenats'i, *History of the Armenians*, 2.90–91), separated the two districts: Daranaghik' to the west and Ekegheats' to the east. It must be noted, however, that both Agat'angeghos and Khorenats'i refer to the place as "the mountain called the Caves of Manē". Mount Sepuh, also known as Mount Gohanam, is identified with modern Kara Daghi.

§30

[1]Here begins the praise of Mount Sepuh, in twelve parts (§§30–41), each beginning with "Rejoice. . . ." The praise culminates with a postlude (§42). This lengthy exaltation of Mount Sepuh has a lesser parallel in Vardan Vardapet Arewelts'i (*Sop'erk'*, 5:73–76).

[2]According to Gen. 8:4. Earlier Armenian tradition, however, identifies the site with Mount Sararad south of Lake Van, on which see the second comment at §29.

[3]Likewise, in his hymn *"Lerink' amenayn . . ."* (All [you] mountains . . .) (*Sharakan*, p. 278; trans., Selection XII), Erznkats'i pronounces Mount Sepuh superior to Masis since St. Gregory himself is the life-saving ark who came to rest there (alluding to Noah's ark).

[4]Another reference to the pre-Christian faith of the Armenians; cf. §§13, 27, 33.

[5]There is an echo here of John 12:24–25.

offering sacrifices to the living and only true God, when dried from filth and cleansed of sin.

31 [*Part II*]

Rejoice, superior mountain, most exalted place, like the mountain of the Amorites, the place of Abraham's offering, where he was to sacrifice his beloved son to the One who is true love; and by obtaining the ram in place of his beloved, he made the Giver of blessings a debtor to the world.[1] Whereas on you, the father of our faith, the enlightener of our souls, Saint Gregory, offered to God the fruit of the Spirit—the virtues—and endurance of the body earth-born in nature and purity of mind.[2] And in return he received a purified people and chosen for their piety. And becoming like a debtor himself, he pleaded with them constantly to guard scrupulously that very seal of faith, through the Orthodox confession of the Only-begotten Son.

32 [*Part III*]

Rejoice, holy mountain, station of sanctity, honored with the grace of Sinai, the site of the Ark which was covered with gold inside and out and contained the golden jar and the tablets of the covenant, above which the cherubim of glory made a canopy.[1] As for you, rejoice all the more, you that became the place of the golden ark: the pure and watchful person of Saint Gregory,[2] who was overlaid with sanctity, inwardly, as regards the soul, and

§31

[1]Alluding to Gen. 22:17-18, attaching to it the commonplace understanding of Abraham's act as prefiguring the Father's giving of His Son for the salvation of the world.

[2]The classical *"mens, corps, spiritus"* in reverse order.

§32

[1]*the Ark.* Alluding, as earlier (§29), to the injunctions given at Sinai regarding the Ark of the Covenant (Ex. 24-25). Also, as earlier, the author may be thinking about the presumed concealment of the Ark (by Jeremiah) on Mount Sinai—hence the analogy with Mount Sepuh. In the *Panegyric* by Vardan Vardapet Arewelts'i, the plains of Ararat are graced with the glory and grace of Mts. Sinai and Horeb (*Sop'erk'*, 5:54).

[2]On the adjective "watchful" as the meaning of the Saint's Greek name, see above (§15).

outwardly, as regards the body. And upon his five bodily senses and the corresponding faculties of his soul,[3] the indelible statutes of the divine Law were inscribed.[4] And, like the golden jar,[5] he was full of the manna of God's grace. And his heart, a censor emitting the fragrance of incense, lies in you, kept as a cherished relic of the holy martyr.[6] Wherefore nations and tribes coming from afar honor you. Your blessed soil they present as gift for the healing of their fellow countrymen.[7]

33 [*Part IV*]

Rejoice, highest mountain and head of the mountains. For as Moses ascended the Araboth of Moab, even Mount Nebo, from where God showed him the land of blessings and where, upon his death, he was protected by angels, so also our Moses:[1] the leader of the new people,[2] the high priest Saint Gregory, when he crossed the sea of sin and drowned the falsehood of idolatry.[3] And rallying the streams of the Twelve Apostles' [teaching], he eradicated the vain teachings of paganism;[4] and through his suffering he gave us inheritance with the saints and the eternal world for a

---

[3]Reference to the fivefold powers of the soul, as in Aristotelian theory, related to the five physical faculties: rational, irascible, appetitive, nutritive, and sense-perceptive. Cf. Philo of Alexandria, *Quaestiones in Genesim*, 4.186, a fragmentary work extant only in Armenian, with which our author was well acquainted.

[4]Drawing perhaps on Jer. 31:33 (38:33 LXX): "I will put my law in their inward parts, and write it in their hearts." In *"Leṙink' amenayn . . ."* (Sharakan, p. 279; trans., Selection XII), Mount Sepuh is said to be superior to Mount Sinai since St. Gregory came there with a shining face (alluding to Moses' experience in Ex. 34:29–35).

[5]Allusion to the jar filled with manna and kept in the Ark of the Covenant (Ex. 16:33–34).

[6]On St. Gregory's "martyrdom," see the seventh comment at §1.

[7]Pilgrims apparently took of the soil of the site for healing purposes.

§33

[1]*so also our Moses*. Alluding, once more, to Deut. 34:1–8 (cf. §29). According to Khorenats'i, St. Gregory's remains were concealed like those of Moses (*History of the Armenians*, 2.91; cf. 3.68). A similar point is made in the *Panegyric* by Vardan Vardapet Arewelts'i (*Sop'erk'*, 5:73, 75).

[2]That is, of the Armenian people as New Israel (see the first part of the Introduction and the preceding references to Zion, especially at §§3, 8, and 11).

[3]Allusion to the Exodus experience at the Red Sea (Ex. 14:15–29).

[4]Again referring to the pre-Christian faith of the Armenians (cf. §§13, 27, 30). For comparisons with Moses elsewhere in this document, see the second comment at §13.

promised land.[5] And he ascended your very high peaks, ever to contemplate that very land of the living; and he prayed within the clefts of your rocks for the preservation of his people and for their becoming worthy inheritors of the abodes of the righteous.[6] And when he died, the watchful shepherd was found by shepherds,[7] protected by the fiery hosts.[8] And now he distributes from you to us the remedy that cleanses from filth and the hope for the forgiveness of sins.

[5]The Armenians as God's people, begotten through the suffering of St. Gregory, is a recurring theme; see below, §§52, 55. So also in the *Panegyric* by Vardan Vardapet Arewelts'i, the Saint begot the Armenian people for God through his suffering (*Sop'erk'*, 5:57, 61). On the Saint bringing his people to heaven as their promised land, cf. the *Panegyric* attributed to St. John Chrysostom (*Sop'erk'*, 4:12) and that of Yovhannēs Sarkawag Vardapet (*Sop'erk'*, 5:33–34; trans., Selection VI).

[6]Allusion to John 14:1–3.

[7]The adjective "watchful" (*hskogh*), used also at §24 with reference to the Saint, reflects the meaning of his name (see the second comment at §15, where other synonymous adjectives reflecting the meaning of *Gregorios* are used). For the legends surrounding St. Gregory's death, burial, and the discovery of his remains, see Khorenats'i, *History of the Armenians*, 2.91 (detailing how shepherds found and buried the Saint's body without knowing who he was, and how after a long time his relics were revealed to a certain ascetic named Garnik "who took them and buried them in the village of T'ordan"); cf. the anonymous *"Patmut'iwn yaghags giwti nshkharats' Srboyn Grigori Hayots' Metsats' Lusaworch'i"* (History of the Discovery of the Relics of St. Gregory the Illuminator of Greater Armenia), *Ararat* 35 (1902) 1178–83. See also the Karshuni version of Agat'angeghos (*Vk* 293–299) which, as mentioned earlier, was written in *ca.* 600; cf. M. Van Esbroeck, "Témoignages littéraires sur les sépultures de S. Grégoire l'Illuminateur," *Analecta Bollandiana* 89 (1971) 387–418, who argues that the story about St. Gregory's relics and the invention of his cult does not predate the sixth century (so also *idem*, "Un nouveau témoin du livre d'Agathange," p. 162). It seems, however, that the relics of St. Gregory were discovered in the time of Emperor Zeno (474–491), and their earliest cultic use is attested by Ghazar P'arpets'i who wrote his *History* in 500/1 (Arm. text, G. Tēr-Mkrtch'ean and S. Malkhasean, eds., *Patmut'iwn Hayots'* [Armenian History] [Tiflis: Martiroseants', 1904], pp. 55, 176; Eng. trans., R. W. Thomson, *The History of Łazar P'arpets'i*, Scholars Press Occasional Papers and Proceedings: Columbia University Program in Armenian Studies/S. D. Fesjian Academic Publications 4 [Atlanta: Scholars Press, 1991], especially pp. 95 n. 2, 238 n. 2). For later versions of what became of St. Gregory's relics, see the panegyric by Vardan Arewelts'i (*Sop'erk'* 5:75–76; trans., Selection IX) and Kirakos Gandzakets'i, *History of the Armenians*, 1 (trans., Selection X).

[8]That is, the angels (cf. §36).

34 [*Part V*]

Rejoice, Mount Sepuh, and exult in majestic glory alongside Zion, where the fame of the Lord's valor is declared, [the place] fortified by David and made beautiful by the magnificent Temple of Solomon.[1] As for you, the gathering place of multitudes of believers, along with your acknowledged fame is told also that which pertains to the amazing virgin, Saint Manē, who was here in your cavernous rocks.[2] Through her heavenly life while in the body, in her enduring solitude, she demonstrated the fellowship of the incorporeals; and she was preoccupied with priestly, unsullied and pristine prayers. Your broad locations and the tiniest crevices of your rocks she transformed into a glorious temple, a mystical altar, a defined dwelling place for the One beyond definition by nature. To this place came the priceless sacrifice,[3] pleading for his people the Father's conciliation and the

§34

[1]See the various Psalms exalting Zion (e.g., Pss. 87, 125, 128, 147 [86, 124, 127, 146–147 LXX]) and the chronicle of the establishment of the Solomonic temple in Jerusalem (2 Chr. 3–7), alluded to in §29 above. In no uncertain terms our author claims for Mount Sepuh what the Scriptures hold for Mount Zion: "this mountain where God dwells" (§§12, 36).

[2]St. Manē is one of the virgins or nuns traditionally associated with Sts. Hṙip'simē and Gayanē. She was believed to have taken refuge in these caves prior to the martyrdom of her companions (Khorenats'i, *History of the Armenians*, 2.91; for later embellishments, see B. Outtier, "Movsēs après Movsēs," in D. Kouymjian, ed., *Movsēs Xorenac'i et l'historiographie arménienne des origines,* Catholicossat arménien de Cilicie, 1700ème centenaire de la proclamation du Christianisme en Arménie 7 [Antélias: Catholicossat arménien de Cilicie, 2000], pp. 99–112). Her name appears to be somewhat related to Nanē, a goddess closely associated with Anahit and whose temple stood in nearby T'il in the province of Ekegheats', one of the Gregorid burial grounds in the fourth century (see Russell, *Zoroastrianism in Armenia,* p. 339). Besides Khorenats'i, the Karshuni version of Agat'angeghos (*Vk* 291) is the only ancient source that refers to Manē in association with the other nuns; stating, however, that she escaped at the time of her companions' martyrdom. Later in this panegyric, the author draws upon subsequent tradition whereby St. Gregory is credited with burying her remains when he came to the same region for his ascetic withdrawal (§41; cf. the above cited article by Outtier, also M. Awgerean, *Liakatar Vark' ew Vkayabanut'iwn Srbots'* [The Complete Lives and Testimony of the Saints], 12 vols. [Venice: S. Ghazar, 1810–1815] 3:130–138). For literary motifs in accounts on discoveries of relics and subsequent or secondary burials, with reference to the narratives on St. Gregory, see the article by Van Esbroeck, "Témoignages littéraires," cited in the seventh comment at §33.

[3]Alluding to St. Gregory and the closing years of his life at the same place.

mercy of the Son and the bestowal of the grace of the Spirit. To this very temple inundated with light converge the faithful children, established in the same hope and asking by faith to find the same salutary gifts through the intercession of their father.

35 [Part VI]

Rejoice, Mount Sepuh, place of praise, exultant in songs. For as on the mountain of the Gibeonites Solomon the King offered burnt offerings and sacrifices to God and asked for wisdom whereby to govern his kingdom and to shepherd the Lord's people, whom he received with incomparable sublimity,[1] so also on you, Gregory, in royal appearance, the seer and the preacher of the Kingdom, offered rational sacrifices—raising the fruit of the vine and the pure body of the Lord God—and sought to apprehend the higher wisdom of Him who is true and perfect.[2] When imparting the Word at the paternal altar, the promise, in accordance with the good news, which he had mastered with incomparable distinction, he moved from the "mirror" to the "face to face": from the lesser knowledge to the greater.[3] And now he shepherds his people, enlightened through the God-given wisdom of his luscious teaching.[4]

§35

[1] According to 2 Chr. 1:3 (contemplated earlier, §29).

[2] While drawing a parallel between Solomon's sacrifice and quest for wisdom at Gibeon and St. Gregory's offering the Eucharistic sacrifice, Erznkats'i underscores a tenet in medieval sacramental theology wherein the Divine Liturgy is seen as a means of mystic ascent to God (see the first comment at §4). A comparable understanding of the Divine Liturgy may be seen also in Frik, a contemporary of Erznkats'i (text in T. M. Mushkambarean, ed., *Frik Diwan* [New York: AGBU, 1952], pp. 332–333). On God as perfect in love, see Matt. 5:48.

[3] Allusion to 1 Cor. 13:12. Erznkats'i has moved from contemplating the liturgy of the Eucharist to contemplating the liturgy of the Word, from the second part of the Divine Liturgy to the first part devoted to the reading of the Scriptures and the ensuing homily. A good homiletician moved from the Old Testament Lesson (often referred to as "a mere shadow of what is to come," Col. 2:17; cf. Heb. 8:5) to the New Testament Lesson, focusing ultimately on the person of Jesus Christ as revealed in the Gospel, "the good news."

[4] As found in *The Teaching of Saint Gregory*, a work repeatedly referred or alluded to in the panegyric; see the second comment at §6.

36 [*Part VII*]

Rejoice, Mount Sepuh, perfect and blessed like Mount Carmel, atop which Elijah arose to pray and to torment with fire and drought the violators of God's Law,[1] though the bread and the oil of the widow of Sarepta he made to overflow from her home.[2] Whereas on you our father Gregory, adorned with prophetic grace like Elijah and apostolic honor,[3] chased away with the fire of the Spirit the legions of demons and with grave calamities chastised the violators of God's Law, though the divine oil of anointing and the bread that comes down from heaven[4] he made to overflow in the churches of Armenia. And like Elisha, who like his teacher performed miracles and saw the heavenly armies descend toward him, who through prayer opened the eyes of the lad to show him the mountain full of fiery chariots and riders,[5] so also Saint Gregory surrounded you with prayers,[6] O mountain where God dwells, where the corporeal seraph had hosts of the incorporeal seraphim descend from the heights of heaven into your deep valleys, those whom God sent in his honor, to come and witness his austere asceticism and to report to the fiery hosts the courageous perseverance [borne] in the

§36

[1]Referring, as earlier (§29), to 1 Kgs. 18. According to Yovhannēs Sarkawag Vardapet, the testimony of the Armenian martyrs is far more effective than that of Elijah when he spoke against iniquity and brought drought upon the land (*Sop'erk'*, 5:7).

[2]Referring to 1 Kgs. 17:9–16, where the Hebrew name is Zarephath; cf. Luke 4:26, where the Greek name Sarepta appears (modern Sarafand, eight miles south of Sidon).

[3]A similar point is made in the *Panegyric* by Vardan Vardapet Arewelts'i, *Sop'erk'*, 5:74 (trans., Selection IX). In the *Panegyric* attributed to St. John Chrysostom, St. Gregory, because of his virtue, was taken to heaven as with Elijah's chariot (*ibid.*, 4:30; trans., Selection II). In that attributed to Theophilos, a disciple of St. John Chrysostom, St. Gregory's resemblance to Elijah is limited to the manner in which both of them were fed, miraculously (*ibid.*, 4:116; cf. 1 Kgs. 17:9–16, alluded to in the immediately following context). St. Gregory combining the prophetic and apostolic offices in himself is a recurring theme in these panegyrics (see, e.g., the third comment at §15).

[4]Combining elements of Baptism and the Lord's Supper, the two most important rites of the Church (the latter from "The Bread of Life" discourse of Jesus, delivered at the synagogue in Capernaum, John 6:25–59), while alluding to the miracle performed at Elijah's hand (1 Kgs. 17:9–16).

[5]Referring, as earlier (§29), to 2 Kgs. 6:8–23.

[6]In *"Lerink' amenayn . . ."* (All [you] mountains . . .), Mount Sepuh is said to be superior to Mount Carmel since St. Gregory's prayers there were like chariots of fire (*Sharakan*, p. 279; trans., Selection XII).

feeble nature of his body.[7] As on the mountain the Lord taught His disciples and prayed on the mountain,[8] so the one faithful to the Lord demonstrated the same in his person: ascending, at the end of it all, to the top of this mountain, where he was occupied in prayer and asceticism.[9]

37 [Part VIII]

Rejoice, praised mountain, place of thanksgiving. Golgotha glows in grandeur, resplendent, where the Lord was lifted up because of the wickedness of us all, attaining our redemption through the Cross while thanking the Father who sent Him—the Only-begotten—for redemption, which He, the Son, accomplished with love on the summit of Golgotha. Whereas on you, honored mountain and praised summit, our father was gloriously adorned by the Father, the veritable son was commissioned by the Son, and the spiritually sapient was chosen by the Spirit. Gregory, the witness praised by all, after doing all the good that he did following his unbearable tortures, having enlightened the northern tribes through his copious teaching[1] and having established the Church of Armenia, he ascended you,

---

[7]The author seems to be contemplating a local tradition detailed in the *Panegyric* by Vardan Vardapet Arewelts'i (*Sop'erk'*, 5:73; trans., Selection IX). According to the latter, St. Gregory wanted to make a pilgrimage to Jerusalem on his knees and to die there. When he thus descended from the place of his seclusion on Mount Sepuh, he was met in the valley by two angels who told him that Christ had considered the extent of his devotion and that he should return to the mountain to end his life there. The Saint did accordingly, but not before erecting crosses at the site where the angels were encountered (cf. §37); wherefore the village there is called Serovbēk' (Seraphim) "to this day" (see Thierry, "Le Mont Sepuh," pp. 407–409 and 438–439, figs. 17–19). According to Arewelts'i, however, at one time St. Gregory and King Trdat went to Jerusalem and there they met with Pope Sylvester and Emperor Constantine, at which time the holy places were divided by lot among their custodians; thus, explaining how Armenians in the Holy Land came to possess their sacred places, which he lists: the Manger, Golgotha, the Monastery of St. John the Forerunner, and that of Sts. James (*Sop'erk'*, 5:78). For a far more dramatic description of an alleged meeting of these four leaders in Rome, see *ibid.*, pp. 66–68; cf. Agat'angeghos, *History*, 873–880.

[8]Referring to the Lord's Prayer as taught in the Sermon on the Mount, in Galilee (Matt. 6:9–13).

[9]Cf. Agat'angeghos, *History*, 886–891.

§37

[1]The "teaching" here, as elsewhere in the panegyric, seems to refer to *The Teaching of Saint Gregory;* see the second comment at §6 where the same adjective (*bazmaban*)

having given thanks to the Father, blessing the Son, and to glorify the Most Holy Spirit[2] through whom he performed great and wondrous miracles. And he erected the redemptive sign of the Cross in prominent places. And with that powerful weapon he marked many valleys and rocks. That imperial weapon, the instrument employed to kill the King of Life, he made into an instrument of life; and it is now kept on you,[3] O fortunate Sepuh and praised by all, a place of sanctification and loved by men who love sanctity.

38 [*Part IX*]

Rejoice, Mount Sepuh, graceful and abundant in gifts, resembling the bountifully blessed Mount Olivet. For as the Lord blessed the disciples there at the time of His ascension and bestowed on them the grace of high priesthood and ascended to His own glory,[1] so also on you the image of the Lord, the high priest worthy of honor, Gregory, built with his own hands the holy shrine resembling the Wood,[2] in the name of the Sun of Righteousness, the Morning Star,[3] and [in the name] of John the Fore-

---

is used with reference to the Saint's "teaching." "The northern tribes," here, as elsewhere, refers to the Armenians and the surrounding nations (§§20 [and the third comment in particular] and 24).

[2]The past, present, and future tenses are noteworthy in this Trinitarian statement.

[3]The immediate preceding context refers to the cross employed by St. Gregory (cf. §39), which seems to have been enshrined in one of the chapels on the mount. Some similar wording is found in the hymn *"Lerṙnk'amenayn..."* (All [you] mountains ...), where Golgotha is linked with Mount Sepuh through the mystery of the Cross. The thought seems to be based upon a special cross displayed at the latter place, perhaps with a relic believed to be of the true Cross (*Sharakan*, p. 280; trans., Selection XII).

§38

[1]As earlier (§29), referring to Luke 24:50–53; Acts 1:1–11.

[2]That is, the Cross; cf. §14, where the Cross is referred to as "the immortal Tree," and §2, "the Tree of Life" in the paradisiacal Church. Agat'angeghos, *History*, 813 and 816 simply suggest that St. Gregory "took the sign of the Lord's Cross," or that he set out with the power of the Cross to destroy temples and to build churches. Cf. the end of the preceding section. Here, however, the allusion is to the cruciform architecture of the Church of the Holy All-Savior (*Surb Amenap'rkich'*), near the Great Monastery of the Holy Illuminator (*Mets Surb Lusaworch'i Vank'*); see Thierry, "Le Mont Sepuh," pp. 400–401. The claim that St. Gregory built the church belongs to a later tradition.

[3]The appellation must stand for the Church of the Holy All-Savior (*Surb Amenap'rkich'*), on which see the preceding comment. "Sun of Righteousness" as a Messianic epithet derives from Mal. 4:2 (see the fifth comment at §1). The common

runner.[4] And in the same sanctuary he bestowed the grace of high priesthood on his son Aristakēs,[5] committing to him [the care of] the rational flock while he occupied himself only with the life of angelic piety.

imagery of the sun serves as a fitting symbol in the transition from Zoroastrianism to Christianity in ancient Armenia, as J. R. Russell observes: "The image of the Sun of Righteousness would have been familiar to Armenian proselytes from Zoroastrianism" ("Here Comes the Sun: A Poem of Kostandin Erznkats'i," *Journal of the Society for Armenian Studies* 3 [1987] 122). The following is from *The Teaching* questionably attributed to St. Gregory: "Who is the sun of righteousness if not He who humbled Himself and cast his rays on all the infirm and those who had fallen by sin into woe? He is the same who proceeded from the Father. For it is only He who can illuminate the darkened spirits of men and bring joy to the souls who sit in the shade. He Himself it is who visited our destruction, by whose rays all creatures live who by Him came into being. Similarly the ornament of heaven, that is the luminaries [Gen. 1.14; 2.1], make their light to shine by looking at his rays in the midst of creation, to give light to the earth; and the heavens and the world are full of his light. His Spirit is the reflection of the rays of the being of the same one who humbled Himself by the will of his compassion and came to illuminate the creatures; for they were in darkness, and He came to give and cast his light" (566; trans. Thomson). "The Morning Star" is likewise a Messianic epithet, as found in 2 Pet. 1:19 and Rev. 22:16 (derived from Num. 24:17).

[4]A common name for St. John the Baptist and a further appellation here for the Church of the Holy All-Savior (*Surb Amenap'rkich'*), on which see the preceding comments and the third part of the Introduction. The shrine built by St. Gregory and dedicated to St. John the Forerunner (*Surb Karapet*) is invariably linked with that of St. Athenogenes (Surb At'anakinēs), the burial of their relics at Ashtishat in Tarōn and Bagawan in Bagrewand (Agat'angeghos, *History,* 810–816, 836). Erznkats'i follows the local tradition that claims too much for Mount Sepuh in placing there the shrine built by St. Gregory for St. John the Forerunner. A similar claim is made in a colophon of the year 1201 by the scribe Yovhannēs Daranaghts'i, with reference to as yet another chapel by the same name (*Surb Karapet*) within the Main Monastery (*Awagavank'*) at the foot of the mountain, some seven kilometers to the south-east of the Great Monastery of the Holy Illuminator (*Mets Surb Lusaworch'i Vank'*). See A. S. Mat'evosyan, ed., *Hayeren Dzeṙagreri Hishatakaranner XIII dar* (Colophons of Thirteenth-Century Armenian Manuscripts) (Erevan: Arm. Academy of Sciences, 1984), pp. 14–17, from Jerusalem manuscript no. 3274, repr. by Bogharian [Pogharean], *Grand Catalogue,* 10:73; see also Thierry, "Le Mont Sepuh," pp. 416–417 (cf. p. 401).

[5]Aristakēs. The ordination of St. Aristakēs, the younger son, as bishop by his elderly father is recorded in Agat'angeghos, *History,* 861–862. This was in 320 (St. Aristakēs died in 327, apparantly a year before his father), at the place where St. Gregory was found: "in the province of Daranaghik', on the mountain called the Caves of Manē." Agat'angeghos also records the presence of St. Aristakēs at the Council of Nicaea of 325 (*History of the Armenians,* 884–885; cf. Khorenats'i, *History of the Armenians,* 2.89–91; *Buzandaran Patmut'iwnk',* 3.10).

39 [*Part X*]

Rejoice, holy mountain, reveling in beautiful light, and exult in the likeness of Senir and Hermon, from where the sources of the Jordan flow,[1] where the Lord was baptized and where He gave us second birth and spiritual enlightenment. Whereas from you two fountains flow besides the numerous streams of water: the Fountain of Light and the Sweet-tasting Water.[2] And like the waters of Siloam, which received the naked, pure body of the holy prophet Isaiah,[3] where healing for maladies was found, so also from you flows this fountain of water: the prayers of the Illuminator spreading round about and close to him, who rests from his meritorious perseverance, by whom the very nature of the water is empowered to give sight to the blind; wherefore at present [the fountain] is called Light.[4] And

§39

[1]On the relation of Senir to Hermon—if not their identity—see the seventeenth comment at §29. In *"Leřinkʻ amenayn . . ."* (All [you] mountains . . .), Mount Sepuh is said to be the place where, like Senir and Hermon, streams of light and refreshing waters flow (*Sharakan,* p. 280; trans., Selection XII).

[2]On the naming of these fountains and the traditions associated with them, see further below.

[3]Erznkatsʻi has the pseudepigraphical *Lives of the Prophets* in mind, a Jewish work from the First Century AD, which begins with the martyrdom of Isaiah: "Isaiah, from Jerusalem, died under Manasseh by being sawn in two, and was buried underneath the Oak of Rogel, near the place where the path crosses the aqueduct whose water Hezekiah shut off by blocking its source. And God worked the miracle of Siloam for the prophet's sake, for, being faint before he died, he prayed for water to drink, and immediately it was sent to him from it; therefore it is called Siloam, which means 'sent'" (1:1–2; trans. D. R. A. Hare, "The Lives of the Prophets," in J. H. Charlesworth, ed., *The Old Testament Pseudepigrapha,* 2 vols. [Garden City, NY: Doubleday, 1983] 2:385). The Pool of Siloam, at the southern end of the Spring of Gihon which feeds it through Hezekiah's tunnel, was constructed by King Hezekiah (724–695 BC) during the prophet's lifetime (2 Kgs. 20:20; 2 Chr. 32:30). Tradition places the prophet's burial place near there. Erznkatsʻi, like the author of the *Lives,* takes Isaiah as the patron spirit of the spring. It was to this pool that Jesus sent the man who was blind from birth to wash his eyes in order to see (John 9:1–7). Erznkatsʻi makes one other connection between Isaiah and St. Gregory in *"Leřinkʻ amenayn . . ."* (All [you] mountains . . .), in claiming that the Saint beheld, like Isaiah, the six-winged seraphim (Isa. 6:2; *Sharakan,* p. 279; trans., Selection XII).

[4]*Light.* This name, given to the local fountain, enables the author to connect the site with the story of the man born blind (see the preceding comment), whose healing comes as a sequel to Jesus' claim to be "the light of the world" and to the ensuing disputation with His opponents (John 8:12–20). Healing powers were apparently ascribed

as the great Moses made sweet the bitter waters of Marah through the mystery of the Cross,[5] so also by the hand of the holy Illuminator was stamped, with the sign of the Cross, this other fountain which was transformed from murkiness to sweet-tasting [water]; wherefore it is called by this very name.[6]

40 [Part XI]

Rejoice, magnificent mountain, desirable to the prophetic spirit[1] who

to the local waters—as was the case at Jerusalem. A unique story is preserved in Jerusalem manuscript no. 1650 (published by Bogharian, *Grand Catalogue*, 5:475), according to which "the emperor of the Greeks" sent princes to look for the remains of St. Gregory. As their search proved to be disappointing, one of them asked a Kurdish shepherd, who was blind in both eyes, about the place. He responded: "Take me to Mount Sepuh, for at night there burns a light like the sun, at a famous spot where there is a small fountain." When taken there, he washes his eyes and begins to see and goes on to point out a place nearby. The princes marvel at the Saint's ability to perform miracles even in death. This story lends some historical validity to likely Byzantine expedition(s) for relics of the Saint in the past, which were brought to the Byzantine capital. These were probably among the sacred relics carried away when the treasures of Constantinople were plundered by the Fourth Crusade in 1204. Substantial relics of our Saint may thus have ended up in various Italian cities, including his skull—as so venerated—in the city of Naples. In 2001, on the occasion of the seventeenth centenary of the proclamation of Christianity as the state religion in Armenia, certain of the Saint's relics were ceremoniously returned by Pope John Paul II to visiting Armenian hierarchs at St. Peter's in the Vatican.

[5]Referring to Ex. 15:23–26. The place was about three days' journey from the Red Sea crossing, where the Hebrews found bitter water. When they complained, God directed Moses to a plant whose foliage sweetened the water. This plant is taken symbolically to represent the Cross. *The Teaching of Saint Gregory* places great emphasis on the significance of the Cross of Christ, the sign of which came to have the greatest power in the context of early Christianity. The old instrument of torture is related to several "symbols" in the Old Testament; e.g., Jacob's ladder, as a link between heaven and earth (303, 629); the four corners of the altar of sacrifice, as cosmic or universal dimension embracing the whole world (488–490); the seven-branched candlestick or Menorah, as the light of the world (683); etc. Hence the light of the Cross shines to all creatures in darkness (585, 683), and the Cross itself to the ends of the world (471). For comparisons with Moses elsewhere, see the fifth comment at §13.

[6]The description of the fountains here, however allegorized, seems to be factual; see the preceding comments on this section.

§40

[1]*the prophetic spirit*. St. Gregory is repeatedly considered to be a prophet by the

sought your coveted place: "Lord, who shall stand in your sanctuary, or who shall dwell on your holy mountain?"[2] Having received the Spirit's answer and having looked at you with his very eyes near the end [of his life], he ascended you, Saint Gregory, the one spotless in life and righteous in spirit, the one ever truthful and enlightening in word, the one guileless and holy in heart, who as a friend never rendered evil in return.[3] For this reason he was never reviled by those who approached him, the one who is praised by all and who praises those who fear the Lord, who never wrapped and hid away the silver of his Lord but brought it to the bankers.[4] These and more than these he did, and on steady feet he died on you[5] and granted you to us, a place for vows and petitions.

41 [*Part XII*]

Rejoice, you bright cave, more desirable home in the rock, where virtue dwells, than awe-inspiring palaces plated with gold. You are chosen in accordance with the mystery of Bethlehem,[1] where the pride of virgins, the mother of the incarnate Word gave birth in immaculate virginity to the One indescribably begotten of the Father and invited the daughters of Eve to become the mother of Christ through virginity, as the Lord affirmed

author (§§15, 36, in addition to the numerous comparisons between the Saint and several of the Hebrew Prophets by name).

[2] Ps. 24:3 (23:3 LXX). The quotation seems to be by way of recall, for it differs considerably from that in the Armenian Bible which together with the Septuagint reads: «Ո՛վ ելցէ ի լեառն Տեառն, կամ ո՛վ կացցէ ի տեղւոյ սրբութեան նորա» (Who shall ascend the mountain of the Lord, and who shall stand in his holy place?). Cf. *"Leṙink' amenayn . . ."* (All [you] mountains . . .), where the same verse is quoted paraphrastically by the author (*Sharakan*, p. 281; trans., Selection XII).

[3] That is, he complied with the Lord's command as found in the Sermon on the Mount, Matt. 6:43–48 (cf. Luke 6:31–36).

[4] Alluding to the parable of "The Talents" in Matt. 25:14–30, contemplated also at the end (§60).

[5] Echoing the tradition that St. Gregory remained standing in death, till his body was found. For a more detailed version of this tradition, see the *Panegyric* by Vardan Arewelts'i, *Sop'erk'*, 5.76 (trans., Selection IX).

§41

[1] The Cave(s) of Manē is here compared with the Grotto of the Nativity in Bethlehem. So also in *"Leṙink' amenayn . . ."* (All [you] mountains . . .) (*Sharakan*, p. 280; trans., Selection XII).

through His divine saying: "The one who does My will is My mother, brother, and sister."[2] In this manner did the bright mystery blossom on you, she who was called to this hope and who attained the highest position, the one immaculate in thought, the one humble in spirit, the one pure in body, Saint Manē,[3] shining like the western light.[4] Seeking the highest good and crossing many mountains and valleys, she came up to you, choosing you to be a covering roof and a home where she could find rest. And submitting herself to the will of God, she constantly longed for the heavenly rest. And when she died in you, she was taken up in spirit to the One whom she desired. And her body, chaste and comely, was gathered up by the holy high priest Gregory, who mediates rest to the souls and bodies of those who now resort in faith, and hope of forgiveness to debtors.

42 [Postlude]

Morover, O mountain full of every beneficent goodness, a cloister for the true ascetic, a haven for the most humble father, a lodging place for his blessed person, a station for his pure feet, a stretching space for his holy hands, a seat for the toiling laborer, a chariot for him who gazes into the heavens,[1] a field for the sweating tiller,[2] a threshing-floor for the sheaves of virtue, a storehouse for the bounteous wheat, a receptacle for the precious gold, a safe for the rare pearl[3] for whose sake believers assemble on you, deeming it better to dwell on you for a day than for a thousand [days] in royal quarters.[4] In your deep gorges they raise their voices in prayer, in the crevices they ask for forgiveness of their sins, at the fountains they shed

[2]Matt. 12:50; cf. Mark 3:35. In both instances Jesus refers to the Father's will. Again, the quotation comes by way of recall, for it differs considerably from the text of the Armenian Bible.

[3]On St. Manē, see the second comment at §34.

[4]Cf. the "Ode to St. Gregory" by Catholicos Grigor III Pahlawuni (in office 1113–1166), where the imagery is applied to St. Gregory (trans., Selection VII).

§42

[1]Allusion to 2 Kgs. 2:1–13; applying the experience of Elijah to St. Gregory. Cf. the *Panegyric* attributed to St. John Chrysostom, *Sop'erk'*, 4:30; trans., Selection II.

[2]St. Gregory is so described earlier, §18.

[3]Echoing the twin parables of "The Hidden Treasure" and "The Precious Pearl" in Matt. 13:44–46, contemplated also in §3.

[4]Echoing Ps. 84:10 (83:11 LXX).

their tears, into the depth of the wilderness they go with confessions. And would that we could come worthily, or that we could be like the beloved! It would behoove us to be purified for three days like the people of Israel[5] and to be cleansed from every bodily filth and to abstain even from foods, lest we bring any useless excesses to you; for it is not proper to defile your fragrant site, to spoil your incense-like rocks, to disturb with drunkenness your place of sobriety. But rather to be cleansed at the foot of the mountain and then ascend your height. But because the nature of the body is weak[6] and few are those who comprehend spiritually your supreme honor, while those who are carnal and think carnally are many, and since our considerate father is compassionate and longs to forgive our transgressions, [let us say]: "Receive us hospitably and dismiss us in peace."

[VII. Praise to the land, the people, and the Church]

43 [*Part I: Praise to the land*]

Rejoice, most beautiful and desirable land,[1] praiseworthy district of Daranaghik‛, with blooming mountains, well-watered valleys, welcoming the Edenic stream of the mighty River Euphrates,[2] concerning which wonders are told. In caverns where its water drips in the heat of the summer season, when the thick snow on the summits of the mountains is gone and the hard ice is melted, at that time the dripping water freezes like rock,

---

[5]Alluding to Ex. 19:10–11 and thus claiming for Mount Sepuh the sanctity of Mount Sinai.

[6]Echoing Matt. 26:41; cf. Mark 14:38.

§43

[1]This three-part "praise" of the land, the people, and the Church of Armenia (§§43–46), with each part beginning with the word "Rejoice" (the part on the Church has a sequel addressed to the hierarchs of the Church, likewise beginning with "Rejoice"), is followed by a more formal or solemn three-part "lament" (introduced at §47) over the same entities (§§48–50), with each part beginning with the word "Weep." Although no such introduction is given here as at §47, the parallelism is equally weighty.

[2]Armenians have traditionally understood Gen. 2:10–14 as referring to their land; see §20.

drops piling upon drops. And if within the first [few] days [one could cover] a journey of many days, [the ice] would be taken for the health needs of kings because of its medicinal power. Conversely, when all waters naturally freeze in the winter season, its waters stay swift and warm. Moreover, in the gorges of your mountains, deep in the ground, you have reserves of deposited salt rising from the depths; with the solvent waters evaporated from the salt by the sun's intense heat, the tasteful and aromatic salt left neatly exposed. For this development you are called *Daran-aghi* ["Storage of Salt"],[3] which you bestow upon many districts.

And this is not your only palpable praise—your natural resource, nor that for which alone you are to be called praiseworthy, desirable district and land. You are more praiseworthy, for you became the district where Saint Gregory dwelt; and a desirable land, since the one desired by the hosts above sojourned in you and was interred in you. Besides, gravesites were established in three places in you, [each] a place for the remains of his sacred body and [marked with] a tombstone.[4] He, himself, is your esteemed glory, the goodly blossom of your highest peaks, the bubbling brook of prayer in your deepest valleys, the river streaming beautifully, gushing forth from Eden,[5] spiritual salt, a seasoning to souls,[6] the healing

---

[3]The mineral waters and the salt deposits of the region were well known in antiquity; see, e.g., the ancient source on Greater Armenia utilized in the *Ashkharhats'oyts'* (*Anania Shirakats'i: Matenagrut'yun*, trans. and annotated by A. G. Abrahamyan and G. B. Petrosyan [Erevan: Sovetakan Grogh, 1979], pp. 291–292); Eng. trans., R. H. Hewsen, *The Geography of Ananias of Širak (Ašxarhac'oyc'): The Long and the Short Recensions*, Beihefte zum Tübinger Atlas des vorderen Orients, Reihe B (Geisteswissenschaften) 77 (Wiesbaden: Reichert, 1992), pp. 59–60.

[4]The three gravesites referred to here are all within the district of Daranaghik', as the context suggests. The number seems to allude to the primary, secondary, and tertiary places for the burial of the Saint: (1) where he died all alone, (2) where his unrecognized remains were buried by shepherds who discovered them, and (3) where his remains were removed for the final burial in T'ordan, by the ascetic named Gaṙnik after he was miraculously led to them (on this last place, see the third part of the Introduction). The second site was marked within the Church of the Illuminator's Resting Place (*Hangist Lusaworch'i*), within the Great Monastery of the Holy Illuminator (*Mets Surb Lusaworch'i Vank'*), on the ruins of which see Thierry, "Le Mont Sepuh," pp. 397–400.

[5]Cf. §§18 and 20, and the respective comments on St. Gregory being likened to the Euphrates River.

[6]Alluding to Matt. 5:13 (and parallels); the metaphor is used earlier, near the end of §27.

and refreshing water in the hot and scorching hours, the warmth and the cheering sound in the harsh and depressing winters. This is your praise-worthy beauty and the crown with which you are adorned. Thus you have been found superior to many districts.

44 [*Part II: Praise to the people*]

Rejoice, nations and tribes of Armenia, you who are called by the name of the mighty Hayk.[1] You were healed from deadly and unbearable pains—the maladies of the soul—with the medicine of the artful and knowledge-able physician.[2] You were freed by the undying bouquet of flowers—those gently spoken admonitions in his teaching.[3] You were prevented from death by the sincere supplications of the entreating high priest. You were forgiven the debt of sin through prayers offered like those by Moses.[4] You were reconciled to the Father by the blood and incense offered by the new Aaron: the blood flowing from the tortures of the martyr for Christ,[5] Saint Gregory, who presents your sins before the Lamb of God together with the fragrant incense of his prayers—offered as from a golden censor [waved]

§44

[1]Hayk is the legendary ancestor of the Armenians, according to Khorenats'i, *History of the Armenians*, 1.10–12. Erznkats'i seems to acknowledge here the diverse origin of the Armenian people. The phrase *azgk' ew azink'* ("nations and tribes") occurs three other times in the panegyric (§§24, 32, and 49), compelling us to translate it similarly here.

[2]Cf. §58 and Erznkats'i's *"Aysor zuarchats'eal ts'ntsay ekeghets'i . . ."* (Reveling today the Church rejoices . . .), where the Saint is called "healer of souls" (*bzhishk hogwots'*) (*Sharakan*, p. 267; trans., Selection XI); so also in the *Panegyric* attributed to Theophilos, (*Sop'erk'*, 4:100) and in Narekats'i's "Ode to the Holy Illuminator" (*Tagher*, p. 176; trans., Selection IV).

[3]The "teaching" here, as elsewhere, refers possibly to *The Teaching of Saint Gregory;* see the second comment at §6. In all likelihood, John 8:32 ("You shall know the truth, and the truth shall make you free") is contemplated here.

[4]Alluding to the intercessory prayer of Moses in Ex. 32:32; for other comparisons with Moses, see §13 (and the fifth comment).

[5]On St. Gregory's suffering whereby he is considered a martyr, see the seventh comment at §1. There is an echo here of the Epistle to the Hebrews (especially chs. 5 and 7), where the high priesthood of Jesus is compared with that of Aaron. Jesus is said to be a greater or better high priest since He made atonement with His own blood and since He had no earthly ancestry. St. Gregory, here called "new Aaron" and repeatedly referred to as "high priest" in this panegyric (§§33, 38, 41, 48, 56, 58), is likewise deemed a greater high priest than Aaron since he—like Jesus—offered his own blood.

by the elderly man, the liberator of debtors.[6] You who were in shameful nakedness, by his worthy hands were made to put on Christ as garment of redemption.[7] You obtained the image of the likeness of Christ from him who through his birth-pangs gives second birth to souls. You were armed for the battle of martyrdom by the captain of our faith.

45 [Part III.1: Praise to the Church]

Rejoice, Church of Armenia, erected by the most ingenious and wise architect—the new Bezalel.[1] You were founded on the Word of God's Wisdom, built on the firm rock of faith,[2] gathered by the labors and sweat of the persevering father, born of the most magnificent word—the luminous teaching of Saint Gregory.[3] [Yours are] the ready soldiers of the mighty captain,[4] the rooted plants of the diligent sower,[5] the members joined to the perceptual Head by the hand of him who fully adorns the entire Church—adorned and decked with garments radiant like gold.

[6]The "golden censer" is symbolic of the Saint's heart (§32; cf. §18, the Saint himself). For another description of St. Gregory as an "elderly man," see the beginning of §49. *Azatarar* ("deliverer" or "liberator") as an attribute of the Saint is used earlier (§27).

[7]A baptismal imagery, echoing Rom. 13:14; Gal. 3:27. Cf. §§15, 59 (to put on God).

§45

[1]The craftsman in charge of building the tabernacle which Moses pitched in the wilderness (Ex. 31:1–11; 35:30–39:31). St. Gregory is likewise described as an architect in the *Panegyric* attributed to St. John Chrysostom (*Sop'erk'*, 4:82).

[2]Echoing Matt. 16:18 and its usual interpretation in Greek and Armenian patristic sources.

[3]As found in *The Teaching of Saint Gregory,* a catechism referred or alluded to repeatedly in the panegyric; see the second comment at §6 and the references there to *Vardapetut'iwn*; cf. the first comment at §7 and the references there to the *Yachakhapatum* collection of homilies.

[4]Cf. §4, St. Gregory as a renowned captain; so also in the *Panegyric* attributed to St. John Chrysostom (*Sop'erk'*, 4:83).

[5]On St. Gregory as a diligent sower here and in the next section, cf. the *Panegyric* attributed to Theophilos (*Sop'erk'*, 4:97).

46 [*Part III.2: Praise to the hierarchs*]

Rejoice, priestly heads and chiefs,[1] overseers[2] of the flock of Christ, you who inherited the lot of the apostle-like father and became bishops[3] over the sees of spiritual authority and rights, shepherds of the chosen flock and of the lambs born of the [baptismal] font, caretakers and nurturers of the living plants of the fervent and diligent sower, guardians and keepers of the hedge made strong,[4] you who adorn and clothe with finery the beautiful bride—the Church,[5] messengers of conciliation, high priests of expiation.[6]

§46

[1]This section, in praise of the hierarchs, is to be treated thematically as an integral part of the preceding section on the Church; however, because of its opening words, and for the sake of consistency in our respect for the form established by the author, we treat it as a separate yet indistinct unit. This is further justified by the author's devoting a three-part admonition to the hierarchs (§§51–53) following his parallel lament over the Church (§50).

[2]The word *veratesuch'k'*, like the word *veraditoghk'* in the immediate context, corresponds with the Greek compound *episkopoi* (bishops), here rendered literally by us.

[3]See the preceding comment.

[4]Allusion to the parable of "The Vineyard and the Tenants" (Matt. 21:33–46; especially vs. 33, and parallels).

[5]Lit., "the bride of beauty." These words echo Rev. 21:2. The Church as the bride of Christ has a long history in both Testaments: in the Hebrew Bible, in the repeated prophetic descriptions of Israel as God's spouse (e.g., Hos. 1–3, Ezek. 16 and 20), and in the New Testament, beginning with the parable of "The Ten Virgins" (Matt. 25:1–13), through St. Paul's admonitions to wives and husbands (Eph. 5:22–33), and ending with the reception of believers into heaven in the Apocalypse (Rev. 19:7; 21:9, 17). For the image among the Fathers, see the selections by T. Halton, *The Church*, Message of the Fathers of the Church 4 (Wilmington: Michael Glazier, 1985), pp. 47–51. This traditional image is found also in *The Teaching of St. Gregory* (441) and in the mystical *Commentary on the Song of Songs* by St. Grigor Narekats'i, among Armenian sources. Note the parallelism here with the end of the preceding section.

[6]These notices resound with several patristic admonitions on the role of the bishop. For a fine collection of comparable sayings by the early Church Fathers, see A. Cunningham, ed., *The Bishop in the Church: Patristic Texts on the Role of the Episkopos*, Theology and Life 13 (Wilmington: Michael Glazier, 1985).

[VIII. Lament over the land, the people, and the Church]

47 [*Introduction*]

And now, I wish to introduce a form of the musicians' art here:[1] [not only] to make delightful music as at times and to subject the listeners to exuberant joy, [but also] to play the string of a dirge at times,[2] to bring forth tears for misfortune and calamity. As for the latter, I have this to say:

48 [*Part I: Lament over the land*]

Weep, land and people of Armenia. You who were at times filled with bright stars as in heaven, you are dimmed again with darkness today, covered, I mean, with clouds of sin and oppressors.[1] You who blossomed like

§47

[1]After so many preceding sections that begin with "Rejoice . . . ," the author is about to compose three lamentations that begin with "Weep . . ." (§§48–50, addressed to the land, its people, and the Church, and corresponding to the same tri-partite arrangement as in §§43–46). Here, as elsewhere, he is introducing a special unit of his overall composition (see the first comment at §10, for the other instances).

[2]Given his talent and training in music, as we gather from his autobiographical remarks in the *Hawak'umn Meknut'ean K'erakani* (Compilation of Commentary on Grammar), Erznkats'i probably sang this dirge as he played a stringed instrument. As for the words, the author was obviously inspired by Khorenats'i, who laments the deaths of St. Sahak and St. Mashtots' as well as the end of the Arshakuni (Arsacid) Dynasty in 387 and that of the line of St. Gregory's descendants with the death of St. Sahak in 427 (*History of the Armenians, 3.67–68*; Khorenats'i, in turn, was inspired by the threnody on St. Nersēs I the Great in 373, found in *Buzandaran Patmut'iwnk'*, 5.30). It should also be noted that from here on the panegyric becomes more hortatory, resembling the author's homilies and exhortations in his other works.

§48

[1]The "oppressors" are the "people of a foreign tongue," "the wicked" mentioned further below. The sweeping reference is to the invasions of Greater Armenia and Cilicia by the Tatar and Mongol hordes, or the Turkmen raiders in general, who wreaked havoc throughout the land, as well as to the Egyptian Mamluks who plundered Cilicia in 1266, under Baybars (1260–1277), and again in 1292, under Sultan al-Ashraf (1291–1293). The references to the invader(s) as "malicious beast(s)" (§49, where more difficult times for the nation are prophesied in an oracular manner) and "wild boar(s)—Satan and evil-loving demons" (§50) agree with other contemporary descriptions of the Asiatic conquerors; e.g., Kirakos Gandzakets'i, *History of the Armenians*, 20–35 (ed.

a pleasant garden [tilled] by the wise gardener, today you have become unattractive like a field [full] of decay.[2] You dwell in sadness and are unadorned, for our own ancestral districts are ruled by people of a foreign tongue and the scepters of the wicked have penetrated the lot of the righteous,[3] because the righteous allowed their hands to accomplish acts of injustice.[4] Though you recovered from the chronic illnesses of many years, you now lie perplexed by worrisome illnesses, unattended by physicians with cures. When we were enemies [of God], we were reconciled to God through the Christ-like high priest;[5] but now we who were loved have become estranged from the bosom of the mother and the compassion of the benevolent Father,[6] as it is written: "Sinners have gone astray from their mother, they were deceived from the womb and have spoken lies."[7] When

Melikʻ-Ohanjanyan, pp. 231–284; trans. Bedrosian, pp. 193–246), and Vardan Areweltsʻi, *Historical Compilation* (text in *Vardan Vardapet Metsn: Hawakʻumn Patmutʻean Vardanay Vardapeti, lusabaneal* [Vardan Vardapet the Great: The Collected History of Vardan Vardapet, Annotated (by Gh. Alishan, unnamed editor)] [Venice: S. Ghazar, 1862], especially pp. 155–159, on his meeting with Hulagu Khan); Eng. trans., R. W. Thomson, "The Historical Compilation of Vardan Arewelcʻi," *Dumbarton Oaks Papers* 43 (1989) 125–226. See also Grigor Vardapet Aknertsʻi, *Patmutʻiwn Tatʻaratsʻ* (History of the Tatars), N. Pogharean, ed. (Jerusalem: St. James Press, 1974); also known as *Patmutʻiwn vasn Azgin netoghatsʻ*; Eng. trans. (with Arm. text), R. P. Blake and R. N. Frye, *Gregory of Agner: History of the Nation of Archers* (Cambridge, MA: Harvard University Press, 1954), unfortunately translated from a poorer edition of the text. A primary source for all the cited works is the now lost history by Vanakan Vardapet, the teacher of Gandzaketsʻi, Areweltsʻi, and Aknertsʻi—among others (Areweltsʻi, in turn, was the teacher of Erznkatsʻi). For an excellent assessment of the medieval Armenian sources of the period, see R. Bedrosian, "Armenia during the Seljuk and Mongol Periods," in R. G. Hovannisian, ed., *The Armenian People from Ancient to Modern Times. Vol. I: The Dynastic Periods: From Antiquity to the Fourteenth Century* (New York: St. Martin's Press, 1997), pp. 241–271. For non-Armenian sources and the difficult times in general, considered to be consequences of religious laxity on the part of the Christian population, see S. Vryonis, Jr., *The Decline of Medieval Hellenism in Asia Minor and the Process of Islamization from the Eleventh through the Fifteenth Century* (Berkeley, Los Angeles, London: University of California Press, 1971), pp. 80–85, 155–160, 244–249, 418–421.

[2]Possible allusion to the vision of the field full of dry bones in Ezek. 37.

[3]Echoing Hab. 1:13, while reflecting historical conditions in Erznkatsʻi's day (on which see above).

[4]Echoing Ezek. 3:20; 18:24–26; 33:18; etc.

[5]Echoing Rom. 5:10.

[6]In such paired analogies, the mother, as always, is the Church, and the Father, God (see §§3, 8, 11, 14, and 50); elsewhere, the father is St. Gregory (*passim*).

[7]Ps. 58:3 (57:4 LXX). The quotation (except for the preposition xi) is in keeping

we were transgressors, we were delivered from indebtedness to sin through the petitions of our lawgiver who taught about God.[8] Slave-servants honored with freedom, we returned to filth and were obligated again to pay back the debt of ten thousand talents.[9]

49 [Part II: Lament over the people]

Weep, children deprived of parental compassion,[1] for we have been orphaned and have no father who in his old age and virtue of yore would move the Heavenly Father into compassion, or would submit himself—free of debt—to die for children indebted to death, or would spill his blood as a price for our redemption, or with the sweat of his body he would wash those smeared with filth, or by the slaughter of the fattened bull would prevent the penalty for sin, or with incense-like prayers would ask remission for the sins of the guilty.[2]

Armenian nation, the youngest child of our Jacob and the last-born of tribes and nations:[3] You were adorned by your enlightening father with a

with the Armenian Bible, which at this point differs somewhat from the Septuagint, which reads: *Apēllotriōthēsan oi amartoloi apo mētras, eplanēthēsan apo gastros, elalēsan pseudē*. The Armenian translators of the Psalms seem to have read *mētros* ("mother") instead of *mētras* ("womb") and have added *kai* ("and") to the third part of the tricolon.

[8]As "lawgiver" here and in §58, St. Gregory is once more compared with Moses; for other comparisons with the prophet, see the fifth comment at §13. In the *Panegyric* attributed to St. John Chrysostom, St. Gregory is said to have ascended the mountain to receive the spiritual law (*Sop῾erk῾*, 4:12).

[9]Allusion to the parable of "The Unforgiving Servant" in Matt. 18:21–35.

§49

[1]Cf. the author's subsequent laments and his "Ode to St. Gregory" (Selection XIII), where he likewise bewails the lack of spiritual leadership in his day.

[2]Echoing the central theology of Leviticus and the Christological application in Rom. 5:7.

[3]St. Gregory is here compared with the biblical patriarch Jacob and the Armenian people with his son Joseph. What follows echoes Gen. 37. The Armenian people are orphaned and deprived of their father's compassion, just as Joseph, the beloved of his father Jacob, was deprived of fatherly love and admonitions. The words "last-born" are not so much to underscore the status of the Armenians among the nations as to dwell further upon the example of Joseph. Although Joseph was not the youngest son of Jacob (Benjamin was the youngest), the two sons of Joseph, Ephraim and Manasseh, became the last two of the Twelve Tribes of Israel and were especially blessed by Jacob (Gen. 48:8–20).

garment in the color of blossoms, to the extent that you were envied by your brothers. Now, how have you fallen prey to malicious beasts, and [how] has your bright garment become stained with blood? And the elderly father Jacob is no longer in our midst to compose a lament on the calamity, saying: "Some malicious and ferocious beast . . ."[4] Understand "malicious beast" as you will, whether as those who kill or enslave the body or as those who tear apart or suffocate the spirit, for we have been endangered by both.

Gregory, likeness to the Heavenly Father and image of parental compassion: Would you speak to your erring children—we who have taken off the pure and immaculate robe of [the baptismal] birth—saying: "My children, whom again I bear in travail until Christ be portrayed in you."[5] For we have no one to counsel us again with yearning compassion and to bear us once more in travail, unto repentance. Behold, it is time for war, gathering of masses. But your ready soldiers are deserted and have become weary. We have no brave and ingenious captain to rally the soldiers for battle on the frontline.[6]

[4]Gen. 37:33. What follows is addressed to the beastly enemy, on whom see the first comment at §48.

[5]These oracular words put in the mouth of the Illuminator are from Gal. 4:19, verbatim. The author could not resist the temptation of having St. Gregory address the political situation and the spiritual condition of the time. The turbulent decades at the close of the thirteenth century are contemplated here, perhaps also the ill-fated military exploits of King Levon II of Cilicia (1269–1289), who in 1281 invaded Syria with the Mongol ilkhans of Persia, and ended up agreeing to a very costly settlement with the victorious Mamluks. The nearly constant military preoccupations of the Cilician kings overshadowed all other policies and made Papal aid even by way of another Crusade highly desirable. Were it not for their coronation oath of loyalty to the Armenian Church (see the sample in Gh. M. Alishan, *Sisuan* [Venice: S. Ghazar, 1885], p. 500), these kings, and more so their non-Armenian successors, could have led the Cilician Armenians to Roman Catholicism, thus nullifying the very traditions associated with St. Gregory. These fears were almost realized during the three-year reign of Philip (1222–1224, married to Zabēl before she was married to Hetʿum I in 1226), the son of Bohemond of Antioch, and again during the Catholicosate of Grigor VII Anawarzetsʿi (in office 1293–1307), a staunch Chalcedonian who was appointed by the Latinophile King Hetʿum II (reigned intermittantly, 1289–1306, murdered in 1307).

[6]Although apocalyptic in tone, the predicted war is very much in the spirit of the times (see the preceding comment and the third part of the Introduction). If not a reference to the plunder of Cilicia in 1266, under Baybars (1260–1277), it is tempting to see a foretelling here of the 1292 invasion of Cilicia by the Egyptian Mamluks under Sultan al-Ashraf (1291–1293), at which time Hŕomkla was sacked and the Catholicos Stepʿannos IV (in office 1290–1292) taken captive to Egypt, where he died a year later— the very year of the author's death. This catastrophe necessitated the transfer of the

50 [*Part III: Lament over the Church*]

Weep, Armenian Church, mother of many children,[1] who in late hour and being advanced in age, like Sarah, miraculously gave birth to a whole nation.[2] But now resemble Rachel and weep for your children: "Rachel weeping for her children and refusing to be comforted because they are no more."[3] Weep also for your children because they are no longer as they were. Whereas from one parent numberless children were born, none is born nowadays from the multitude of fathers;[4] and those who beget [children] do not teach [them] the nurture of the Law.[5] From a seed you sprouted into a stalk, from a stalk you increased, and from a single shoot you became a well-rooted vine, growing many branches and spreading, filling the earth from sea to sea. But now your strong hedges have been broken down, and you are being despoiled by strangers and foreign nations that pass by, [they reap] the benefits of your material fruit.[6] And the hog of the forest is defiling your rational vineyard and the blossoms of your spiritual seed are being grazed by the wild boar—Satan and evil-loving demons.[7] You were a large flock under one shepherd of the Great Shep-

Catholicosate to Sis. As always, it was believed that the adverse political situation is caused by religious laxity on the part of the clergy, especially the wanton behavior of those in high offices (see the author's "Ode to St. Gregory," trans., Selection XIII).

§50

[1]On the theme of the Church as mother, see the fifth comment at §3.

[2]Allusion to Gen. 18:11. For more on this self-definition of the Armenian people since embracing Christianity, see the first part of the Introduction (cf. §§3, 8, 52, 55).

[3]Matt. 2:18; cf. Jer. 31:15 (38:15 LXX). The quotation does not differ from the Armenian Bible.

[4]That is, St. Gregory, is the "parent" from whom "numberless children were born," a theme repeated further below in this section and elsewhere in the panegyric; cf. the hymn by Erznkats'i, *'Aysōr zuarchats'eal ts'ntsay ekeghets'i . . .*" (Reveling today the Church rejoices . . .), where the Saint is referred to as "a spiritual parent" (*tsnogh hogewor*) (*Sharakan*, p. 267; trans., Selection XI). The author seems to be critical of the bishops of his day, who collectively fail to produce a single child of God. He has the same corrupt bishops in mind in §55 and in his "Ode to St. Gregory" (Selection XIII).

[5]On the religious education of children in medieval Armenia, see V. Hats'uni, *Dastiarakut'iunĕ hin hayots' k'ov* (Education among the Ancient Armenians) (Venice: S. Ghazar, 1923), pp. 38–78.

[6]Echoing Isa. 5:5.

[7]On the identity of the enemy, the plundering hordes of invaders in Erznkats'i's time, see the first comment at §48.

herd,[8] but now you are scattered around, dispersed into the many winds, roaming and wandering over the mountains, being attacked and wounded by wolves, grazing in hazardous and deadly pastures, destitute and deprived of a green place—the teachings of the Holy Scriptures, not being nurtured with water that soothes, being outside the gathering fold. Nor do you have a shepherd who could shepherd you with both tools, holding a rod and a staff in his hands: to fight against the beasts with the rod and to lead the sheep with the staff.

Divine sanctuary, receptive of the light from the candlestick with seven branches,[9] together with children begotten of light, by our father, the Illuminator:[10] Why are your light-giving lanterns now empty of the oil of wisdom? The captains of your warfare are not equipped with the knowledge of the Law. The physicians on whom your life depends are not diligent in wisdom. The shepherds of your flock are voluptuous, and ambitious for glory. Your pupils are impatient and dislike counsel and are not pleased to hear the voice of a masterful speaker, nor do they accept medicine from a wise provider of medicine; rather, their providers of medicine are in need of a physician's cure, and should anyone give it, they would hate and oppose him.

---

[8]Echoing Heb. 13:20.

[9]That is, the *menorah*, whether of the Tabernacle pitched by Moses in the wilderness or of the Temple built by Solomon at Jerusalem (Ex. 25:31–35; 37:17–20; 1 Kgs. 7:49). This Old Testament object, once allegorized in Hellenistic Judaism as a symbol of the seven planets, is typologically equated with the Cross in early Christian literature, or with Christ's humanity in general (see *"Luxnia"* [Lamp] 2. in Lampe, *Lexicon,* p. 817); note the following from *The Teaching of Saint Gregory* (683): "They (i.e., the Apostles) became lighted torches as on a candlestick, that is, on the cross. And by the power of the same they shone and illumined the world; they expelled the obscurity of darkness from all men, to make them receptive to the divine love" (trans. Thomson).

[10]St. Gregory as begetter of children of God or of the Church, is a recurring theme in this section and elsewhere in the panegyric; see above §§16, 52, 55.

[IX. Admonition to the Church]

51 [Part I]

And although you deserve lamentations for all of these,[1] and even though aliens have wasted away your physical attraction, and your children of the covenant were taken into captivity, and your delightful ornaments were looted,[2] and the indescribable mystery is today sold for a price,[3] and the heavenly ladder is snatched away by those who prefer the earth,[4] you are still blessed with great and superbly good things and are very joyous. For the light of the Orthodox faith was never dimmed, the defiling tares were not mixed with the good seeds of wheat.[5] The murky water of alien teachings[6] did not contaminate the clear fountain of your traditions. In your

---

§51

[1]This section marks a turning point: from a lament to a more joyous recitation, giving hope to the Church.

[2]Desecration of churches by the enemy, abduction and martyrdom of monks, and looting of precious objects with total disregard for anything sacred are reported lamentingly by nearly all Armenian chroniclers of the thirteenth century. Some even report enslavement of the inhabitants of certain towns.

[3]The practice of buying an ecclesiastical office, called "simony" after the account in Acts 8:14–24, is condemned again in the panegyric (§55), as also in Book I (ch. 4) of the *General Epistles* by St. Nersēs Shnorhali (Arm. text: * Endhanrakan T'ught'k'* [Jerusalem: St. James Press, 1871], especially p. 48; Eng. trans. of Book I, A. Aljalian, *St. Nersēs Šnorhali: General Epistle* [New Rochelle: St. Nersess Armenian Seminary, 1996], p. 52) and by several writers of the thirteenth century. The selling and buying of ecclesiastical offices was a major concern for the reform-minded religious leaders in eastern Armenia who longed for the return of the Catholicosate to the cradle Ējmiatsin; see K. Maksoudian, *Chosen of God: The Election of the Catholicos of All Armenians from the Fourth Century to the Present* (New York: St. Vartan Press, 1995), p. 70. A bishop who bought his office had to tax the faithful either to recoup or to make payments to the ruler who appointed him, or else he would ordain for money. A priest thus ordained would, in turn, recoup by charging for the sacraments administered by him, even for the Eucharist—as the text implies.

[4]Allusion to Jacob's "ladder" in Gen. 28:10–12. The author is referring to the misbehavior of worldly churchmen who lack heavenly insights.

[5]Allusion to the parable of "The Sower" in Matt. 13:24–30.

[6]Most notably the Grecizing efforts and the Latinizing influence of the time rather than the waning heresy of schismatics such as the Tondrakians, whose divergent teachings preoccupied the ecclesiastical authorities for centuries prior to Erznkats'i's time; see V. Nersessian, *The Tondrakian Movement: Religious Movements in the Armenian*

living bread of certainty and truth the deadly yeast and the baneful heresy of vinigary dilution were not mixed.[7] In the gold of undefiled faith and the silver of enlightened reason neither corroding copper nor tarnishng lead was found. And these, through the petitions of the great martyr for Christ,[8] Saint Gregory, were granted to you by Him who is the Fountainhead of all good things and the Foundation of life eternal.[9]

52 [*Part II*]

Wherefore, you, high priests and heads of the Church:[1] Rejoice with ecstasy and shake with fear and much trembling, lest you who are elevated heads and knowledgeable about heaven should become like swine that crawl on earth and wallow in ashes, thinking only of the earthly. And you, who are overseers of metropolitan and rural sees: Do not become careless watchers, falling into sloth or sleep.[2] For if you see the sword of God's wrath coming and you do not forewarn, you shall be found accountable for blood, for letting people perish in death.[3] Presiders for uncorrupt justice: Do not desire

---

Church from the Fourth to the Tenth Centuries, Princeton Theological Monograph Series 15 (Allison Park, PA: Pickwick Publications, 1987), p. 90.

[7]While echoing Matt. 16:6–12 and parallels, the statement is a direct reference to the Eucharistic gifts, the leavened bread and the diluted wine used in the Greek or Byzantine Church. The practice was considered heretical by the Armenian Church (whose Eucharistic bread is unleavened and wine undiluted) during the post-Chalcedonian polemics (after 451). The Byzantines tried repeatedly to impose their tenets upon the Armenians, but to no avail. Such efforts continued in the author's time. On the non-Chalcedonian posture of the Armenian Church, see K. Sarkissian, *The Council of Chalcedon and the Armenian Church* (London: SPCK, 1965), and more recently, N. Garsoïan, *L'Église arménienne et le grand schisme d'Orient*, Corpus Scriptorum Christianorum Orientalium 574, sub. tom. 100 (Leuven: Peeters, 1999).

[8]On St. Gregory as martyr, see the seventh comment at §1.

[9]Echoing 1 Cor. 3:11 and Johannine theology in general.

§52

[1]This specific address to the heads or bishops of the Church marks the beginning of a formal and lengthy admonition (§§52–53) and appeal (§§55–57, introduced at §54). The addressees are referred to with a variety of related ecclesiastical terms: high priests and heads of the Church, presiders over justice, and guides along the heavenly path (§52); and again with another trilogy, as sailors, husbandmen, and healers (§53).

[2]Echoing Matt. 25:5.

[3]Allusion to Ezek. 3:16–21; so also in the *Panegyric* attributed to St. John Chrysostom (*Sop'erk'*, 4:43).

injustice and be not eager to grab. And you who are great in heavenly matters: Let not your hearts crave for carnal and vain greatness. Guides to the heavenly path and shepherds of Christ's flock and of the precious lambs whom the Only-begotten of the Father inherited through blood and death, whom He received as a special people through the fifteen-year suffering of our Illuminator[4] and gave them over to you freely and without price, as an inheritance: Do not mislead them over the mountains and the untraveled path, and do not betray to wolves and beasts those whom the Good Shepherd carried over His shoulder and lifted up to heaven and added them to the number of those who did not stray.[5] Do not become like the hirelings who sow for the body and those who overlook the souls of the rational sheep. Do not become inattentive, pitiless, or heedless toward those who are pierced, wounded, for whose sake Christ took upon Himself the piercing and the wounds. Do not become ruthless and cruel superiors who love titles of glory, handing some over to the anguish of despair.

53 [Part III]

Sailors of the ecclesiastical ship:[1] Do not abandon the ecclesiastical ship

[4]On the Armenians as God's people, begotten through the suffering of St. Gregory, see above, §33 (cf. §55). The fifteen years seem to cover the period of St. Gregory's imprisonment in the pit, his release, consecration as bishop at Caesarea, and the ensuing baptism of the king and the people. There is a discrepancy on the length of this period in our document; cf. §55, where the period of the Saint's confinement is said to be thirteen years (so also in the other panegyrics on St. Gregory: in that attributed to Theophilos, a disciple of St. John Chrysostom, e.g., St. Gregory spends fourteen years in the dungeon, Sop'erk', 4:104, 111; elsewhere, pp. 113 and 115, the period of his imprisonment is given as fifteen years). A similar discrepancy exists in the *History* of Agat'angeghos: in 122, 124, and 132 it is thirteen years; in 215 and 233 it is fifteen (fourteen in the sixth-century Greek translation [*Ag*] from the extant Armenian text, ed. Lafontaine; fifteen in all three authors in the Appendices provided at the end of this book). The origin of the discrepancy could be traced to early scribal error(s).

[5]Alluding to John 10:11–18; Matt. 18:12–14 and parallels.

§53

[1]The popular symbol of the ship for the Church, especially in early Christian art and literature, has quite a history that goes back to the canonical gospels (see E. Hilgert, *The Ship and Related Symbols in the New Testament* [Assen: Van Gorcum, 1962]). By means of this powerful symbol, the Church depicts its vital role in salvation history—just as contemplated by Erznkats'i.

to wrecking storms that gather over the sea of life or to tumultuous winds. Lest, by letting drown those whom you personally should have rescued from the suffocating sea, you should become losers of innocent souls. You who were designated cultivators and guardians of the rational and heavenly plants in the divine vineyard and who partake of the fruit of the vineyard and expect a denarius as payment from the most gracious Lord:[2] Do not allow the beast to spoil the divine vineyard,[3] the well-bearing branches of the rooted, True Vine.[4] Do not disturb the watchtower of God's commandments, do not trample upon the canons of the covenant of faith established by God, do not tear down the protective hedge of traditions established by the fathers,[5] lest you should be smitten with incurable evil [inflicted] by the serpent. Rational physicians and overseers of souls,[6] who possess the divine manual of healing: Do not become pitiless, uncaring toward those bitten by the lurking serpent, lest you should be overcome by natural and unnatural pains. Do not become resuscitators of evil instead of dissipaters of pains.

[X. APPEAL TO THE HIERARCHS]

54 [*Introduction*]

The divine Paul has written an admonition to you and to all believers, saying: "Remember your leaders who spoke the Word of God to you. And having considered the course of their conduct, be imitators of their faith."[1]

---

[2]Echoing one or another of the parables on the vineyard found in the gospels, especially "The Laborers in the Vineyard" (Matt. 20:1–16), contemplated also at the end of the panegyric.

[3]Echoing Cant. 2:15.

[4]Alluding once more to John 15:1–17: "The Vine and the Branches" (cf. §§2, 13, 21).

[5]Echoing Deut. 19:14; 27:17; etc.

[6]On bishops as spiritual healers, see Book I (ch. 1) of the *General Epistles* by St. Nersēs Shnorhali (especially pp. 15–17 of the Arm. text; pp. 23–24 of the Eng. trans.).

§54

[1]Heb. 13:7. Except for the added preposition end and the conjunction ;u5 the quotation corresponds with the text of the Armenian Bible. It must be said that the Pauline authorship of the epistle is seriously and convincingly rejected in New Testament scholarship. The quotation serves as an introduction to the tri-partite appeal made to

55 [*Part I*]

Now,[1] therefore, remember the leader of your life and salvation and bear in mind the unbearable suffering of the father full of divine compassion, the Illuminator of souls, the persevering martyr for Christ,[2] Saint Gregory. Do not forget the one over whom the heavenly host marveled, over the endurance of his earthly body. Revere him for the excessive modesty of his life, you who currently enjoy what came forth through blood-like sweat and tears mingled with dew,[3] the fruit of the land sowed with the seeds of faith. Consider now the course of his conduct, how he sojourned in this world and what the course of his conduct was; for that is the gate of the sheepfold, of shepherding, through which he entered.[4] He received his people through suffering. Through the flaying of the bones of his body and the blood flowing from his side, he made this nation a church for God, as the Lord made the nations and the whole world His, through the blood gushing from His side.[5] Through the affliction by fire he was roasted for his beautiful lambs.[6] Through ingenious tortures he was brought to the

the hierarchs of the Church; they have to follow the example of their leader, St. Gregory. This is the last of the seven introductions to specific units within the overall composition (see the first comment on these introductions at §10).

§55

[1]The next three sections begin with "Now . . ." As he is about to conclude his task, the author is reverting to a favorite form used frequently in the first half of the panegyric ("And now . . ."), especially in the three invocations near the beginning (§§8–10).

[2]On St. Gregory's "martyrdom," see the seventh comment at §1. The designation "persevering martyr" recurs at §57.

[3]Echoing Luke 22:44.

[4]Echoing John 10:1, 9. Erznkats'i is not unscrupulous in his choice of words and ascriptions here. St. Gregory's life is an ideal example of shepherding; cf. §18 ("a true shepherd"), §§16, 24 ("shepherd for . . . the True Shepherd"), and the similar terms further below: "This is the gate of spiritual shepherding." The recurring references and allusions to John 10 in this section and the following two, as in those just cited, seem to have been inspired by the Gospel reading (John 10:11–16) for the feast day of the discovery of St. Gregory's remains (cf. §§16, 24).

[5]Echoing John 19:34. On the Armenians as God's people, begotten through the suffering of St. Gregory, see above, §§33 and 52. The *imitatio Christi* motif is overwhelmingly strong at this juncture.

[6]An allusion, it seems, to the eleventh torture of St. Gregory, when molten lead was poured over him "and his flesh was completely burned" (Agat'angeghos, *History*, 119:

gallows,[7] and he kept praying for his faithful flock. He spent thirteen years in the dungeon of darkness and among tortuous snakes[8] because of the pitfall of sin and the strike of the serpent, and the venomous filth into which we had fallen.[9] This is the gate of spiritual shepherding, and whoever does not come in through this gate is a thief and a robber.[10] This is the example by which the inheritance is appropriated and not through blood relation, as they lord it over the flock of Christ.[11] This is the ransom for the lambs

«*և այրեցին զմարմինս նորա առ Հասարակ*»). Erznkats'i uses a more dramatic verb, «*խորովեցաւ*».

[7]An allusion to the first two of the twelve tortures of the Saint (*ibid.*, 69–99).

[8]There seems to be some confusion in the number of years St. Gregory spent in the dungeon, the last of his twelve tortures; see the discussion above, at §52, where the number of years is fifteen. In a hymn by Erznkats'i, *"Aysōr zuarchats'eal ts'ntsay ekeghets'i . . ."* (Reveling today the Church rejoices . . .), dedicated to St. Gregory, he is said to have coped with the snakes in the pit so as to save us from the dragon (*vishap*), whose head he crushed in the pit (*Sharakan*, pp. 271, 276; trans., Selection XI; cf. the *Panegyric* attributed to St. John Chrysostom, *Sop'erk'*, 4:29; trans., Selection II). According to the *Panegyric* attributed to Theophilos, a disciple of St. John Chrysostom, St. Gregory's fourteen-year survival is a greater miracle than that of Daniel in the lions' den, since snakes are deadlier (*Sop'erk'*, 4:104, 111; cf. 110, where the snakes tell how their venomous nature was transformed in the presence of the Saint; and 113 and 115, where the period of his imprisonment is given as fifteen years). See also the *Panegyric* by Yovhannēs Sarkawag Vardapet, where St. Gregory is said to have tamed the snakes in the dungeon so they couldn't bite (*Sop'erk'*, 5:31; trans., Selection VI).

[9]Allusion to the fall in Gen. 3.

[10]Echoing John 10:1, 8. Erznkats'i wishes to disqualify religious leaders who do not follow the example of St. Gregory in willingness to suffer for the flock of Christ.

[11]Erznkats'i may have had the Pahlawuni heads of the Armenian Church in mind, several generations of whom held the Catholicosate: Grigor II Pahlawuni, also known as Vkayasēr or Martyrophile (in office 1066–1105), his nephew Barsegh I Anets'i (in office 1105–1113) and grand-nephews Grigor III Pahlawuni, who was elevated to the Catholicosate at the age of twenty (in office 1113–1166), and his brother St. Nersēs IV Klayets'i, also known as Shnorhali or the Gracious (in office 1166–1173). The latter was succeeded by his nephew, Grigor IV Pahlawuni, also known as Tghay or the Youth (in office 1173–1193), who was succeeded by his twenty-two-year-old nephew, Grigor V, also known as K'aravēzh (in office 1193–1194), for falling to his death from the walls of the castle of Kopitaṙ where he was imprisoned on Prince Levon's orders. He was succeeded by another nephew of Grigor III and Nersēs IV, a cousin of Grigor IV, the elderly Grigor VI Apirat (in office 1194–1203). But since these hierarchs preceded the author and were remotely related to St. Gregory (see *Vipasanut'iwn Haykazants'* [Epic History of the Descendants of Hayk] by St. Nersēs Shnorhali), the criticism may have been aimed more at contemporary bishops and their kin who tried to retain their offices by some improper means (see the next sentence). Moreover, the anti-catholicoi of Aght'amar, who were related to the Artsruni dynasty, also held to the same princi-

of Christ, not the abundance of silver—for they shall be spurned who are elected by it.[12]

56 [*Part II*]

Now, [regarding] the one who thus entered through the gate of the sheep-fold,[1] consider the course of his conduct and marvel. For after receiving his people, after ascending the high-priestly throne,[2] he denounced the world, withdrew to the wilderness, into uninhabited regions, distancing himself from honor, eschewing glory, conversing with God, joining the chorus of angels, uttering sacred utterances with the seraphim.[3]

57 [*Part III*]

Now, be imitators of the compassionate shepherd—as he is of his Lord and Christ[1]—and take upon yourselves the example of the persevering

---

ple of hereditary succession (Maksoudian, *Chosen of God,* pp. 44–46). The author's uneasiness with the hierarchs of his day is also reflected in another of his compositions dedicated to St. Gregory (Selection XIII).

[12]This age-old corruption of buying an ecclesiastical office, called "simony" after the account in Acts 8:14–24, is condemned earlier (see the third comment at §51).

§56

[1]Further allusion to John 10:1–18, underscoring the faithful shepherding of St. Gregory (see the fourth and tenth comments on the preceding section).

[2]When referring to the consecration of St. Gregory, Erznkats'i follows the early tradition found in Agat'angeghos where the Saint is referred to as *k'ahanayapet* and *episkopos* (*History*, 793, 805) and not the later, anachronistic references to him as *kat'oghikos* (*ibid.*, 862, 884); so also in a hymn by our author, *'Aysōr zuarchats'eal ts'ntsay ekeghets'i* . . ." (Reveling today the Church rejoices . . .), dedicated to St. Gregory (*Sharakan*, p. 266; trans., Selection XI).

[3]The alliteration here echoes a line from the Anaphora of the Divine Liturgy, preceding the "Sanctus": "And singing the *sanctus* in accord with the seraphim and the cherubim, to make melodies and, boldly crying out, to shout with them and to say) (ed. Findikyan, pp. 29–30). Such ecstatic/prophetic utterances were deemed a major gift of the Spirit, foremost of the *charismata* of 1 Cor. 12–14.

§57

[1]Echoing the words of St. Paul in 1 Cor. 11:1; cf. the *Panegyric* attributed to St. John Chrysostom, where the same verse is applied to St. Gregory (*Sop'erk'*, 4:16).

martyr.² Bring into your souls the equal of such a faith, and be afflicted though not by oppressors but by a voluntary way of life. Let nothing disrupt the shepherding of God's flock: no threat of the sword, no aches of the body, no tempting incidents, nothing that the times might bring—especially now that there are no afflictions by oppressors,³ no conflicts with schismatics,⁴ but honor and glory. For the father of faith bore the afflictions and the toil, and you are relishing some of the fruit, and have been adorned beautifully at the divine sanctuary, in the midst of the people, in the priesthood established by God.⁵

[XI. PRAYER TO ST. GREGORY]

58 [*Part I*]

And you, O divine and priestly head¹—for I am talking with you as I would with someone truly living, you who have put on divine and immortal life, O holy high priest, equal in rank to the higher, angelic priesthood. On our immortal altar, where Jesus is sacrificed, [you offered] the sacrifice of your virtue,² with which the Heavenly Father is well pleased. You are the

²On St. Gregory as martyr, see the seventh comment at §1.

³The relative and albeit temporary peace was apparently that obtained at a costly price in the settlement between King Levon II of Cilicia (1269–1289) and the Egyptian Mamluks (see the last comment at §49). Otherwise, the allusion is to a short-lived, interim peace. See, however, §48 on foreign domination, and §49 on a predicted, imminent war.

⁴As of this time the Armenian sources nearly cease to speak of the Tondrakians whose divergent teachings preoccupied the ecclesiastical authorities for centuries; see Nersessian, *The Tondrakian Movement*, p. 90.

⁵Here ends the author's appeal to the bishops and heads of the Church; for its beginning, see §54.

§58

¹Here begins a prayer in three parts, to St. Gregory, each part beginning with the exclamatory "O . . ." (*Ո՛*) followed by the vocative (§§58–60); cf. the three-part prayer to the Trinity at §8.

²Eucharistic thought, reminiscent of the hymn *"K'ristos patarageal . . ."* (Christ is sacrificed . . .) in the Divine Liturgy. The thought that St. Gregory offered his virtues as sacrifice, occurs earlier (§31: "[He] offered to God the fruit of the Spirit—the virtues"). In the *Panegyric* attributed to St. John Chrysostom, it was St. Gregory's virtue that took him to heaven, like Elijah (*Sop'erk'*, 4:30; trans., Selection II).

demonstrator of the true likeness of His image in Adamic nature, through clear and simple purity.[3] Of all the saints of our nature, who are chosen for the beauty of that image in their character, you are the most noticeable of all because of your profoundly resplendent life that brings the two [likenesses] marvelously into one through your most noble deeds and thoughts—that are untouched by any lowly thing—and through your meek, good-tempered conduct, your sorrowful heart, soft-spoken and pleasant speech, your angelic face. To the whole world and [all] nations and age-groups and classes, you are a source of benevolence: bringer of pious virgins to the glorious Bridegroom,[4] counsel of wholesome thoughts to the ranks of the married, heaven-reaching projectile to those living in solitude, lawgiver for the stability of civil life,[5] delightful teacher to those who conduct themselves unpretentiously, deeply probing theologian to thoughtful sages, restraining reins to ostentatious princes, consoling comforter to the utterly poor, a stable cane to those advanced in age, teacher of discretion to the young in years, glorious bounty to those miserably impoverished, treasurer to those resplendent in divine things, guardian to widows, impartially compassionate father to orphans, healer to the sick—those in excruciating pain—both spiritual and physical,[6] preserver of health to the true in faith and the virtuous in deeds—those persistent in fasts and prayers, kin to those neither of flesh nor of blood[7]—those who sing psalms without ceasing, like the fiery spirits, like the vigilant spirits, tireless and unyielding in steadfast wakefulness.[8]

---

[3]Echoing Gen. 1:27.

[4]Allusion to the parable of "The Ten Virgins" (Matt. 25:1–13).

[5]As "lawgiver" here and in §48, St. Gregory is once more compared with Moses; for several other comparisons with the prophet, see the fifth comment at §13.

[6]Or physician, as in §44. In the hymn by Erznkats'i, *"Aysōr zuarchats'eal ts'ntsay ekeghets'i . . ."* (Reveling today the Church rejoices . . .), dedicated to St. Gregory, he is similarly called "healer of souls" (*bzhishk hogwots'*) (*Sharakan*, p. 267; trans., Selection XI); cf. the *Panegyric* attributed to Theophilos, a disciple of St. John Chrysostom (*Sop'erk'*, 4:100).

[7]So also in the *Panegyric* attributed to Theophilos (*Sop'erk'*, 4:92). The thought echoes John 1:13; 1 Cor. 15:50.

[8]That is, angels, "those neither of flesh nor of blood" mentioned earlier.

59 [*Part II*]

O [blessed] person who is close to God and has put on God:[1] Please consider with compassion and love this nation and Church whom you have presented to God, those brought to God as spoils of war [obtained] through your perseverance and triumph of martyrdom.[2] And beseech for us the heavenly peace, and for our lives full of temptations, the calmness of the sea,[3] and guidance to those who strive in the path of goodness.

60 [*Part III*]

Moreover, O blessed image of divine kindness, compassion, and benevolence, holy father of our souls: Consider me also, pitiable and wretched in spirit, one who has found mercy through your benevolence but who has lost it because of unworthiness, who has put on the garb of priesthood with shame but not the works of justice, one who has hidden many talents in the ministry of the Word,[1] without gain, squanderer of the things of my Lord which were to be managed, one who lends unjustly and not faithfully.[2] And my life has been consumed with vanity and I was unable to do [what I should have done]. And if I were to come yonder begging, who would have mercy on me, the one willfully deprived of good things? My only hope and means of deliverance, a sufferer that I am, is to trust in your mercy, from which [comes] even this gift of rational offering.[3] Please accept it through your fatherly compassion. If there is any worthwhile thing for your Church

§59

[1]So also at §15; echoing Rom. 13:14; Gal. 3:27 (cf. "put on Christ" at §44).
[2]On St. Gregory's "martyrdom," see the seventh comment at §1.
[3]Allusion to Matt. 8:23–27 (and parallels).

§60

[1]Allusion to the parable of "The Talents" in Matt. 25:14–30.
[2]Echoing the judgment scenes following certain Matthean parables, as that of "The Talents" (25:14–30), contemplated in the preceding contrition and earlier (§40), or that of "The Unmerciful Slave" (18:23–35). There seems to be a reflection here on an injunction in the third canon attributed to St. Gregory that forbids priests to lend money with interest (see V. Hakobyan, ed., *Kanonagirk' Hayots'* [Canon Law of the Armenians], 2 vols. [Erevan: Arm. Academy of Sciences, 1964–1971] 1:245).
[3]A reference to the panegyric itself, dedicated to the Saint; cf. §6.

to receive, it is a gift from you, and from your own to you is presented.[4] If there were no forgiveness of one's manifold and recurring sins, would someone—condemned as I—have such daring of his own free will and desire? As for my few remaining days of life, please make me worthy to carry out my humble service to your Church, that I may find mercy and reward with the laborers cultivating your living plants,[5] [and at the end] to behold you with your Christ, in unequalled glory, because you partook of His suffering and therefore should revel in indescribable glory with Him; and that I may be worthy with the pious children of your Church to glorify the most holy Trinity: the Father, the Son, and the Most Holy Spirit, now, always, and forever. Amen.

[4]Echoing Rom. 11:36. Cf. the following line from the Anaphora of the Divine Liturgy: "And we offer to you yours of your own . . ." (ed. Findikyan, p. 32).

[5]Contemplating the parable of "The Laborers in the Vineyard" (Matt. 20:1–16).

Selections

I. Hymn to St. Gregory the Illuminator

By Movsēs Bishop of Siwnikʻ (*ca.* 670–731)[1]

I.

O happy lord, Saint Gregory, minister of sanctity and leader of the rational flock, we have you for a mediator with Jesus—the Only-begotten—and an intercessor on behalf of those who have allied themselves with you. Hasten to ask for forgiveness of sins, for us, discipled by you.

O blessed lord, Saint Gregory, we have you for a mediator with Christ on our behalf. You who are not ignorant of the misleading ways of the tyrant, we have you for a mediator with Christ on our behalf. You who are ranked with the disembodied ones, we have you for a mediator with Christ on our behalf.

True substance of the divine precepts and foundation of faith for the human race, lord Saint Gregory, beseech Christ for us through your intercessory prayers. Chosen of God, true high priest and spiritual shepherd of the rational flock,[2] lord Saint Gregory, beseech Christ for us through your intercessory prayers.

Wreath of decorum of the church of Christ and leader unto life eternal, lord Saint Gregory, beseech Christ for us through your intercessory prayers. Chosen of God, true high-priest, and spiritual shepherd of the rational flock, beseech Christ for us through your intercessory prayers.

You, who through your calling, your dedication to Christ, rose like a sun[3] and enlightened the land of Armenia with the knowledge of God, lord Saint Gregory, mediate for us without ceasing. You, who were translated to the heavenly tabernacle of light after your virtuous perseverance, mediate for us without ceasing.

The Christian churches were made glorious through you, ever glorifying the union of the Holy Trinity, lord Saint Gregory. Mediate for us without ceasing.

II.

We bless you always, God of our fathers, who sent your beloved and faithful servant, Saint Gregory, and enlightened the land of Armenia at his hand.

We bless you always, God of our fathers, who granted patience to Saint Gregory throughout his unbearable tortures and enlightened the land of Armenia through his forbearance.

We bless you always, God of our fathers, who lifted the darkness of idolatry from the land of Armenia because of his sanctified prayers and brought forth worshipers of your most Holy Trinity.

III.

Bless the Lord and magnify him always.

Come now, you faithful ones and those called to adoption by Saint Gregory, bless and magnify the God of all.

Let us celebrate with joy the memory of our patriarch and together with him let us praise and magnify Christ our King.

Priests and ministers, together with the holy patriarch praise and magnify with spiritual utterances the Holy Spirit of Truth.[4]

IV.

Most merciful God, save us through the intercession of your high-priest and martyr.[5]

You, who alone are most merciful, hear us through the petitions of Saint Gregory.

Lord, forgive us our sins by means of the prayers of the one through whom we learned the way of life.

V.

Guide to faith and illuminator of our souls, lord Saint Gregory. Let us come, we who have become believers through him, to give thanks to God.

Great confessor of Christ, who suffered personally for our sake, lord Saint Gregory. Let us come, we who have become believers through him, to give thanks to God.

High-priest of God and communicator of divine precepts, lord Saint Gregory. Let us come, we who have become disciples, to sing with him glory to God in the highest.

VI.

Glorious God and always beneficent, who through your foreknowledge preordained the redemption of the Armenian people by granting us an illuminator from the sinful Parthian nation,[6] because of his mediation, Savior, deliver us now and at your awe-inspiring coming.

With wonderful amazement the blessed Saint Gregory took unbearable tortures upon himself, and for fifteen years dwelt among venomous creatures in the forbidding recesses of the pit. Because of his mediation, Savior, deliver us now and at your awe-inspiring coming.

By your miracle-working word and great mercy he went about healing those stricken by the afflictions inflicted by demons, bringing forth worshippers of your most Holy Trinity. Because of his mediation, Savior, deliver us now and at your awe-inspiring coming.

VII.

O blessed lord Saint Gregory, who were called unto adoption by the heavenly Father and became a true martyr of Christ our God, ask of the Lord atonement for your people.

Who through your patience received unto yourself a special and chosen people, and adorned them anew through the birth of the holy font, ask of the Lord atonement for your people.

Who opened the gate of light, of the true knowledge of God, to us who had strayed into darkness and made us worthy to be heirs of the life eternal, ask of the Lord atonement for your people.

VIII.

Brave shepherd of the rational flock, lord Saint Gregory, you established the foundation of the church in the land of Armenia, upon the foundation of the holy apostles.

Good shepherd and guide to eternal life, lord Saint Gregory, establish our souls in the true faith, upon the foundation of the holy church.

We beseech you now, father, teacher, and lord, intercede with Christ our God to save our souls.

II. St. Gregory in the Pit

From the *Panegyric* attributed to St. John Chrysostom (*ca.* 350–407)[7]

Indeed, how could have they hoped to find him there in that unbearable place, after such a long time? But there were unexpected things, surprises not anticipated. "But with God all things are possible" (Matt. 19:26). For He who kept Jonah alive in the belly of the whale and saved Paul from the depths of the abyss[8] kept Gregory the Great incorruptible in that deep pit. And the Lord used to reveal the future to him, not like He did before, from the storm and the cloud, to those who kept pleading with Him.[9] Rather, He used to appear visibly to him, face to face, and was with him daily and never departed from him, as He says: "He who loves me observes my word . . . and I and the Father will come and will lodge with him" (John 14:23). And "To whom shall I give rest but to those who are humble and lowly and tremble at my word?" (cf. Matt. 11:28–29). Wherefore the Compassionate One and the Lover of humankind called His martyr, saying: "'Come, you who are asleep, and rise from the dead, and Christ again shall be the Giver of light to you' (Eph. 5:14). Come, my brave martyr, for through your great endurance you trampled upon and destroyed the contending accuser. Come, you who persevered bravely against the enemy and were martyred. Come, you who toppled under foot and killed Beliar,[10] the evil one of old. Come, you the firmly established pillar of my Church[11] and the pride of the universe. Come, you teacher of orthodoxy and beauty of the world. Come, you preacher of faith and leader of humankind on the way to the Kingdom. Come and be strong, come and gird yourself bravely.[12] You did not drown in the turbulent waves.[13] Wake up and be watchful, for behold 'I shall renew your youth like the eagle's' (Ps. 103:5 [102:5 LXX]). Come and preach my Gospel, for the sake of which you patiently bore much suffering. Come and rejoice, for 'I will make you into a great nation' (Gen. 12:2) like Abraham before. Come and receive the fruit of your labor. It was for this reason that I prolonged the pain of your unbearable tortures, so as to make you 'the father of many nations' (Gen. 17:4); 'for I will multiply your children like the stars of heaven and like the sand of the sea . . . such that you will not be able to count them' (Gen. 22:17; 32:12). For you shall emerge as righteous, for you shall be glorified, for you shall be distinguished before angels and men. I could have crowned you [with martyrdom] in the course of your ordeal. Even though much danger was there for you, I was patiently bearing [with you] when it came to your suffering, that I may make you worthy for the highest glory, that I may elevate you to yet greater honor and rank. You did receive the crown of martyrdom. Now you shall receive a patriarchal throne.

In your virtue you were taken up in the chariot with Elijah;[14] receive now the grace of his foreknowledge. You endured with Jonah in the harshest solitude; cry out with him 'the voice of the one crying in the wilderness' (Matt. 3:3). You were tortured in shackles with Paul in prison;[15] receive with him the unhindered preaching of my word throughout the universe.

Peter received from me the keys of the Kingdom;[16] receive the same authority from me, to bind and to loose in heaven and on earth. My twelve disciples parceled out the world between them by lot,[17] but to you alone is allotted to preach my Gospel throughout the inhabited world. For this reason you have received the name I had in my incarnation: you shall be called 'the Sun of Righteousness' (Mal. 4:2) universally."[18]

III. St. Gregory's Reward

From the *Panegyric* attributed to Theophilos (5th cent.?)[19]

Besides praise we shall tell what happened afterwards. When he was brought out of that pit, the king and all the deluded people, naked and ridiculous, came to meet him. They stood outside the city, waiting for him. And when they saw him coming from afar, they began, in their delusion, to bite their bodies, to scream and to say: "Come, embodied angel, and chase away our disembodied and darkness-loving persecutors. Come, persecutor of those who control us, those who incite our fervent hearts to persecute their mighty persecutors. Come in your visible body and chase away the invisible darkness of our souls . . ."

And now, it is impossible to praise the blessed ones as much as they deserve; yet my desire made me think it is possible. I have said precious little, and there is so much more!

The Creator said to His faithful servant: "Heedful, good, and faithful servant. Do not think of anything [as a reward] for your love for mankind. For you are planted as a second Paul, and I shall nurture you. 'Come, enter the joy of your Lord' (Matt. 25:21, 23). Fear not, second Moses, for you are designated to remove unbelief from among the nations. You loved me more than your body, and I shall give you the rest that I have prepared for those who love me. Come, new Daniel, rest from all your labor. Come into the bridal chamber, which I promised you earlier. Come, be ranked among the apostles, you, a twofold apostle, who preached the word of truth to a proud nation. Come, dance with the bands of angels, for your life on earth resembled theirs. Come, rejoice with the patriarchs, and be planted like a holy palm tree in the house of the Lord and blossom in the courtyards of your God.[20] Come, be crowned with the martyrs and rejoice in my holy nuptial chambers with the ranks of those who were martyred for me. Come, revel with the bands of anchorites who loved the mountains and the deserts, for in your ceaseless prayers you were crucified with me. For this reason I sent bands of my angels, gathered you unto myself, and brought you into Paradise, where the bandit entered with his cross.[21] For you lifted up your cross and followed me.[22]

Blessed are you among the patriarchs, holy father, an angel in the body; and when out of the body, you are ranked with the disembodied ones. Blessed are you, brave overseer, who found the lost sheep of your King that were outside the fold; and you gathered them into His fold.

IV. Ode to St. Gregory the Illuminator

By St. Grigor Narekats'i (951–1003)[23]

Գ 1–13

With overwhelming joy the children of Zion[24]
celebrate your memorial day,[25]
with passionate zeal, O great confessor
and shepherd of the rational flocks, Saint Gregory.
With earnest petitions, heartfelt tears,
we beseech you, O good teacher and father,
to have tender compassion on your children,
to whom you gave birth in travail, through the womb and the bosom
of the [baptismal] font, the mother of us all.
Please present with entreaties the petitions of the present celebrants,
constituents brought together by the power of the Word,
that He may grant His gift of atonement and grace of mercy
to the rational flocks, the children of men, we plead.

Բ 14–27

Of all tribes and nations,
　　　you were found to be superior among Adam's descendants.
By an amazing miracle, to evil ancestors who murdered their master,

you were a God-given child, a virtuous son,
a rose grown from a thorny bush,
saffron and graceful lily of the valleys,
a plant from dried up roots
planted along the fertile windings of rivers,
feeding the children of New Zion,
      those starving for the heavenly Bread of Life;[26]
a refreshing cup [of water], delicious, gushed forth from the rocks
for the panting children of Eve, the tribes descended from Hayk.[27]
Please petition the Lord, who chose us,
who called and crowned you,
to grant His gift of atonement and grace of mercy
to the rational flocks, the children of men, we plead.

Ի   28–39

From the dense darkness of godlessness,
a nursling infant, you were brought to the edifice of light,
where you were doubly nursed from the breasts extending from Zion,
the New and the Old Testaments for a spiritual drink,
with which you were amazingly fed.
You attained to mature manhood in Jesus, the Savior of all.[28]
You arrived at His deep mystery like Paul, in full command,[29]
a revealing teacher and preacher of the inscrutable, hidden mystery.
With a benevolent will, mediate with God,
the Creator from non-existence, the Provider and Restorer,
to grant His gift of atonement and grace of mercy
to the rational flocks, the children of men, we plead.

Լ   40–52

Superior to the band of the Eleven,[30]
      a preacher for the world and seasoning salt,[31]
filled with the intelligible light, you appeared from the West[32]
to the regions of the North,[33]
      to the sons of T'orgom[34] dwelling in darkness;
willing to die for them, brave shepherd,

you offered yourself courageously, like the Lord upon the cross.
You took upon yourself the agony of tortures, twelve in number,[35]
corresponding to the cardinal sins of all humanity.
You dwelt in the snake-infested dungeon
      for six-times-two-plus-one symbolic years.[36]
You neutralized the deadly venom of the serpent.
Disembodied, you ruled over the snakes there.
Beseech the heavenly Father that we may be cleansed
      from the venom of the tortuous dragon;
to grant His gift of atonement and grace of mercy
to the rational flocks, the children of men, we plead.

Ո   53–67

To the children of men abiding in darkness,
from a dark region you shone, a shining light, intelligible and sunlike;[37]
a cure for the torments of demons and a healer of our souls.
You ascended into the ranks of the incorporeals,
you were set apart and were given for our redemption.
You brought the king back from his irrational nature,
      changed him to a man.[38]
You brought the princes, together with the elders and the troops,
      to their senses.
You freed from demonic powers all the inhabitants of the land,
consigning them to the heavenly Father as children of light,
[born] of the womb of the [baptismal] font.
By your own blood and the travail of your ordeals,
you appropriated a people to yourself.
Would you earnestly beseech Jesus,
      the Hope of everyone and Lord of all,
to grant His gift of atonement and grace of mercy
to the rational flocks, the children of men, we plead.

Ո   68–87

Good teacher, thoughtful mentor,
proclaimer of the Word of Life, lord Saint Gregory,

renowned in your fine progress, bearer of good tidings to Zion,
recounter of the unreachable things and revealer of those not found:
You revealed the infinite God to the nation gone astray,
the union of the Three Persons, along with the nature of the Divinity,
by whom the totality of things was wrought.
You taught ignorant people in darkness
about the descent of the Son into a body,
        the One whose birth is without when and where.
You made the uninformed knowledgeable.
You talked about eternal life and the second death,
about His death on the cross for the human race.
You preached about becoming heirs of God and brother[s] of Christ[39]
through resurrection after death.
By the grace of the Spirit, by whom you were renewed,
you summoned again, in a glorious fashion,
        Adam with his progeny.
Please beseech with heartfelt love the grace-imparting Spirit of God
to be with us always,
to grant His gift of atonement and grace of mercy
to the rational flocks, the children of men, we plead.

բ   88–105

Truly called from on high, with a specific decree,
you were appointed patriarch and bridegroom
        of the Church of Christ, lord Saint Gregory,
distributor of the graces of the Holy Spirit to all [your] children,
to whom you gave birth, children of the daughter of Zion,
spread like a flowing river through the land of Armenia.
You cleansed, enlightened and perfected
        the grandchildren of Ashkenaz.[40]
Those alienated, as those at home,
        and those distant, as those who are near,
you led to Jesus' door, to the Spirit's home,
        and to the Father's bosom;
bringing, like a father, your children to God,
nurturing with milk, like a mother,

the countless children born through your travail.
The One who once died and who is alive for evermore,[41]
you offered as Eucharistic gift for the reconciliation of men to God,
as He offered Himself on the cross.
You went into seclusion at the end of your life;[42] at the end of it all,
you were taken to the Father's bosom by the grace of Christ's love.
Beseech the One to whom you are intimately close,
    the Three Persons and One Divinity,
to grant His gift of atonement and grace of mercy
to the rational flocks, the children of men, we plead.

ꝗ   106–129

Appearing in superior purity,
you shone on the children of Zion, lord Saint Gregory,
rising in the fullness of the sun—more than that of the stars;
universal preacher, greater than the band of the Eleven,
superior to the patriarchs who followed them,
    brave and courageous shepherd.
You obtained your flocks through your own blood,
O great among the confessors and altogether incomparable
    among those who were crowned with blood,
you, who knew the mystery of Jesus more than the Prophets,
true leader and head of ascetic clerics,
heavenly man and earthly angel,
Seraph of clay and corporeal Cherub,
corporeal seat and resting place for the will of the Great God:
I plead earnestly with you to appeal to the Lord
on behalf of all earthly humanity:
For patriarchs, right doctrine;
for bishops and priests, impeccable share of grace;
for deacons, readers, and all dedicated children of the Church,
sanctity, holiness, and righteousness;
for kings and princes, courage and just judgement;
for soldiers and commanders, and for all men and women,
health and true confession;
for those asleep, rest and resurrection unto life.

Please, remember and have mercy upon those fallen asleep
in the hope of the resurrection, we pray.

Ա   130–131

Moreover,
grant us [to abide by] the admonitions to love
        and to [do] good deeds, we pray.

Բ   132–133

To rededicate ourselves and one another,
to submit ourselves to the Lord God Almighty, we plead.

Գ   134–158

With entreating voice, tearful pleading,
we ask you, Lord of All, Holy Trinity,
Creator of all creatures that came into existence from nothing,
Fashioner of our nature from two constituents made into one:
corporeal and incorporeal, spiritual body, in your image and form,
provident Provider, Restorer of the immaterial and the material,
Reviver of our fallen nature and Redeemer of the first man, Adam,
Merciful, Lover of mankind, generous Benefactor:
Through the intercession of the truly blessed Mary,
        the bearer of God,
mother of the incarnate Word,
through the intercession of John the Forerunner,
the baptizer of your Son, hearer of the Father's voice,
seer of your Spirit in the form of a dove,[43]
through the entreaties of the blood of Stephen the Protomartyr,
who saw you at the right hand of the Father,[44]
through the intercessory perseverance of Saint Gregory,
        who is commemorated today,[45]
through the petitions of the Apostles and the Prophets,
and the brave and blessed martyrs made perfect,
through the constantly outstretched arms

of the pure, ascetic bands of hermits,
grant peace to the world and stability to the Church,
guidance to leaders and sanctity to priests,
and atonement and mercy to all people.
And now, may the Lord our God have mercy on us
according to His great mercy.

V. Prophet and Apostle

From the *Discourse* of Grigor Sarkawagapet Erusaghēmats'i (12th century, perhaps earlier).[46]

This our blessed patriarch Saint Gregory, who led you to faith and became your illuminator, through whom we came to know our Creator from whom our ancestors strayed long ago, was found to be most loved by Christ. For he became unto us the way of life, appearing with prophetic credentials and apostolic wonders and preaching, and as a teacher of truth. Though the prophets performed many miracles, in our land greater wonders were performed by the will of God, at the hand of St. Gregory. There were also powerful manifestations by the Apostles, as is known to all. But nothing like this was ever witnessed or reported, even at the hands of the Apostles. For under their auspices healing was brought to the sick and there was resurrection of the dead. But through the prayers of our patriarch, the king who was transformed into a boar was restored to being human and health was restored to many.[47] Likewise, demons were chased away and great and magnificent temples made of stone were destroyed without a trace being left, as were also their priests.[48] We know of nothing like this happening anywhere else. Nowhere among the mighty acts of God was such a crop of converts brought into adoption by God in a single day. The flow of the Euphrates stopped, as did the Jordan of old.[49] But more than that, the light shone brighter here than it did on Israel.[50] Moreover, the canopy of cloud[51] was surpassed by the light radiating from the exalted cross; so also the previous record of endurance, through his diverse and bitter tortures and the unimaginable stay for so many years in the deep pit, in the midst of poisonous snakes. Neither I nor anyone else could tell from where such power comes. Now, am I belittling the former things by telling this? God forbid that such a thought should cross my mind. Rather, I want to say that God had shown more mercy on Armenia. For with thankfulness we give glory daily to the Most Holy Trinity for making known to us His love for humankind in such a powerful way. We bless His name every hour for granting us such a patriarch, Christ-loving and one who cares for the people.

Like Jesus, he prayed for those who hanged him on the appalling and horrible gallows.[52] As for his teaching, he addressed every conceivable issue. Moreover, he sought [God's] help in his patriarchal role for his lot which he received beyond his expectation, and he brought to us the heavenly gifts. And after his teaching he passed on to us his counsel on every aspect of life, in many sermons,[53] so that we who were to come after him would not be denied of the counsel of his lips.

I know how joyous it is for me to recount these remembrances of our teacher, and what a delight to you listeners. For we all know him very well. He is a Parthian by nationality, from the district of Bahl, from the Arsacid clan, from the Surēnian household, Anak his father's name.[54] He spread the light of his teachings openly in the northern regions, into our hearts submerged in darkness, and made known to us the Sun of Righteousness risen upon the earth. For this reason it behooves us to love and honor him with joyous memorials and merry feasts and to exalt him as a prophet and an apostle, martyr and confessor, patriarch and leader, teacher and hermit, and as an ascetic. He was perfect in every personal virtue. After all his miracles, he withdrew into seclusion on the mountain so as to talk with God daily, without distraction, like the proto-prophet Moses the Great and Elijah the Tishbite who ascended mountaintops to pray for Israel.[55] So did also Saint Gregory for the land of Armenia, making petitions with much tears and deep sighs to Him whose eye is over the righteous and whose ear is inclined to their prayers, listening to do them good. And he spread the Benefactor's compassion over us, from the start of his petitioning to this day.

VI. Like unto Moses

From the *Panegyric* of Yovhannēs Sarkawag (*ca.* 1050–1129)[56]

As for words to compare him [i.e., St. Gregory], there are countless words to show his superiority, and there are countless instances of coincidences.

But let us focus on the one of whom we read today, the worker of miracles, the first of the prophets, and the lawgiver, I mean Moses the Great, the lesser of those who truly saw the glory of the Lord and whose face was made glorious.[57] For he saw the burning bush which was not consumed, or that which was a theophany. And this was for real, whether in his approach or in his vision; for only the voice prevented him from approaching the mystery. He was told to untie the strings of his sandals, as one who is unworthy to stand thus in a divine place. And he was given orders to bring the children of Israel out of Egypt with signs and wonders. This propels those who are infants into the circle of instruction in what pertains to Christ . . . And to help his slowness of speech, as a mouthpiece for eloquence, God granted him his brother Aaron,[58] which means "spirit," symbolic of additional spirit and gifts.[59] But as for this one, by divine foresight he was given the heavenly brides from the Roman world, including the beautiful virgin with her midwife, those who challenged the mighty ones.[60]

See, for a fact! Three led out the Exodus of Israel: Moses, Aaron, and the staff from God. Truly these too were three: the martyr, the saintly girl, and the elderly [woman] with virtuous thoughts.[61] The former were foreshadows, but these, ministers of the Truth . . .

Lest we should deviate by mistake from words of comparison, let us go back to such words. With the staff from God he turned the water into blood and in the midst of the palace he made the same staff appear like a serpent, and by stretching his hand again, made it revert to its nature.[62] By such miracles he was able to bring out the children of Israel and to have them dwell in the blessed, Promised Land. But this one, in the depth of the pit, in the midst of the venomous [snakes], restrains their consuming nature or neutralizes their venom. And he does not strike the water with the staff but the very person of the king with the word of God, and transforms his human appearance into the worst kind of an animal, which was abominable even to the Babylonians, which was unclean according to the Law and unacceptable for divine sacrifices.[63] But then, by extending to him the sign of the cross that he held in his hand, he transformed him to normalcy and his wickedness to piety. And he brought the people of the tribe of Aram and the whole of the north out of the darkness of ignorance to the light of the knowledge of God. The other tormented the Egyptians with a dozen blows and delivered the children of Israel from the iron smelting furnaces, but this one, taking upon himself scores of diverse torments, thrice victorious, with as many victories, tormented the rebel's invisible power.[64] And he lifted us up from baneful and hellish Egypt,[65] from unimaginable darkness, and from consulting with demons to the rays of the intelligible and unapproachable Sun. The other divided the Red Sea with the staff, led the children of Israel by a pillar of fire and a cloud, and caused Pharaoh to drown deep in the abyss.[66] But this one turned around the flow of the Euphrates with his heel and caused the rising of the brightest light from heaven, brighter than the rays of the sun. And he enlightened the multitudes of our people at such a depth: with the mystery of the [baptismal] font, by the power of the One who in the waters of the Jordan crushed the head of the invisible Pharaoh.[67] The other fed the people with manna in the desert,[68] but this one with the true Bread that came down from heaven,[69] whom he introduced. The other smote the massive rock with the staff, made streams to flow, and quenched the thirst of the people.[70] But this one opened up the fountainhead of the divine admonitions, made the living waters flow like a river,[71] and inundated with spirituality the parched fields of the souls of the people. The other, by his uplifted arms, empowered Joshua and defeated Amalek;[72] but this one, with the sign of the wooden cross, put to the flames the sanctuaries of demons and made the demons flee as exiles to the Caucasus.[73] The other brought up the people to Palestine, the Promised Land; but this one leads us by true shepherding to the intelligible world to come or, one may say, to the more perfect one, to see God—provided each of us is taught by precept and example and the right teaching of the Word so as to see God.

VII. ODE TO ST. GREGORY THE ILLUMINATOR

By Catholicos Grigor III Pahlawuni (Catholicos, 1113–1166)[74]

The sun, from the rising of the sun,
From the rising of the sun, the sun
Shone on us from the West,
Shone on us even from the West.[75]

The bridesmaid[76] of the immaculate Bride[77]
Brought good news to the groomsman:
      "Wake up, you 'wakeful' by name,[78]
      "And awaken those slumbering in sin.

"Arise, you who are sleeping in the pit,
"You who are sleeping in the pit, come forth,
      "Illuminator of our homeland, Armenia;
      "Illuminator of Armenia, our homeland.

The cloud that covered the sun,
Yes, the cloud that covered the sun
      Oppressed Peter's flock,
      [It oppressed Peter's flock].[79]

The earth is watered with blood.
Sow the seed, you spiritual sower.[80]
      The one who was bound came out of prison,
      Released the bonds of the one who had him bound.

From irrational state of being
The king was restored to reason;
      The throngs of common people
      From demonic scourge delivered.

Like the band of the Eleven[81]
He proclaimed the Bread of Life;[82]
      With the prophets he saw
      The Only-begotten descend from heaven.[83]

The shepherd of the flock newly formed
Established it through his heavenly calling.
      Thus, with the heavenly beings we sing
      Blessings to the One Divinity.

VIII. Ode to the Holy Illuminator

By Catholicos St. Nersēs Shnorhali (Catholicos, 1166–1173)[84]

Ս With cherubic voices we chant today
    in memory of our father and *teacher:*

Բ The chief of *teachers* who made rise, amidst darkness,
    the light of the *Word* of Wisdom upon Armenia –

Գ That *Word* who, descending from the Father, redeemed the world.
    By that [Word] he raised us, the fallen ones, unto *uprightness.*

Դ In that *uprightness* he was found pleasing to the Beholder;
    he was a rosebud *bursting* from thorny branches.[85]

Ե Vast and meritorious knowledge was *bursting*
    in *his* heart, from youthful years onward.

Զ Cause of salvation for *his* fellows,
    he became a life-line cast in the sea of sin.

Է *He became* a witness in a court of justice,
    like Jesus before the *assembly* of Pilate.

Ը By the head of the *assembly,* King Trdat, he was interrogated
    with thick rods—an oblation to *fanciful* musings.

Թ He was unmoved by the *fanciful* decepions,
    enduring with patience the pain of the *scourge.*

Ժ The deadly *scourge* as with an incorporeal body
    he bore upon his *blessed* self—all twelve [tortures].[86]

Ի *Blessed* was he deemed by the higher host gathered in heaven;
    their *assembly,* descending, was astonished at that [sight].

Լ The ungodly *assembly* laid [blocks of] salt on his sacred body
    at the start of the tortures he took *upon himself.*

Խ *Upon himself* [he took] the disdainful water poured [into him]
    and the *iron* [nails] driven through the soles of his feet.

Ծ The skin of the Saint was scraped with *iron* scrapers
    and the saintly *teacher* was struck on the eyes.

Կ The knees of the *teacher* were hit hard with hammers
    and he was suspended from hooks, *his chest* fettered.

Գ. *His chest,* (full) of fresh air, breathed the furnace ash.
    In place of water *he* drank vinegar with his Lord.[87]

Ի The very sharp spikes on which *he* was laid
    were colored with streams of *his* blood.

Ի Over *his* mouth, whence goodness flowed,
    they poured the *painful,* boiling lead.

Ե The *painful* tortures insufficient seemed;
    wherefore the *teacher* was bound, hung from the foot.

Ր The good *teacher,* by nature akin to the One who is good,
    never *ceased* to pray for his torturers' forgiveness.

Ս When the deadly tortures which he bore were *ceased,*
    he was thrown *in that very* dungeon deep.

Ի *In that very* pit, dark, the venomous snakes,
    restraining their venom, embraced his feet with *love.*

Ս His **love** for God brought the Most High down [to him],
    transformed the abyss of the pit into a fiery *heaven.*

 Է The King of *Heaven,* with the ranks of angels,
    was with his servant for fifteen years.

IX. The Death of St. Gregory on Mount Sepuh

From the *Panegyric* of Vardan Vardapet Arewelts'i (*ca.* 1200–1271)[88]

And he [i.e., St. Gregory] died altogether unbeknown, like Moses, lest his newborn children, the Armenians still lacking in faith, should worship his bones.[89] Moreover, he dwelt on Mount Sepuh, which nowadays is called *Srboyn Grigori* ["St. Gregory's"]. From there, they say, he wanted to go to Jerusalem on his knees, to die there. And he thus descended from the mountain and crossed one of the valleys. Christ his Lord sent two Seraphs to meet him, to tell him: "I am impressed by your unbearable perseverance. Stand on your feet and ascend the mountain from where you descended, for there you shall die and for a while no one shall know of your death. The people whom you so well instructed shall perform no [funeral] service for you." He did accordingly. He erected crosses at that place and called them

"Seraphs." There is a small village nowadays at that place, where the miracle-working crosses are found. And the village is called *Serovbēkʿ* ["Seraphs"] to this day. This tradition which I told is very well known.[90]

He then ascended this accessible mountain, this tangible mountain, following the Lord's command through His messengers, the Seraphs. And he used to meditate there, like Elijah at Carmel.[91] And he remained there, crucified each day and night. And when every mystery was made known to him and all good gifts and perfect bounties had come down to him from above,[92] it was time for him to depart from his crucified and much tormented body and to go to his Lord, unto the indescribable glory that was in store, when he completed his thirty years of high priesthood, having fought the good fight, having kept the faith, having completed his course, and having attained to the wreath that withers not.[93]

Thus, the Lord's command led him to the summit of Mount Sepuh. And He showed him the Promised Land, the Heavenly Jerusalem, the Church of the Firstborn, those who were waiting for Him. Just as Moses the Great saw Palestine from Mount Nebo and died,[94] so also our Moses. After seeing the heavenly glory and the boundary of his lot, which he blessed with the sign of the cross, he committed himself to God, with familiar prayers and much tears. He then yielded his impeccable soul into the hands of God, the One and Only God. And the countless armies of his sons and daughters were left longing and thirsting for the remains of his body. And the loving and affectionate posterity of the nuptial chamber and the children of his spiritual travail were unable to hear his last admonitions so as to be comforted. They did not prepare his corpse nor did they weep over him for thirty days, as the House of Israel did over Moses and Aaron.[95] In place of these, a fiery pillar and armies of angels surrounded his body acceptable to God. And there was indescribable joy among the ranks of the heavenly beings over his pure and Christ-adorned soul. And the body of our brave shepherd, canopied by heavenly glory, was discovered by fortunate shepherds and buried unrecognized.[96] They noticed him because he was standing straight, leaning over his staff, his arms outstretched.[97] However, because of the glorious light, they came to realize that he was a great servant of God. He was afterwards discovered by the holy ascetic Garnik, who brought [his remains] to Tʿordan. From there Emperor Zeno [474–491] brought them to Constantinople. Afterwards they were brought to Armenia by the patrician Grigor [Mamikonean],[98] who placed half of them in the four pillars of the rugged [church] of Saint Gregory.[99] And the rest were kept in churches and various places. And his light-receiving and grace-distributing right arm, with other remains, and the altar on which he used to celebrate the Eucharist, and his staff, are at his holy See, at the citadel established by God, called Hŕomklay.[100]

X. More on the Death and the Relics of St. Gregory

From the *History* of Kirakos Gandzakets'i (*ca.* 1203–1272)[101]

Worthy of every praise and acclaimed with good remembrance, our spiritual father and begetter through the Gospel, Saint Gregory, after enlightening the land of Armenia with the knowledge of God and all Orthodox ordinances and canons, and after ordaining more than four-hundred-thirty bishops, he went with King Trdat the Great to Rome, to see the relics of the holy Apostles Peter and Paul and to make a sworn alliance with King Constantine the Great [324–337] and the holy Patriarch Sylvester [314–335].[102] Saint Constantine and the great Patriarch received Saint Gregory at the imperial court with great honors, befitting the confessor and martyr for Christ, full of apostolic grace. They gave him patriarchal honor, like that of the vicar of Peter. They also gave him some of the relics of the Apostles, including the left arm of the Apostle Andrew, and other gifts; and in Jerusalem, Golgotha, the place of Christ's crucifixion, [the cathedral of] Saint James, and a place to celebrate the divine liturgy adjacent to the Holy Resurrection [Rotunda].[103] (They say that Saint Gregory hung a lantern over the tomb of Christ and asked God in prayer to light it with immaterial light on the feast of the holy Passover; that miracle continues to this day.) Trdat the Great was honored likewise, as befits his valor. By the blood of Christ and by faith in Him, they made a treaty to keep the love that exists between the two nations inviolable after themselves.

Constantine asked Saint Gregory: "How great is the angels' joy over the reclaiming of so many lost sheep?" He answered: "Considerably great; however, the heavenly hosts consider us, the descendants of Adam, as one[104] sheep." And the Emperor said: "And the redeemed are one. Let us resolve, on the occasion of your visit, to be with them."

And he commanded the whole city to celebrate with the slaughtering of sheep. But the Jews and the pagans who had persisted in unbelief stayed away from the blessed salt, for Saint Gregory and Sylvester had blessed salt. And Saint Gregory said to the Jews: "You make circumcision into uncircumcision when you break the Law" (Rom. 2:25).[105] And he added: "Animals brought as sacrifice to God, or as offering to the saints, or in memory of those who are asleep, are like the holocausts of the pagans when offered without the blessing of salt."[106]

And upon their return to our land with great joy and spiritual jubilation, they adorned our land greatly with all the Christian ordinances.

During his life he ordained his son, Saint Aristakēs, chief bishop of the Armenians, the Georgians, and the [Caucasian] Albanians, and gave himself fully to the ascetic rules, that he may be crowned severally: in apostolicity, martyrdom, patriarchy, and asceticism, which accustoms man to be closer to God, by talking to Him without ceasing. And after Aristakēs returned from the Council of Nicaea, Saint Gregory was not seen by anyone. Having lived his full time, he rested in Christ, having served thirty years in the patriarchal office. When shepherds found him dead, they heaped a pile of rocks over him.

Later, under the influence of the Spirit, a certain Gaṙnik, an ascetic and holy man, found him. And they brought and laid him in the village of T'ordan. And in the days of the Emperor Zeno [474–491], they brought some of his remains and of those of the Hṙipsimian saints to Constantinople. And they made a silver reliquary in which they placed the relics of the saints; and after they wrote each name on it, they placed it in a marble sarcophagus and sealed it with a ring. It was left there for a long time, unknown as to whose it was, except that it was of some saint.

In the days of the Emperor Basil [867–886] and the Bagratid Ashot [862–890], King of the Armenians,[107] it came to light in this manner: A youth possessed by an evil spirit was praying in the church where the relics of the saints were. The demon lifted the youth and threw him over the sarcophagus of the saints, and he began to scream, saying: "Saint Gregory, Illuminator of the Armenians, do not torment me; and you, Lady Hṙipsimē, have come to torment me; and you, Gayanē, are tormenting me." And he was screaming like this for a long while.

When the multitude heard this, they made it known to the Emperor,[108] and he ordered that the sarcophagus be opened. As soon as they opened it, a great light shone forth from the relics of the saints. And the Emperor ordered to overlay the sarcophagus with gold and to write the names of the saints over it, so that everyone would know whose sarcophagus it is. A certain eunuch of the Emperor came and related all this to King Ashot, and when he heard it, he gave glory to God. And they assigned that day to be the feast day of Saint Gregory, which is the Saturday of the sixth week in the Lenten period—observed to this day.[109]

XI. Hymn to St. Gregory the Illuminator

By Yovhannēs Erznkats'i (ca. 1230–1293)[110]

Ա A

Reveling today the Church rejoices, this God-planted garden now blossoming, from where lord Gregorios was given to us as the plant of immortality that filled the entire world with its fruit.[111]

Բ B

Fruitful branch of the True Vine, cultivated by the fatherly right arm of God, from which derives the cup of joy for the nations in despair, drinking from which we are thrilled with spiritual gladness.[112]

Գ G

The breeze of the southern wind that ushers in the spring season was powered by the fire of the divine Spirit, by which the ice of the northern nations' idolatry was melted;[113] and they blossomed in divine knowledge.

Դ D

A garden of renewed joy was planted in the land of Armenia by the many efforts and sweat of lord Gregorios, watered by the flowing streams of the truly proclaimed Word, filled with beautiful, blossoming plants.

Ե   E

You revealed the heavenly light that dawned upon the earth, brightened by the glitter of the Sun of life,[114] by which the utter darkness of the Armenian nation dissipated; and it beheld the light of the grace of the Holy Spirit.

Զ   Z

The fiery hosts of the disembodied ranks rejoice, dancing together with us who are of earthly nature, whom lord Gregorios presented to the Lord God; for by him are children dedicated to the glory of the Orthodox faith.

Է   Ē

Good image of the goodness of the Self-existent, good chief-shepherd lord Gregorios,[115] who with a pleasant voice turned the straying flock around, gathering it to the flock of the true Shepherd.[116]

Ը   Ĕ

Blameless high-priest,[117] chosen of God, proclaimer of the true word of God, you did present to the Lord God a sanctified, new people, invited to the glory of Zion above.[118]

Թ   T'

By virtue of your apostolic life, lord Gregorios, you are the crown of pride prepared for the Arshakuni dynasty,[119] composed of multi-colored gems derived from martyrdom; a fitting wreath woven for the holy Church.

Ժ   ZH

You inherited the paternal, special flock entrusted by lot to the holy Apostle Thaddaeus, a gifted child of his living remains, a descendant asked for through the grace of prayer.[120]

ṗ I

A red rose blossoming from a thorny plant,[121] you received the apostolic grace, lord Gregorios. You filled Armenia with pleasant scent, revealing to us the fragrance of knowledge.

ּ L

You were revealed to the world as a brilliant blossom, healer of our souls, lord Gregorios, and a delicious date palm planted in the house of God, laden with the fruit of your children in faith.[122]

խ KH

Confessor of Christ and true witness, a martyr who suffered much,[123] lord Gregorios. You bore in your body the remainder of the Lord's suffering;[124] wherefore the Church rejoices in the glory of the children of Zion.

ծ TS

Spiritual parent,[125] God-like in love, compassionate father, much to be proud of, lord Gregorios. Through your corporeal suffering you cleansed us from the filth of sin and begot children through your enlightening word.[126]

կ K

Image of the glory of the Only-begotten Son, victorious martyr, lord Gregorios. Your sacred, heaven-bound feet were wounded with iron nails,[127] so that you might fix us to the fear of God.

հ H

Chosen author, father of the faith of Armenia, you led a tireless life, lord Gregorios. By virtue of your bleeding legs, twisted in shackles,[128] part of your body nurtured in holiness, we are established upon the rock of faith.

Ձ DZ

With petitioning voice we commemorate you, illuminator of our souls, father Gregorios. The iron fetters and the dreadful suspension from the gibbet notwithstanding,[129] you bowed down by bending the knees of your sanctified body.

Ղ GH

You crossed the sea of this world with the rudder of faith, in a grief-bearing body, lord Gregorios. Your God-lifting and sacred arms were broken,[130] so that you might restore again the disjointed members of our souls.

Ճ CH

You were filled with the wisdom of the Spirit of Truth, the grace gushing forth, lord Gregorios. You were suspended head-down, patiently enduring torture by the inrushing of water,[131] so that you might cleanse us from the filth of sin.

Մ M

You became the cleansing and the seasoning salt of Armenia, valiant watchman, lord Gregorios. As a bearer of God's law,[132] you bore on your back the heavy salt,[133] whereby you lifted the burden of sin from our midst.

Յ Y

With precious gems held together with gold, in a row of pearls we weave the number of your tortures,[134] lord Gregorios, afflicted with ropes on pulleys and devices of evil contrivance, with bridles and muzzles on your mouth speaking of God.[135]

Ն N

Good martyr, chosen of God, soldier of the King, lord Gregorios. Suspended with your head down and breathing the stench,[136] you endured valiantly so that you might direct the course of our feet to heaven.

̃ȝ   SH

Pathway adorned with lights that leads to the Way of life,[137] traveler to the Promised Land, lord Gregorios. You were compelled to breathe ashes, had vinegar poured into your life-breathing nostrils,[138] imparting to us the salve of joy.

ɲ   O

In spirit resembling the most honored head cast in gold, father Gregorios. Your divinely adorned head, smitten with blows, was placed in vises[139] so that the heads of those lost in sin might be lifted up.

ǫ   CH'

To us who are of earthly nature, an object of pride from the pleasant land, enduring suffering, lord Gregorios. You were tortured with iron thistles, sharp scrapers, and melted lead.[140] The sacred remains of your bones were charred.

ƞ   P

[You are] part of the circle of the heavenly host of spirits, dressed in shining garments of holiness, lord Gregorios. You were lowered into the deep dungeon, into the mire, among vile snakes,[141] so as to deliver us from the evil dragon.

ǳ   J

With fervent prayers and spiritual love, with hope rewarded, lord Gregorios, lift us up to be with you in the heavenly sanctuaries, we who are fallen from heaven into the depths of the valleys, being wounded by sin.

ɽ   R'

Soothing balm, granted to us from on high, you who were secluded in the dungeon for fifteen years.[142] You were released because of that divine revelation, to heal the one stricken with demonic ailments, whom you brought to faith by the flow of the luminous word.

ʊ S

Through the marvelous prophetic spirit you became a seer of that awe-inspiring vision revealed from above, of the open altar in the upper realm and of the heavenly light.[143] You mingled humanity with the fiery hosts.

Վ V

By the pink blood of the martyrs for the Lord, our land was cleansed from the filth of sin; and there you laid the foundation of an altar for the deep mystery, a divinely constructed sanctuary,[144] from where the spring of our atonement flows.

ʂ T

Good overseer of the household of God, worthy of grace, lord Gregorios. By the power of the Cross you destroyed shrines and dismantled temples,[145] you who are a high-priest chosen by divine revelation.

ր R

By the summons of the Teacher you were called above, to an apostolic throne,[146] lord Gregorios. With abundant wisdom and spiritual birth you enlightened the land of Armenia, building sanctuaries everywhere to the glory of God.

ȝ TS'

Worthy of cherubic, incorporeal life, in impeccably pure body, lord Gregorios. By living in solitude you became a hermit like unto John and Elijah and Moses, the great lawgiver of the divine commandments.[147]

ի   W

To us who are vexed by sin, suffering children, you manifested the compassion of God, father Gregorios. Through your prayers to the heavenly Father, ask that we complete our journey in the Orthodox faith.

փ   Pʿ

By virtue of the salvific death of the life-giving Word, living martyr, lord Gregorios, beseech the one born of the Father, the Only-begotten Son, the true Light,[148] to enlighten each of us with his divine knowledge.

ք   Kʿ

Melodious harp of the divine Spirit,[149] by whom your body and the parts of your soul were constituted, petition the Holy Spirit, the one emanating from the Father and equal in honor to the Son, to cleanse us from our sins.

XII. Hymn to Mount Sepuh

By Yovhannēs Erznkatsʿi (*ca.* 1230–1293)[150]

All you mountains, rejoice today at the magnificent glory of Sepuh, the most exalted mountain, for Saint Gregorios dwelt here, the pillar of light[151] of the holy Church of Armenia, because of whom she rejoices with the glory of Zion above.

This mountain exults with far deeper mystery than the Araratian summit of Masis, for Saint Gregorios rested here, the ark which saved the lives of the people of Armenia caught in the torrents of sin and by which we are constantly saved from the torrential waters.[152]

Rejoicing in superior light, Mount Sepuh is exalted alongside Sinai; for here lighted the vaulted cloud, Saint Gregory, adorning it—like Moses—

with superior light that makes our faces shine with the grace of the Holy Spirit.[153]

The mountain where Saint Gregory retired, as in the vision at Carmel, is guarded round about by fiery hosts who shield the living chariot,[154] the sacred prayers of the holy Illuminator, the spiritual father whom we always have as an intercessor with the Lord.

Lord Gregorios, the one like unto Isaiah the son of Amoz, the holy prophet purified by lightening, who by the living Spirit became a seer of the fiery Cherubim, the living creatures with six wings;[155] he transformed the crevices of the deep valleys into heavenly arches.

The grace-imparting hand of Jesus has honored Mount Sepuh like Senir and Hermon.[156] From it gushes the Spring of Light, its tasty water and currents streaming; because of which the earth rejoices with bountiful harvest.

By the birthing of the holy Virgin in the cave of Bethlehem the daughters of Eve were admonished to become like the mother of Christ in virginity. On this heaven-like mountain, in the cave of Manē, who led a sanctified life, a bright mystery was revealed, by which we are always cleansed from the filth of sin.[157]

The mystery of the One crucified at the most magnificent site of Golgotha is seen tacitly at this very mountain: that imperial weapon, the instrument employed to kill the King of Life, is now employed as an instrument of life—by which He shall save us from eternal death.[158]

The mystery of the special glory of Sepuh was made known by the Holy Spirit to the prophet who was asking: "Who shall dwell in the tabernacle of God and on the mountain of the Lord?"[159] This we see fulfilled in Saint Gregory.

The one unblemished in life, righteous in spirit, truthful in word, and holy in heart, lord Gregorios, whom the hosts of Seraphim—those fiery mouths descending from heaven to earth—desired to behold, the one enduring in the flesh, in whose honor this place is named.

The shepherds became followers of the watchful shepherd, who is in the likeness of the true and good Shepherd. They gathered up his pure body, near the cave of Manē, as a remedy to cleanse us from the passions.[160] By him our souls are cleansed from the venom of the dragon.

XIII. Ode to St. Gregory the Illuminator

By Yovhannēs Erznkatsʻi (*ca.* 1230–1293)[161]

 Գ. Brothers, today we are celebrating the release of Gregorios
    from the pit, the saint who suffered much.

Բ The happy virgins who came from the West
    have given a festal joy to the people of Armenia.

Ի At the site of their death, where their sacred blood flowed,
    heavenly tabernacles were created upon earth.

Գ. Arches of light joined pillars of fire and cloud,
    their bases golden and colored red.

Ո The dusty earth blossomed in expanses
    of celestial blue, the tint of heaven;

Բ The earth was suddenly dotted with sacred altars,
    numberless, like the stars of heaven.

Ի A spring of water gushed forth amid the tabernacles,
    coursed like rivers, with waves as of the sea.[162]

Ո Flocks of black goats, passing by, were dyed like lambs
    with sparkling fleece, those who put on Christ,

Ս Being crucified with the Son in the water of the holy font,
    cleansed by the Holy Spirit, through faith in the Father.[163]

Լ Father Gregorios, illuminator of our souls,
    look at us, pierced and wounded unto death.

Ո We, your rational flock,[164] moaning, in tears,
    are deprived of shepherds and caring lords.

Ի Your faithful children[165] have wasted away,
    enslaved, scattered among foreign nations.

Ս The sacred tabernacles, once founded by you,
    lie in ruins, desolate, dark, uninhabited.

Վ The lambs of Christ's flock, once purchased by blood,
    have become flocks of black goats because of sin.[166]

Տ Wolves have taken the place of the shepherds of the flocks,[167]
    scattering[168] the sheep obtained with pain.

Ր The covenants of the Law and the injunctions of canon law,
    these your commandments are being shattered.

Ց There is a dearth of wise teachers' prudence,
    diminished by a malevolent way of life.[169]

Ւ Those destined to be among the heavenly ranks
    are ruled today by those destitute of wisdom.[170]

Փ We have neither caring nor compassionate mediators[171]
    to recount the release of the happy seer.

Ք Most compassionate father, image of the Heavenly Father,
    we plead with you, intercede[172] with the Lord

Վ To bring back from captivity the fallen and scattered sheep
    allotted to you and to grant forgiveness of sins.

Օ Regarding the one who sits on your lordly throne today,[173]
    ask of Christ to grant us an illuminator [like you].

Ր As for the crowned king of the descendants of Aram,[174]
    ask of the Spirit to keep him always strong.

Օ While rejoicing today and gladdened by your feast,
    we give thanks and glory to the Trinity.

NOTES

[1]Text in *Sharakan Hogewor Ergots' Surb ew Ughghap'ar̄ Ekeghets'woys Hayastaneayts'* (Hymnal of Spiritual Songs of the Holy and Orthodox Church of Armenia) (Jerusalem: St. James Press, 1936; reprinted New York: St. Vartan Press, 1986), pp. 554–560.

[2]These are recurring attributes of St. Gregory in the panegyrics.

[3]On St. Gregory as "sun," see the opening of the panegyric by Erznkats'i and the fifth comment at §1; cf. the panegyric attributed to St. John Chrysostom, *Sop'erk'*, 4:31 (trans., Selection II), and Narekats'i's "Ode to the Holy Illuminator," *Tagher*, p. 179 (trans., Selection IV).

[4]"Spirit of Truth," as in John 14:17.

[5]On St. Gregory as "martyr," "confessor," and related attributes, see the panegyric by Erznkats'i and the proper comment at §1.

[6]On the Parthians, see the panegyric by Erznkats'i and the comment at §20.

[7]Text in *Sop'erk'*, 4:27–31; *Oskeberani . . . Meknut'iwn T'ght'ots'n Pawghosi*, 2:801–803. Without ruling out the possibility of a Greek original, there is reason to suspect that the work is of Armenian authorship from the twelfth century. See the first colophon translated in the second part of the Introduction, p. 31; cf. A. Terian, "The Ancestry of St. Gregory the Illuminator in the Panegyrical Tradition," *St. Nerses Theological Review* 7 (2002) 45–65. The expanded title purports that it was written during St. John Chrysostom's exile at Cucusa (Koukousos) in Armenia, between 404 and 407, and upon the request of a certain bishop and vardapet, his Armenian-born compatriot named Dioscoros.

[8]Alluding to the shipwreck at Malta, Acts 27.

[9]Alluding to the theophanies in Exodus and elsewhere in the Pentateuch.

[10]Name given to Satan in the intertestamental Jewish literature; cf. "accuser" in the preceding line (Rev. 12:10). In the hymn *"Aysōr zuarchats'eal ts'ntsay ekeghets'i . . ."* (Reveling today the Church rejoices . . .) by Erznkats'i, dedicated to St. Gregory, he is said to have coped with the snakes in the pit so as to save us from the dragon (*vishap*), whose head he crushed in the pit (*Sharakan*, pp. 271, 276; trans., Selection IX).

[11]An apostolic designation, according to Gal. 2:9: "James, Peter and John, those reputed to be pillars."

[12]Allusion to the angelic words to Peter in Acts 12:8.

[13]Allusion to Peter's experience in Matt. 14:25–33.

[14]Allusion to 2 Kgs. 2:1–13; cf. the panegyric by Erznkats'i (§42).

[15]Allusion to Acts 16:16–40.

[16]Allusion to Matt. 16:19.

[17]The Acts of Thomas 1; cf. Eusebius, *Historia Ecclesiastica*, 3.1; *The Teaching of St. Gregory*, 609, 688.

[18]See comment at §1 of Erznkats'i's panegyric, on the same appellation being used for both Christ and St. Gregory.

[19]Text in *Sop'erk'*, 4:120–124; *Oskeberani . . . Meknut'iwn T'ght'ots'n Pawghosi*, 2:839–841. Without ruling out the possibility of a Greek original, there is reason to suspect that the work is of Armenian authorship, from eleventh/twelfth-century Cilicia. See the second and longer colophon translated in the second part of the Introduction, p. 32; cf. Terian, "The Ancestry of St. Gregory the Illuminator," pp. 46–47. The comparison with the Prophets and the Apostles in this selection is a recurring theme in most of these panegyrics.

[20]Allusion to Ps. 52:8 (51:8 LXX).

[21]Allusion to Luke 23:43.

[22]Allusion to Matt. 16:24; cf. Luke 9:23; 14:27.

[23]Text in Grigor Narekats'i, *Tagher ev Gandzer* (Odes and Hymns), A. K'yoshkeryan, ed. (Erevan: Arm. Academy of Sciences, 1981), pp. 173–183. The composition in poetic prose, entitled *"K'aroz Grigori Narekats'woy, asats'eal i Surb Lusaworich'n Grigor"* (Litany by Grigor Narekats'i, Composed upon Saint Gregory the Illuminator), is intended for liturgical use, as the word "k'aroz" (used in Armenian and Syriac liturgical rubrics) and the structure of the composition indicate. However, since the text has been treated as an ode by K'yoshkeryan and versified accordingly, I have followed her arrangement. Acrostically, the sections yield ԳՐԻԳՈՐԻ ԳԱՆՁ (Hymn by Grigor). Narekats'i's homage to St. Gregory the Illuminator must have had considerable influence on the subsequent panegyrics surveyed in the second part of the Introduction (pp. 31–40).

[24]Same as "New Zion," "children of the daughter of Zion," and "children of Zion" below; a recurring designation for the people of God in the Prophets, appropriated by first-century Christians.

[25]Cf. line 149. On the feast day(s) of St. Gregory, see the Introduction, pp. 45–47.

[26]Echoing John 6:25–59.

[27]The legendary ancestor of the Armenians; see below, n. 34, and the first comment at §44 of Erznkats'i's panegyric.

[28]Cf. Eph. 4:13.

[29]Arm. *hazarapet*, literally, "commander of a thousand men," is a military term, corresponding to Gk. *chiliarch*.

[30]A recurring designation in this selection, it refers to the Disciples after the exclusion of Judas Iscariot; cf. Selection VII, the ode by Catholicos Grigor III Pahlawuni.

[31]Echoing Matt. 5:13 (and parallels), "seasoning salt" is a common metaphor in the genre, used by Erznkats'i (§§27, 43 and Selection XI) and others. The universal role of St. Gregory is a recurring theme in the panegyrics; see especially §§21–22 and 24 of the panegyric by Erznkats'i and the respective comments.

[32]Although of Eastern origin, St. Gregory came to Armenia from the West, from Cappadocian Caesarea, where he was raised; for a similar view, see §24 of Erznkats'i's panegyric and Selection VII, the ode by Catholicos Grigor III Pahlawuni.

[33]Referring to Armenia and the Caucasus in general, as in §§20, 24, 37 of Erznkats'i's panegyric (see the respective comments), and Selections V, VI, XI below.

[34]Referring to the Armenian people, believed to be descended from Togarmah (Arm. T'orgom; Gen. 10:3), who begot Hayk, the legendary ancestor of the Armenians (Movsēs Khorenats'i, *History of the Armenians*, 1.5, 9, and 12; Eng. trans., R. W. Thomson, *Moses Khorenats'i, History of the Armenians*, Harvard Armenian Texts and Studies 4 [Cambridge, MA: Harvard University Press, 1978]). The claim, however, is not original with Khorenats'i, for Togarmah/T'orgom is identified as the progenitor of the Armenians in Agat'angeghos, *History*, 16 (Eng. trans., R. W. Thomson, *Agathangelos, History of the Armenians* [Albany, NY: State University of New York Press, 1976], p. 29) and in Hippolytus, an early third-century bishop of an unknown see whose *Chronicle* survives partly in Greek and wholly in Latin and Armenian (*Werke*, A. Bauer and R. Helm, eds., Die Griechischen Christlichen Schriftsteller der ersten drei Jahrhunderte 46 [Berlin: Akademie-Verlag, 1955], p. 12). The identification derives from references to the House of Togarmah in Ezek. 27:14 and 39:6, along with Jer. 51:27 (28:27 LXX): "Summon against her these kingdoms: Ararat, Minni, and Ashkenaz." Moreover, owing to Gen. 10:3, where Ashkenaz is an elder brother of Togarmah, a confusion seems to have risen that led to the interchangeable use of their realms deemed as adjacent lands in the northern region of the ancient Near-Eastern world, between the Black and Caspian Seas. Hence the rise of an alternate tradition making the Armenians descended from Ashkenaz; so further below in this selection (line 93), as also in Koriwn, *Life of Mashtots'*, 1 (*Vark' Mashtots'i*, M. Abeghyan, ed. [Erevan: Haypethrat, 1941]; reprinted with an "Introduction" by K. H. Maksoudian [Delmar, NY: Caravan Books, 1985], p. 22; Eng. trans., B. Norehad, *The Life of Mashtots* [New York: AGBU, 1965], p. 21; so also Movsēs Kaghankatuats'i, *Patmut'iwn Aghuanits' Ashkharhi*, 1.14 (V. Aṙak'elyan, ed. [Erevan: Arm. Academy of Sciences, 1983], p. 32; Eng. trans., C. J. F. Dowsett, *The History of the Caucasian Albanians* [London and New York: Oxford University Press, 1961], p. 19). A similar confusion seems to have existed in Jewish sources; see H. R[osenthal] and L. G[inzberg], "Armenia," in *The Jewish Encyclopedia*, I. Singer et al., eds., 12 vols. (New York and London: Ktav, 1901–1906) 2:117–118; cf. M. L. M[argolis], "Ashkenaz," ibid., 2:191–192.

[35]On the twelve tortures of the Saint, culminating with his being thrown into the pit or dungeon of Khor Virap, see Agat'angeghos, *History of the Armenians*, 69–122 (cf. the "Ode to the Holy Illuminator" by St. Nersēs Shnorhali [Selection VIII]).

[36]A play on numbers replete with allegorical significance, as in Hellenistic Jewish numerology, such as found in the works of Philo of Alexandria and adopted by the Church Fathers. See the references in A. Terian, "A Philonic Fragment on the Decad," in F. E. Greenspahn et al., eds., *Nourished with Peace: Studies in Hellenistic Judaism in Memory of Samuel Sandmel*, Scholars Press Homage Series 9 (Chico, CA: Scholars Press, 1984), pp. 173–182. On the varying number of the Saint's years in the pit, see the fourth comment at §52 of Erznkats'i's panegyric.

[37]Cf. below, line 108. On St. Gregory as "sun" (*aregak*), see the fifth comment at §1 of the panegyric by Erznkats'i and the references there.

[38]King Trdat's punishment as a wild boar is described in Agat'angeghos, *History,* 211–225.

[39]Alluding to Rom. 8:17; Gal. 3:29; etc.

[40]See above, n. 34.

[41]Echoing Rev. 1:18.

[42]Agat'angeghos, *History,* 858, 861, 888.

[43]Allusion to Matt. 3:13–17.

[44]Allusion to Acts 7:55–56.

[45]The bidding of these four by name: the Blessed Virgin Mary, St. John the Baptist, St. Stephen the Protomartyr, and St. Gregory the Illuminator, is standardized in the liturgy of the Armenian Church. Narekats'i's ode is an early attestation to this usage.

[46]Text in *Sop'erk',* 4:132–137. A comparable account is found in the panegyric by Erznkats'i, §15; cf. §§36, 40.

[47]Summing up Agat'angeghos, *History,* 211–225.

[48]Agat'angeghos, *History,* 813; but cf. 781 and 840, where the pagan priests were made to serve the church.

[49]Allusion to Josh. 3:15–16.

[50]Allusion to the pillar of light that guided Israel by night, Ex. 13:21.

[51]Allusion to the pillar of cloud that guided Israel by day, Ex. 13:21.

[52]Allusion to Luke 23:34; cf. Agat'angeghos. *History,* 75–98.

[53]Allusion to both *The Teaching* and the *Yachakhapatum* collection of homilies traditionally ascribed to St. Gregory.

[54]On St. Gregory's ancestry, see the panegyric by Erznkats'i, §20 and comments.

[55]Referring to the experiences of Moses at Horeb and Sinai and to that of Elijah at Carmel (Ex. 17 and 10; 1 Kgs. 18).

[56]Text in *Sop'erk',* 5:27–34.

[57]Although the allusion is to Ex. 34:29–35, the initial comparison here is between Jesus and Moses, "the lesser" of the two; see John 1:18. However, none of the prescribed readings in the Lectionary for the feast of the discovery of the remains of St. Gregory is on Moses (Ps. 131:9 LXX [132:9 MT also RSV]; the apocryphal Wis. 4:7–15; Mic. 7:7–10; Acts 20:22–32; John 10:11–16), neither any of those for the feast of his release from the pit (Ps. 39:3 LXX [40:2 MT also RSV]; Wis. 5:1–18; Isa. 60:20–61:7; Heb. 13:17–21; Matt. 19:27–29), nor any of those for the feast of his entry into to the pit (Ps. 87:7 LXX [88:6 MT also RSV]; Mic. 7:7–10; Wis. 1:15–2:22; Phil. 1:12–21; Matt. 16:24–28).

[58]Referring to Ex. 4:4.

[59]The etymology of Aaron's name is apparently based on the belief that he was possessed by the prophetic spirit. See Philo of Alexandria, *Questions on Exodus,* 2:105 (comment on Ex. 27:21).

[60]Speaking of St. Hrip'simē and her companions, especially Gayanē, her spiritual "midwife," who are reputed to have challenged the Emperor of Rome (Diocletian) and the King of Armenia (Trdat).

[61]That is, Sts. Gregory, Hrip'simē and Gayanē.

[62]Referring to Ex. 7:8–24.

[63]Lev. 11:7, etc. King Trdat's punishment as a wild boar is described in Agat'angeghos, *History,* 211–225.

[64]Allusion to Satan as a rebel; cf. Isa. 14:12–15.

[65]In Hellenistic Jewish allegory, Egypt is the land of sin; cf. Philo of Alexandria, *Questions on Exodus,* 1 (*passim*).

[66]Referring to Ex. 14.

[67]Alluding to the tradition that at his baptism Jesus crushed the head of Satan, who was lurking as a serpent in the Jordan, and thus fulfilled the prediction made in Gen. 3:15 literally. The Armenian panegyrists drew an analogy between this and what St. Gregory experienced in the snake-infested pit.

[68]Referring to Ex. 16.

[69] Alluding to Jesus' discourse on the "Bread of Life," John 6:25–59.

[70] Referring to Ex. 17:1–7.

[71] Allusion to John 7:37–39.

[72] Referring to Ex. 17:8–16.

[73] Cf. Agat'angeghos, *History*, 780.

[74] "Tagh S. Grigor Lusaworchin ē asats'eal," in T. Palean, ed., *Hay Ashughner, zhoghovrdakan hay ergichner ew taghasats'k'* (Armenian Troubadours, Popular Singers and Song Writers), 2 vols. (Izmir: Tpagr. Mamurean, 1911–1912) 2:236–237. The repetitive lines indicate that it was composed as a song.

[75] On St. Gregory as "sun" (*aregak*), see the fifth comment at §1 of the panegyric by Erznkats'i; cf. Selection IV, the ode by Narekats'i (lines, 54, 108). Here, however, the synonym *arew* is used. Although of Eastern origin, St. Gregory came to Armenia from the West, from Cappadocian Caesarea. For yet another Western connection of the Saint, see the second comment at §24 of Erznkats'i's panegyric. Elsewher in the panegyric (§41) "the western light" refers to St. Manē, a companion of St. Hṙip'simē.

[76] A likely allusion to St. Hṙip'simē, the Christian virgin from Rome, who with her companions took refuge in Armenia, fleeing persecutions under the Emperor Diocletian (284–305) only to be martyred on Armenian soil at the hand of King Trdat IV (298–330). This took place during St. Gregory's imprisonment.

[77] An allusion to the Blessed Virgin Mary—if not to the Church.

[78] While echoing the parable of "The Ten Virgins" (Matt. 25:1–13), the line is a play on the meaning of St. Gregory's name; see the panegyric by Erznkats'i, §15. St. Gregory as the "grooms-man" is seldom attested.

[79] A reference to the Diocletian persecutions late in the third century. They began in Rome, where the Church was founded by St. Peter. These persecutions, by no means the first in Rome, precipitated the flight of the virgins to Armenia and consequently the conversion that followed at the hand of St. Gregory.

[80] Allusion to the parable of "The Sower" (Matt. 13:1–23).

[81] The number of the Disciples after the exclusion of Judas Iscariot, "the betrayer"; cf. Selection IV, the ode by Narekats'i.

[82] Allusion to John 6:33–35; cf. 48, 51.

[83] Allusion to St. Gregory's vision of the descent of the heavenly "man" with a golden hammer (identified with the Only-begotten in later centuries) to mark the site of the cathedral of Surb Astuatsatsin (Holy Theotokos) to be built in the capital Vagharshapat (the name Ejmiatsin was not applied to the site until after the twelfth century), according to Agat'ankeghos, *History*, 735 (see Thomson's note, pp. 478–479). The four lines underscore St. Gregory's Apostolic and Prophetic ranking; cf. Selections IV and V.

[84] Text in *Tn. Nersesi Shnorhalwoy Hayots' Kat'oghikosi Bank' Ch'ap'aw* (Words in Verse by Lord Nersēs Shnorhali, Catholicos of the Armenians [1166–1173]) 2nd ed. (Venice: S. Ghazar, 1928), pp. 499–503. In addition to its acrostic structure, yielding the phrase *Srboyn Grigori erg i nersisē* (To Saint Gregory an ode by Nersēs), the ode abounds in alliteration of a somewhat unique sort, whereby the last word of each line becomes the opening word of the next. These words are italicized for easy recognition.

[85] On St. Gregory as a rose from a thorny bush, see the panegyric by Erznkats'i, §13.

[86] The twelve tortures, described in the rest of this ode, are those recounted by Agat'angeghos, *History*, 69–122.

[87] Alluding to Matt. 27:48 and parallels.

[88] Text in *Sop'erk'*, 5:73–76.

[89] Allusion to Deut. 34:6; cf. the panegyric by Erznkats'i, §33.

[90] See the panegyric by Erznkats'i, §36.

[91] Allusion to 1 Kgs. 18 (as above, n. 32).

[92]Echoing the closing words of the "Prayer of St. John Chrysostom" at the end of *The Divine Liturgy of the Armenian Church* (D. Findikyan, ed. [New York: St. Vartan Press, 1999], p. 53).

[93]Amplifying 2 Tim. 4:7–8.

[94]Deut. 34:1–8. See the panegyric by Erznkats'i, §§29, 33, for further comparison between the death of Moses and that of St. Gregory.

[95]Num. 20:29; Deut. 34:8.

[96]For the legends surrounding St. Gregory's death, burial, and the discovery of his remains, see Khorenats'i, *History of the Armenians,* 2.91 (detailing how shepherds found and buried the Saint's body without knowing who he was, and how after a long time his relics were revealed to a certain ascetic named Gaŕnik "who took them and buried them in the village of T'ordan"); cf. the anonymous *"Patmut'iwn yaghags giwti nshkharats' Srboyn Grigori Hayots' Metsats' Lusaworch'i"* (History of the Discovery of the Relics of St. Gregory the Illuminator of Greater Armenia), *Ararat* 35 (1902) 1178–1183. For more on the death and burial of St. Gregory, see the seventh comment at §33 of Erznkats'i's panegyric.

[97]Cf. the panegyric by Erznkats'i, §40.

[98]Grigor Patrik Mamikonean, the *marzpan* of Armenia (d. 685). On him, see Yovhannēs Draskhanakertets'i, *Hayots' Patmut'iwn* (Armenian History), M. Ēmin, ed., Ghukasean Matenadaran 5 (Tiflis: Aghaneants', 1912), pp. 89–93 (reprinted with introduction by K. H. Maksoudian [Delmar, NY: Caravan Books, 1980]; cf. Kirakos Gandzakets'i, *Patmut'iwn,* 1; Arm. text: K. A. Melik'-Ohanjanyan, ed., *Kirakos Gandzakets'i: Patmut'iwn Hayots'* (Erevan: Arm. Academy of Sciences, 1961), pp. 62–63; Eng. trans., R. Bedrosian, *Kirakos Gandzakets'i's History of the Armenians* (New York: Sources of the Armenian Tradition, 1986), p. 56.

[99]Built by Grigor Mamikonean in his native Aruch, at the foot of Mount Aragats; destroyed during one of the Arab invasions.

[100]The See of the Catholicosate since 1149, till it was moved to Sis after the fall of Hŕomklay to the Mamluks of Egypt in 1293.

[101]*Patmut'iwn,* 1 (ed. Melik'-Ohanjanyan, pp. 10–14; Eng. trans., Bedrosian, *Kirakos Gandzakets'i's History of the Armenians,* pp. 8–11). The translation provided here is mine.

[102]On this alleged visit to Rome, see Agat'angeghos, *History,* 873–880; the panegyric by Vardan Arewelts'i, *Sop'erk',* 5:66–68.

[103]This tradition, explaining how Armenians in the Holy Land came to possess their sacred places, is found also in the panegyric by Vardan Arewelts'i (*Sop'erk',* 5:78), who tells of a second meeting, in Jerusalem, between the four saints, at which time Armenians were given their possessions there. Arewelts'i lists them as follows: the Manger, Golgotha, the convent of St. John the Forerunner, and that of Sts. James.

[104]The text accents *mi* as a prohibitive command here and in the next line; this, however, makes less sense in a paragraph where the thought is on unity: "to be [one] with them [i.e., the redeemed]." Obviously, I have disregarded the punctuation here (unlike Bedrosian, *Kirakos Gandzakets'i's History of the Armenians,* p. 9).

[105]A paraphrase of Rom. 2:25: "If you break the Law, your circumcision becomes uncircumcision."

[106]In the Armenian Church, the blessing of salt precedes the slaughter of sheep brought as *matagh* to this day.

[107]Invested as Prince of Princes in 862 and crowned King in 884, Ashot is customarily referred to as "King" even in earlier sources. The reign of Basil II (976–1025) does not synchronize with any of the Bagratid kings named Ashot.

[108]Literally, "to the King."

[109]On the original feast day of St. Gregory, see the Introduction, p. 46.

[110]Text in *Sharakan Hogewor Ergots',* pp. 264–274; for an arrangement in verse, see A. Erznkats'i Srapyan, *Hovhannes Erznkats'i* (Erevan: Sovetakan Grogh, 1986), pp. 123–139. Cf. the ode in alphabetic acrostic in the author's panegyric, §18.

[111]Cf. the author's panegyric, §2 and comment.

[112]Cf. the author's panegyric, §§2, 13.

[113]Cf. the author's panegyric, §§13, 27, 30, 33; "the northern nations" refers to the Armenians in particular and the people of the Caucasus in general, as in §§20, 24, 37.

[114]On Christ as Sun, see the author's panegyric, §1 and comment.

[115]Cf. the author's panegyric, §16 and comment.

[116]Allusion to John 10:1–18.

[117]On this and related titles of St. Gregory, see the comment at §56 of the author's panegyric.

[118]Allusion to Gal. 4:26; cf. §§3, 8, 11, 33.

[119]The dynasty to which King Trdat belonged; C. Toumanoff, "The Third-Century Arsacids," *Revue des études arméniennes*, n.s. 6 (1969) 233–281.

[120]On the purported miracle surrounding the birth of St. Gregory, see the comment at §5 of the author's panegyric, a subject repeated at §§21–22, 24.

[121]Cf. the author's panegyric, §13 and comment.

[122]These are recurring imageries of St. Gregory: bright blossom (§§2, 43), healer of souls (§§44, 58), and date palm (§20).

[123]On St. Gregory as a martyr, see comment at §1 of the author's panegyric.

[124]As in §24 of the author's panegyric.

[125]As in §50 of the author's panegyric.

[126]Allusion to *The Teaching of St. Gregory*, on which see comment at §13 of the author's panegyric.

[127]A reference to the fourth torture of St. Gregory; Agat'angeghos, *History*, 103.

[128]A reference to the third torture of St. Gregory; *ibid.*, 102.

[129]A reference to the second torture of St. Gregory; *ibid.*, 74.

[130]A variation of the tenth torture, when his knees were broken; *ibid.*, 115. Note also the Eucharistic echoes here.

[131]References to the fifth and seventh tortures of St. Gregory; *ibid.*, 106, 109.

[132]Allusion to St. Gregory as second Moses, a recurring motif in the author's panegyric.

[133]A reference to the first torture of St. Gregory; Agat'angeghos, *History*, 69.

[134]The twelve tortures of St. Gregory are here compared with the twelve-gem breastplate of Aaron (Ex. 28:15–27).

[135]Another reference to the first torture of St. Gregory; Agat'angeghos, *History*, 69.

[136]Another reference to the second torture of St. Gregory; *ibid.*, 74.

[137]Allusion to John 14:6.

[138]Further references to the second and fifth tortures; Agat'angeghos, *History*, 74, 106.

[139]Further references to the fourth and sixth tortures; *ibid.*, 103, 107.

[140]References to the eighth, ninth, and eleventh tortures; *ibid.*, 111–112, 119.

[141]The ultimate of the twelve tortures; *ibid.*, 122.

[142]So also at §52 of the author's panegyric; but at §55, he has thirteen years, as in Agat'angeghos, *History*, 122, 124, 132. On the varying years, even in Agat'angeghos, see the Commentary on the cited sections; cf. Selection I, pt. vi (thirteen), Selection IV (thirteen), Selection VIII (fifteen).

[143]Allusion to St. Gregory's vision as found in Agat'angeghos, *History*, 731–756.

[144]Allusion to the funerary chapels built by St. Gregory, *ibid.*, 756–776.

[145]Allusion to the overthrow of the pagan edifices, *ibid.*, 777–790.

[146]On the apostolic ranking of St. Gregory, see comment at §15 of the author's panegyric.

[147]On the prophetic ranking of St. Gregory, see comment at §15 of the author's panegyric.

[148]Allusion to John 1:9.

[149]Cf. §18 of the author's panegyric; elsewhere, the Saint's lips and church structures are compared to a harp, §27. Note the invocation of the Most Holy Trinity in the last three stanzas.

[150]Text in *Sharakan Hogewor Ergots'*, pp. 278–281; for an arrangement in verse, see Srapyan, *Hovhannes Erznkats'i*, pp. 130–132. Cf. §§28–42 of the author's panegyric.

[151]Echoing Ex. 13:21.

[152]Echoing Gen. 8 (as in the author's panegyric, §29).

[153]Echoing Ex. 34:29–35.

[154]Allusion to 2 Kgs. 6:8–23 (as in the author's panegyric, §29).

[155]Allusion to the prophet's vision (Isa. 6:2).

[156]Often thought to be the site(s) of the Transfiguration (Matt. 17:1–13); cf. §§29 and 39 of the author's panegyric.

[157]Similar analogy is made in the author's panegyric, §41.

[158]Similar wording is found in the author's panegyric, §37, with reference to the cross employed by St. Gregory, enshrined in one of the chapels on Mount Sepuh.

[159]A paraphrase of Ps. 24:3 (23:3 LXX), quoted in the author's panegyric, §40.

[160]On the discovery of St. Gregory's remains by shepherds, see above, n. 96.

[161]Text in Srapyan, *Hovhannes Erznkats'i*, pp. 115–116. The onomastic acrostic yields the words *Grigorios Lusaworich' Hayots'* (Gregorios the Illuminator of the Armenians). Regarding the contents of the ode, cf. §§47–50 of the panegyric. The ode was not included in the hymnal probably because of its tacit criticism of the hierarchy.

[162]Allusion to Ezek. 47:1–12.

[163]These lines are based on the meaning of baptism in Rom. 6:1–14.

[164]Text has *hawatk's* instead of *hawtk's*.

[165]Text has *mangunk'* instead of *mankunk'*.

[166]Allusion to the vision of St. Gregory, referring to the time when many Armenians apostatized (Agat'angeghos, History, 754).

[167]Allusion to Matt. 7:15.

[168]Text has *varaten* instead of *p'araten*.

[169]Text has *yanbarēsēr* instead of *yanbaresēr*.

[170]The author seems to be faulting the ecclesiastical hierarchs and not civil rulers, foreign or native.

[171]Text has *barēkhaws* instead of *barekhaws*.

[172]Text has *barēkhawseay* instead of *barekhawseay*.

[173]Either Yakob I of Hṙomklay (1268–1286), Kostandin II of Katuk (1286–1289), or Step'anos IV of Hṙomklay (1290–1293). Our author had good relations with the first.

[174]Either King Levon II (1270–1289) or King Het'um II, who reigned intermittently (1289–1306, murdered in 1307 with his nephew, Levon III [1301/6–1307], by Bilarghu, the Mongol general in Anazarba).

Appendix

VARIANT READINGS IN THE PUBLISHED EDITIONS OF ERZNKATS'I'S *PANEGYRIC*

S RAPYAN'S TEXT OF Erzenkats'i's *Panegyric* stands in need of numerous corrections. Most of her errors are due to orthographic confusion between Classical and Modern Eastern Armenian spelling. Besides, there are a few obvious corruptions in the manuscripts of the text, seen also in the Venice edition. The following are worth noting in the two editions (the first number in parenthesis stands for the page and the second for the line in the respective edition):

V = VENICE 1853; E = EREVAN 1986

Title   զովետա - զովետափ V (84–2) E (136–2)

§1   աշխարհայոյս - աշխարհայույս E (137–11)
       յիշատակի - Հիշատակի E (137–14)

§2   ողկյզն - ողկյզան V (86–21)
       գյորդաւատ - գՀորդաւատ E (137–27)
       յիշատակաւն - Հիշատակաւն E (138–5)

§3   իմաստութեամբն - իմաստութեամբ E (138–14)
       գխորՀրդաբար - գխորՀրդարար E (138–16)
       տերունական - տերունական E (138–24)
       պայծառացեալն - պայծառաւացեալն V (88–11/12)
       Հայրենի - գՀայրենի E (139–11)

§4   ի Հոգիս - յոգիս V (89–2) Հոգիս E (139–17)
       դխտողն - գխտողն E (139–19)
       զանուանելի - զանվանելի V (89–15)

§6   պարապեալքս - պարապեալքս E (141–14)

§7   գործոցդ – գործոյ V (92–15) E (142–4)

    մասանց – մասաց E (142–19)

    հոգիս – յոգիս V (93–16) E (142–29)

§8   շարայարել – շարահարել E (144–2)

    աւագանին – պատարագին E (144–10)

    նորածնունդ – նորասնունդ V (95–15)

§11   յամենեցունց – յամենեցուն E (146–15)

§12   յուսույն – յուսույն V (97/825/1) E (146–23)

    ուղղեալ – ուղղել V (98–10)

§13   սրովբէական – սրովբեական E (148–1)

§14   մնւցանեն_– omit E (148–20)

    յաւխենականն – հաւխենականն E (149–1)

§15   մարգարէից – մարգարեից E (149–26)

§18   ծաղկաւէտ – ծաղկավէտ E (151–5)

    յորդահոս – հորդահոս E (151–5)

    աստուածագարդ – աստուագարդ E (151–7)

    յոքունց – հոքունց E (151–20)

    գժրողին – գրժողին E (151–27)

    պողաւճտեալ – պողաւետեալ E (151–28)

    կերպարան փառաց – կերպարն փափառաց E (152–1)

    յարփիագեդ – յարփիադէգ E (152–13)

§19   գլխոյն – գլխոյ n E (153–22)

§20   նահապետէ – նահապետէ E (153–27)

    ծնող – ծնող E (154–1)

    աւագանածին – աւագածին V (107–13) աւագանին E (154–5)

    Եփրատէս – Եփրատես E (154–12)

    Պահլաւական – Պահհաւական V (108–3)

    յԱնակայ – ի յԱնակայ V (108–11) ի Անակայ E (154–25)

    կամ – եւ E (155–12)

    արուեստաւորէ – արուեստէ V (109–6/7) E (155–13)

    եւ – omit E (155–26)

    ի – omit E (156–3)

    յեղաշրջեալ – հեղաշրջեալ E (156–6)

§21   տնկոյն – տնկոյ V (110–14)

    առ – առ ի E (156–20)

    գերեզմանի – գերեզմանոյ E (156–20)

    յաշխարհամարան – յաշխարհամատն V (111–2)

գՀայաստանեայց – գՀայաստանեաց E (157–12)

գորենոյն – գորենոյ E (157–15)

գայս – այս E (157–16)

գորենոյն – գորենոյ E (157–18)

Կապադովկացւոյն – Կապադովկացոյն E (157–28)

գոռն – գոռն E (158–1)

§22   քրիստոնէական – քրիստոնեական E (158–18)

անակիտան – անակիտն E (158–24)

տպեցեալ – տպացեալ V (158–26)

§23   գնորին – նորին E (159–8)

գայսոցիկ – գայսոսիկ E (150=27)

§24   գայ առ – գա E (160–14)

դաւանաց – ումիտ E (160–15)

մարմնոյն – մարմնոյ E (160–25)

թուել – թուեալ E (161–3)

գձմարտութիւն – ձմարտութիւն V (117–6)

գձմարտութեան E (161–23)

§25   բանիւ – բանի E (162–3)

§26   անուղղեայ – անուղղայ V (118–7)

§27   եւ – omit E (162–24)

կարկամեալք – կարկամեալքդ V (119–11/12)

աստուածուսոյց – աստուծուսոյց E (164–9)

գակունս – գականս V (120–7/8)

որդւոյն – որդւոյն E (165–16)

բարիան – բարին E (165–18)

ուսցին – ուսիցն E (165–24)

աստուածաբան – աստուածաբար E (165–25)

գանհամուլթիւն – գանմահուլթիւն E (166–18)

§29   իմաստութիւն – իմաստութիւնն E (168–7)

լերին – լերինն E (168–12)

Սանիրայ – Սանիրա E (169–1)

յորմէ – յորում E (169–9)

Արգեոս – Արգեոս E (160–16)

§30   բարձրակարոյցն – բարձրակարուցն E (169–28)

Հանգեաւ – Հանգաւ E (170–1)

կեցուցանէր – կացուցանէր E (170–11)

Բանի – բան ի V (128–11/12) E (170–17)

§31   գերեզմանն – գէշմանն E (170–23)

պարտական – omit E (170–26)

լեալ – լինել V (129–8) լինէր E (171–7)

§32   եղեր – եղէր E (171–17)

եղեալ – եղեալ E (171–27)

§33   ժողովրդեանն – ժողովրդեանս V (130–19/18)

ելեալ – եալեալ E (172–18)

եւ – իսկ E (172–23)

§34   Սինի – Սինայի V (131–15) E (173–2)

անուամբն – անուամբ E (173–7)

Մանէ – Մանի V (131–23) E (173–8)

պարապէր – պարապէր V (132–2/3)

բնակութիւն – բնութիւն E (173–16)

§35   Սողմոն – Սաղոմմն V (132–20)

ողջակէզս – ողջակէզ E (173–27)

արքայութեանն – արքայութեան E (174–5)

որթանց – շրթանց V (133–4) E (174–7)

լուսաւորեալ – լուսաւորել V (133–16/17) E (174–18)

§36   երախտութեամբ – երախշտութեամբ E (174–22)

Սարեփթացւոյ – Սարեփթացոյ V (133–23)

Հատտարիմն – Հատտարիմ E (175–22)

պարապեալ – պարապէր E (175–24)

§37   փայլեալ – omit V (135–9)

կատարեաց – կատարեց E (176–6)

տեղւոջ – տեղւոյ E (176–6)

բարութիւնս գանտանելի – omit E (176–12)

լուսաւորեալ – լուսաւորել V (135–26) E (176–13)

գմեծամեծ – գամենամեծ E (176–18)

ամրակուր – ամրակուր E (176–20)

§38   իւրովք – իւրով E (177–6)

§39   Սանիրայ – Սանիրա E (177–14)

բնութիւնն – բնութիւն V (138–1)

§40   եւ Հայցէր – Հայցէր E (178–14)

Հոգւովն – Հոգւոյն E (178–17)

փառաւորիչն – փառաւորչին E (178–26)

սեղանաւորան – սեղանաւորն V (139–3/4) E (178–28)

գքեզ – քեզ E (179–3)

§41 ԲեղդեՀէյմի – Բեղդեէյմի V (139–12) E (179–7)

Մանէ – Մանի V (139–26) (179–19) E

եւ – omit E (180–3)

§42 արժանեացն – արժանույն E (180–26)

սիրեայն – սիրեան V (141–14/15) E (180–27)

սակաւք – սակաւ E (181–14)

§43 Եղեմարութ – Եղեմական E (181–25)

ելեայ – ելեայ V (143–10)

§44 երկնելովն – երկնելով E (184–7)

Հաւատոյ – Հաւատոց V (145–17)

§45 Հայաստանեայց – Հայաստանեաց V (145–19/20)

§46 զարդարիՀք – զարդարիՀ V (146–22/23) E (185–8)

§47 գողբերգականն – գողբերականն E (185–17)

§48 դարմանողաց – դարմանաց E (196–9)

§49 գՀեղձուցանողան – գՀերձուցանողան E (187–23)

խոսեցայիս – խոսեցաւ E (187–26)

§50 ողջոյն – ողջիւն E (188–12)

ծնողէ – ծնոյէ E (188–19)

եղեր – եղէր E (189–7)

Հոդմոց – Հոլուաց V (151–18) (151–18) E (189–8)

յարոտս – յարոտս E (189–11)

§53 յայեկոծութիւն – յայեկոծութիւն E (192–9)

յամՀնաբարի – յամՀնաբարի E (192–17)

տայք – տաք E (192–18)

§55 աստուածագույթ – աստուածագործ E (193–15)

§56 փախստական – փախստեան E (195–6)

§57 նմանողք – նմանող E (195–10)

քաՀանայութեանն – քաՀանայութեան E (195–28)

§58 խորաքննին – խորաքնին E (197–2)

որբոց – որդւոց E (197–11)

§59 յաղթանակ – Հաղթանակ E (197–26)

Հայցեսցես – Հայեսցես E (197–27)

§60 թէ – եթէ E (198–19)

մի – omit E (198–21)

յոլովից – Հոլովից E (199–1)

եղեց – եղեց E (199–12)

Among other observations regarding Srapian's text, the following are note-worthy (the parenthesized numbers refer to sections in the English trans-lation):

Page 137, line 13 (§2): Wrongly maintains continuity here with the pre-ceding section, disregarding the new section or strophe beginning acrosti-cally with the second letter in the author's name.

Page 140, line 10 (§5): Wrongly maintains continuity here with the pre-ceding section, disregarding the new section beginning acrostically with the fifth letter in the author's name.

Page 141, line 7 (§6): Wrongly maintains continuity here with the pre-ceding section, disregarding the new section beginning acrostically with the sixth letter in the author's name.

Page 143, line 12 (§8): Unnecessarily divides the petition to the Father in this three-part prayer addressed to the Father, the Son, and the Spirit.

Page 144, line 6 (§8): Unnecessarily divides the petition to the Son in this three-part prayer addressed to the Father, the Son, and the Spirit.

Pages 151–153 (§18): Disregards the line arrangement in triplets through-out the poem in alphabetical acrostic. She ignores the author's versification where he intends it, and supplies it where he does not.

Page 159, line 2 (§23): Wrongly maintains continuity here with the pre-ceding section, disregarding the transition from discussing St. Gregory's birth and upbringing, in three parts (ancestral, physical, and spiritual), to discussing his accomplishments in virtue, in three parts (marriage, mission, and forbearance).

Page 166, line 13 (§27): Places the word *zanmahut'iwn* (immortality) at the beginning of the line instead of at the end of the preceding line, creat-ing a confusion between two distinct categories. This last line of the sec-tion ought to begin with *ew* (and).

Page 167, line 11 (§29): Unnecessarily begins a new section with this line, interrupting the comparative disquisition on the biblical mountains.

Page 173, line 3 (§34): Places the words *i Dawt'ē amrats'eal* (fortified by David) at the end of the line instead of at the beginning of the following line, where they contextually and logically belong.

Page 187, line 6 (§49): Unnecessarily begins a new section, interrupting a clearly defined lament, comparable to the preceding and the following laments (all three beginning with the imperative "Weep . . .").

Page 189, line 19 (§50): Unnecessarily begins a new section, interrupting, as in the preceding section, a clearly defined lament over the Church.

Page 192, lines 3–4 (§52): Unnecessarily singles out these last two lines as a separate section, overlooking the absence of addressees—as found in the preceding and the following sections.

Page 193, line 11 (§55): Wrongly maintains continuity here with the preceding section, disregarding the formal beginning of the first of three distinct appeals, all beginning with the adverbial *Ard*... (Now ...).

Page 194, line 12 (§55): Unnecessarily begins a new section, severing the repetitiousness and continuity of thought from the preceding lines on exemplary shepherding.

Page 198, last line (§60): Oddly divides the line after the negative particle *och*' (no), creating two lines needlessly and awkwardly; the particle here cannot be separated from what follows.

Select Bibliography

Limited to the Introduction.
Full bibliographic information is given in all first citations in the Commentary on Erznkats'i's Panegyric and in the notes to the Selections.

Ancient Texts

AGAT'ANGEGHOS (Armenian—*Aa*). G. Tēr Mkrtch'ean and S. Kanayeants', eds., *Agat'angeghay Patmut'iwn Hayots.* Tiflis: Martiroseants', 1909; repr. Delmar, NY: Caravan Books, 1980; Eng. trans., R. W. Thomson, *Agathangelos: History of the Armenians.* Albany, NY: State University of New York Press, 1976.

_____ (Greek—*Vg*). G. Garitte, ed. and trans., *Documents pour l'étude du livre d'Agathange.* Studi e Testi 127. Vatican City: Biblioteca Apostolica Vaticana, 1946.

_____ (Karshuni—*Vk*). M. van Esbroeck, ed. and trans., "Un nouveau témoin du livre d'Agathange." *Revue des études arméniennes,* n.s. 8 (1971) 13–167.

ANANIA SANAHNETS'I. "Eranelwoy hōr Ananiayi hogevarzh p'ilisop'ayi Nerboghean asats'eal i surb Kat'oghikē Ekeghets'i, or ē i Nor K'aghak', or ayzhm koch'i Vagharshapat ..." (Panegyric by the Blessed Father Anania, the Spiritual Philosopher, on the Holy Cathedral in Nor K'aghak', Nowadays Called Vagharshapat ...). In *Girk' or koch'i Zhoghovatsu* (Book Called Miscellarea). Constantinople: Astuatsatur Kostandnupolsets'i, 1747, pp. 441–483; repr. 1793, pp. 403–442, and A. Ayvazean, ed., *Chrak'agh* I (1859) 265–272, 291–298, 323–332, 359–366, 399–406.

ANANIA SHIRAKATS'I. *Ashkharhats'oyts'.* In A. Abrahamyan, ed., *Anania Shirakats'u Matenagrut'yunē* (The Writings of Anania Shirakats'i). Erevan: Matenadaran, 1944, pp. 336–354; E. Arm. trans., in A. G. Abrahamyan and G. B. Petrosyan, *Anania Shirakats'i, Matenagrut'yun* (A. Sh.: Writings). Erevan: Sovetakan Grogh, 1979, pp. 258–312; Eng. trans., R. H. Hewsen, *The Geography of Ananias of Širak (Ašxarhac'oyc'): The Long and the Short Recensions.* Beihefte zum Tübinger Atlas des vorderen Orients, Reihe B (Geisteswissenschaften) 77. Wiesbaden: Reichert, 1992.

ANONYMOUS. "Patmut'iwn yaghags giwti nshkharats' Srboyn Grigori Hayots' Metsats' Lusaworch'i" (History of the Discovery of the Relics of St. Gregory the Illuminator of Greater Armenia). *Ararat* 35 (1902) 1178–1183.

ANONYMOUS (Pseudo-Agat'angeghos). *Nakhneats'n Patmut'iwn* (Primary History). In *Patmut'iwn Sebēosi,* chs. 1–6 (ed. Abgaryan, pp. 47–64). French trans. of chs. 1–4, "Le Pseudo-Agathange: histoire ancienne de l'Arménie," in V. Langlois, ed., *Collection des historiens anciens et modernes de l'Arménie.* 2 vols. Paris: Firmin-Didot,

1867–1869, 1:195–200 (the so-called long version, under the title "Mar Apas Catina: histoire ancienne de l'Arménie," in *ibid.*, pp. 18–53, is the expanded version in Book I of Khorenats'i, *Patmut'iwn Hayots'*); Eng. trans. of chs. 1–4, "Appendix," in R. W. Thomson, *Moses Khorenats'i*, pp. 357–367.

APHTHONIUS. *Progymnasmata.* Eng. trans., R. Nadeau, "The Progymnasmata of Aphthonius in Translation." *Speech Monographs* 19 (1952) 264–285.

BUZANDARAN PATMUT'IWNK'. *P'awstosi Buzandats'woy Patmut'iwn Hayots' i ch'ors dprut'iwns* (P'awstos Buzandats'i's History of the Armenians in Four Registers). 4th ed. Venice: S. Ghazar, 1933; Eng. trans., N. G. Garsoïan, *The Epic Histories Attributed to P'awstos Buzand (Buzandaran Patmut'iwnk').* Harvard Armenian Texts and Studies 8. Cambridge, MA: Harvard University Press, 1989. Also K'. P[atkanean], ed., *P'awstosi Buzandats'woy Patmut'iwn Hayots'.* St. Petersburg: Kayserakan Chemaran Gitut'eants', 1883; repr. Delmar, NY: Caravan Books, 1984, and Erevan: [State] University of Erevan, 1987, with E. Arm. trans.

DIONYSIUS THRAX. *Ars Grammatica.* N. Adonts' [Adontz], ed., *Aruest Dioniseay K'erakani* (Dionysius' *Ars Grammatica*). St. Petersburg: Kayserakan Tparan, 1915.

EGHISHĒ. *Meknut'iun Araratsots'.* L. Khach'ikyan, ed., *Eghishei Araratsots' Meknut'iunĕ* (Eghishē's Commentary on Genesis). Erevan: Zvart'nots', 1992.

———. *Vasn Vardanay ew Hayots' Paterazmin.* E. Tēr-Minasyan, ed., *Eghishēi vasn Vardanay ew Hayots' Paterazmin* (Concerning Vardan and the Armenian War). Erevan: Arm. Academy of Sciences, 1957; Eng. trans., R. W. Thomson, *Ełishē: History of Vardan and the Armenian War.* Harvard Armenian Texts and Studies 5. Cambridge, MA: Harvard University Press, 1982.

EZNIK KOGHBATS'I, *Eghts aghandots'* (Refutation of the Sects). L. Mariès and C. Mercier, eds. and trans., *Eznik de Kołb: De Deo* (Arm. text with French trans.) in *Patrologia Orientalis* 28, fascs. 3–4. Paris: Firmin-Didot, 1959; Eng. trans., M. J. Blanchard and R. D. Young, *Eznik of Kołb. On God.* Eastern Christian Texts in Translation 2. Leuven: Peeters, 1998.

GHAZAR P'ARPETS'I. *Patmut'iwn Hayots'.* G. Tēr Mkrtch'ean and S. Malkhasean, eds., *Ghazar P'arpets'i. Patmut'iwn Hayots'.* Tiflis: Martiroseants', 1904; repr. Delmar, NY: Caravan Books, 1986; Eng. trans., R. W. Thomson, *The History of Łazar P'arpec'i.* Scholars Press Occasional Papers and Proceedings: Columbia University Program in Armenian Studies / Suren D. Fesjian Academic Publications 4. Atlanta: Scholars Press, 1991.

Girk' T'ght'ots' (Book of Letters). Y. Izmireants', ed. Sahak Mesropean Matenadaran 5. Tiflis: Ṙotineants' and Sharadzē, 1901. Revised: N. Pogharean, ed. Jerusalem: St. James Press, 1994.

GREGORY THE ILLUMINATOR. *Vardapetut'iwn.* In Agat'angeghos (*Aa* 259–715); Eng. trans., R. W. Thomson, *The Teaching of St. Gregory,* rev. ed. AVANT: Treasures of the Armenian Christian Tradition 1. New Rochelle: St. Nersess Armenian Seminary, 2001.

———. *Yachakhapatum.* A. Tēr Mik'elean, ed., *Srboy Hōrn Meroy Eranelwoyn Grigori Lusaworch'i Yachakhapatum Chaṙk' Lusawork'* (Often-repeated and Enlightened

Homilies of Our Blessed Father St. Gregory the Illuminator). Ējmiatsin: Mother See Press, 1894.

GRIGOR AKNERTS'I. *Patmut'iwn T'at'arats*. N. Pogharean, ed., *Grigor Vardapet Aknerts'i. Patmut'iwn T'at'arats'* (G.V.A.: History of the Tatars). Jerusalem: St. James Press, 1974; also known as *Patmut'iwn vasn Azgin Netoghats*. R. P. Blake and R. N. Frye, eds. and trans., *Gregory of Agner: History of the Nation of Archers*. Cambridge, MA: Harvard University Press, 1954.

GRIGOR DARANAGHTS'I. *Zhamanakagrut'iwn* (Chronography). Jerusalem: St. James Press, 1915.

GRIGOR MAGISTROS. *T'ught'k'.* K. Kostaneants', ed., *Grigor Magistrosi T'ght'erĕ* (The Epistolary of G. M.). Alexandropol: Gēorg Sanoyeants', 1910.

GRIGOR NAREKATS'I. *Matean Oghbergut'ean* (Book of Lamentations). P. M. Khach'atryan and A. A. Ghazinyan, eds. Erevan: Arm. Academy of Sciences, 1985; Eng. trans., T. J. Samuelian, *Speaking with God from the Depths of the Heart*, 2nd ed. Erevan: Vem Press, 2002.

_____. *Tagher ev Gandzer* (Odes and Hymns). A. K'yoshkeryan, ed. Erevan: Arm. Academy of Sciences, 1981.

GRIGOR (III) PAHLAWUNI. "Tagh S. Grigor Lusaworchin ē asats'eal" (Ode Said on St. Gregory the Illuminator). In T. Palean, ed., *Hay Ashughner, zhoghovrdakan hay ergichner ew taghasats'k'* (Armenian Troubadours, Popular Singers and Song Writers). 2 vols. Izmir: Tpagr. Mamurean, 1911–1912, 2:236–237.

GRIGOR SARKAWAGAPET. *Khosk' i Surb Grigor Lusaworich'* (Discourse on St. Gregory the Illuminator). In *Yovhannu Oskeberani ew Grigori Sarkawagapeti Nerbogheank' i S. Grigor Lusaworich'* (Panegyrics on St. Gregory the Illuminator by John Chrysostom, [His Disciple Theophilos], and Gregory Sarkawagapet). Sop'erk' Haykakank' 4. Venice: S. Ghazar, 1853, pp. 129–157.

HET'UM KOR'IKOSTS'I (Anton). *La Flor des estoires de la Terre d'Orient (Liber Historiarum Partium Orientis)*. M. Awgerean, trans. (from Latin), *Het'um Patmich' T'at'arats'* (Het'um the Historian of the Tatars). Venice: S. Ghazar, 1842.

JOHN CHRYSOSTOM. *Meknut'iwn T'ght'ots'n Pawghosi* (Commentary on the Epistles of Paul). *Yovhannu Oskeberani Kostandnupolsi Episkoposapeti Meknut'iwn T'ght'ots'n Pawghosi* (John Chrysostom, Archbishop of Constantinople: Commentary on the Epistles of Paul). 2 vols. Venice: S. Ghazar, 1862.

[Ps.] JOHN CHRYSOSTOM. *Srboyn Yovhannu Oskeberani Nerboghean Asats'eal yaghags Varuts' ew Nahatakut'ean Srboyn Grigori Hayots' Metsats' Hayrapeti* (Panegyric Recited by St. John Chrysostom upon the Life and Martyrdom of St. Gregory the Patriarch of Greater Armenia). In *Yovhannu Oskeberani ew Grigori Sarkawagapeti Nerbogheank' i S. Grigor Lusaworich'* (Panegyrics on St. Gregory the Illuminator by John Chrysostom, [His Disciple Theophilos], and Gregory Sarkawagapet). Sop'erk' Haykakank' 4. Venice: S. Ghazar, 1853, pp. 5–86. Also among the *Erkbayakan Chaṙk'* (Allegorical Homilies) in *Yovhannu Oskeberani Kostandnupolsi Episkoposapeti Meknut'iwn T'ght'ots'n Pawghosi* (John Chrysostom, Archbishop of Constantinople: Commentary on the Epistles of Paul). 2 vols. Venice: S. Ghazar, 1862, 2:792–826.

KIRAKOS GANDZAKETS'I. *Patmut'iwn Hayots'*. K. A. Melik'-Ohanjanyan, ed., *Kirakos Gandzakets'i, Patmut'iwn Hayots'*. Erevan: Arm. Academy of Sciences, 1961; Eng. trans., R. Bedrosian, *Kirakos Gandzakets'i's History of the Armenians*. New York: Sources of the Armenian Tradition, 1986.

KORIWN. *Vark' Mashtots'i*. M. Abeghyan, ed. and trans., *Koriwn, Vark' Mashtots'i*. Erevan: Haypethrat, 1941; Eng. trans., B. Norehad, *Koriwn: The Life of Mashtots*. New York: AGBU, 1965; repr. of both vols. with introduction by K. H. Maksoudian. Delmar, NY: Caravan Books, 1985. Also G. Fntglean, ed., *Koriwn, Vark' Mashtots'i. Ughgheal ew Lusabaneal* (Koriwn, Life of Mashtots': Emended and Annotated). Jerusalem: St. James Press, 1930.

MKRTICH' NAGHASH. [*Works*]. Ē. Khondkaryan, ed., *Mkrtich' Naghash*. Erevan: Arm. Academy of Sciences, 1965.

MOVSĒS KHORENATS'I. *Patmut'iwn Hayots'*. M. Abeghean and S. Yarut'iwnean, eds., *Movsisi Khorenats'woy Patmut'iwn Hayots*. Tiflis: Martiroseants', 1913; repr. Delmar, NY: Caravan Books, 1981, and Erevan: Arm. Academy of Sciences, 1991; Eng. trans., R. W. Thomson, *Moses Khorenats'i: History of the Armenians*. Harvard Armenian Texts and Studies 4. Cambridge, MA: Harvard University Press, 1978.

NERSĒS SHNORHALI. *Ēndhanrakan T'ught'k' S. Nersisi Shnorhalwoy* (General Epistles of St. Nersēs Shnorhali). Jerusalem: St. James Press, 1871.

———. *"Vipasanut'iwn Haykazants'"* (Epic History of the Descendants of Hayk). In *Tn. Nersesi Shnorhalwoy Hayots' Kat'oghikosi Bank' Ch'ap'aw* (Words in Verse by Lord Nersēs Shnorhali, Catholicos of the Armenians). 2nd ed. Venice: S. Ghazar, 1928, pp. 539–608.

Pataragamatoyts' (Divine Liturgy). D. Findikyan, ed. and trans., *The Divine Liturgy of the Armenian Church*. New York: St. Vartan Press, 1999.

Patrologiae cursus completus, Series graeca. J.-P. Migne et al., eds., 161 vols. in 166 pts. Paris: Garnier, 1857–1966.

SEBĒOS. *Patmut'iwn*. G. V. Abgaryan, ed., *Patmut'iwn Sebēosi*. Erevan: Arm. Academy of Sciences, 1979; Eng. trans., *The Armenian History Attributed to Sebeos*, trans. with notes by R. W. Thomson, historical commentary by J. Howard-Johnston, assistance from T. Greenwood, 2 pts., Translated Texts for Historians 31. Liverpool: Liverpool University Press, 1999 (trans. begins with ch. 7 of Abgaryan's edition [p. 64]).

Sharakan Hogewor Ergots' Surb ew Ughghap'ar Ekeghets'woys Hayastaneayts' (Hymnal of Spiritual Songs of the Holy Orthodox Armenian Church). Jerusalem: St. James Press, 1936; repr. New York: St. Vartan Press, 1986.

Sop'erk' Haykakank' (Armenian Writings). 24 vols. Venice: S. Ghazar, 1853–1934.

STEP'ANOS SIWNETS'I. *Meknut'iwn zhamakargut'ean*. M. Findikyan, ed. and trans., "The Commentary on the Armenian Daily Office by Bishop Step'anos Siwnec'i: Edition and Translation of the Long and Short Versions with Textual and Liturgical Study." Diss., Pontificum Institutum Studiorum Orientalium, Romae, 1997.

THEODORET OF CYRRHUS. *Religious History*. R. M. Price, trans., *A History of the Monks of Syria*. Cistercian Studies Series 88. Kalamazoo, MI: Western Michigan University Press, 1985.

[Ps.] THEOPHILOS. *Eranelwoyn Tʻēovpʻilosi asatsʻeal nerboghean patmagrabar surb hōrn meroy ew lusaworchʻi, kʻahanayapetin Kʻristosi ew vkayi, Metsin Grigori Arkʻepiskoposi Hayotsʻ Metsatsʻ ashkharhi* (Narratively Recited Panegyric by the Blessed Theophilos on Our Holy Father and Illuminator, the High Priest of Christ and Martyr, Gregory the Great, the Archbishop of Greater Armenia). In *Yovhannu Oskeberani ew Grigori Sarkawagapeti Nerbogheankʻ i S. Grigor Lusaworichʻ* (Panegyrics on St. Gregory the Illuminator by John Chrysostom, [His Disciple Theophilos], and Gregory Sarkawagapet). Sopʻerkʻ Haykakankʻ 4. Venice: S. Ghazar, 1853, pp. 89–125. Also among the *Erkbayakan Charkʻ* (Allegorical Homilies) in *Yovhannu Oskeberani Kostandnupolsi Episkopasapeti Meknutʻiwn Tʻghtʻotsʻn Pawghosi* (John Chrysostom, Archbishop of Constantinople: Commentary on the Epistles of Paul). 2 vols. Venice: S. Ghazar, 1862, 2:826–841.

———. *Patmutʻiwn Varutsʻ*. . . *Surb Yovhannēs Oskeberan Hayrapetin Kostandnupolsoy: Tʻargm. i Yunakanē i Hays, i Grigorē Katʻughikosē Vkayasēr Kochʻetsʻeloy* (History of the Life . . . of St. John Chrysostom, Patriarch of Constantinople, Translated from Greek into Armenian by Katʻoghikos Grigor, Called Martyrophile). Venice: S. Ghazar, 1751.

TʻOVMA ARTSRUNI. *Patmutʻyun*. V. Vardanyan, ed., *Tʻovma Artsruni ev Ananun, Patmutʻyun Artsrunyatsʻ Tan*. Erevan: Armenian Academy of Sciences, 1978); Eng. trans., R. W. Thomson, *Thomas Artsruni, History of the House of the Artsrunikʻ*. Detroit: Wayne State University Press, 1985.

VANAKAN VARDAPET. *"Ban Hawatali"* (A Believable Word). In *Girkʻ Tʻghtʻotsʻ* (ed. Izmireantsʻ), pp. 533–535.

VARDAN AREWELTSʻI. *Nerboghean yEritsʻs Eraneal Partʻewn Grigorios Lusaworichʻ Hayastan Ashkharhis* (Panegyric on the Thrice Beatified Parthian, Gregorios the Illuminator of Armenia). In *Yovhannu Sarkawagay, Vardanay Bardzrberdtsʻwoy, Yovhannu Erznkatsʻwoy Nerbogheankʻ i S. Grigor Lusaworichʻ* (Panegyrics on St. Gregory the Illuminator by Yovhannēs Sarkawag, Vardan Bardzrberdtsʻi [read Arewueltsʻi], and Yovhannēs Erznkatsʻi). Sopʻerkʻ Haykakankʻ 5. Venice: S. Ghazar, 1853, pp. 39–82.

———. *Patmutʻiwn*. [Gh. Alishan, ed.] *Vardan Vardapet Metsn: Hawakʻumn Patmutʻean Vardanay Vardapeti, lusabaneal* (Vardan Vardapet the Great: The Collected History of Vardan Vardapet, Annotated). Venice: Mekhitarists, 1862; Eng. trans., R. W. Thomson, "The Historical Compilation of Vardan Arewelcʻi." *Dumbarton Oaks Papers* 43 (1989) 125–226.

Yishatakarankʻ (Colophons). L. Khachʻikyan, ed., *ZhD-dari Hayeren Dzeṙagreri Hishatakaranner* (Colophons of 14th-Century Armenian Manuscripts). Erevan: Arm. Academy of Sciences, 1950.

———. A. S. Matʻevosyan, ed., *Hayeren Dzeṙagreri Hishatakaranner, ZhG Dar* (Colophons of Armenian Manuscripts, 13th Century). Erevan: Arm. Academy of Sciences, 1984.

———. A. K. Sanjian, *Colophons of Armenian Manuscripts, 1301–1480*. Cambridge, MA: Harvard University Press, 1969.

————. G. Yovsep'ean, ed., *Yishatakarank' Dzeṙagrats'* (Colophons of Manuscripts). Antelias: Armenian Catholicosate of Cilicia, 1951.

YOVHANNĒS DRASKHANAKERTTS'I. *Patmut'iwn Hayots'.* M. Emin, ed., *Yovhannu Kat'oghikosi Draskhanakertets'woy Patmut'iwn Hayots'.* Moscow: Vladimir Gotie, 1853; repr. Tiflis: Aghaneants', 1912, and Delmar, NY: Caravan Books, 1980; Eng. trans. and commentary, K. H. Maksoudian, *Yovhannēs Drasxanakertc'i: History of Armenia,* Scholars Press Occasional Papers and Proceedings: Columbia University Program in Armenian Studies 3. Atlanta: Scholars Press, 1987.

YOVHANNĒS ERZNKATS'I. [*Bank' Ch'ap'av*]. A. Erznkats'i Srapyan, ed., *Hovhannes Erznkats'i, Bank' Ch'ap'av* (Hovhannes Erznkats'i: Words in Verse). Hay K'narergut'yun Matenashar. Erevan: Sovetakan Grogh, 1986.

————. *Hawak'umn Meknut'iwn K'erakani* (Compilation of Commentary on Grammar). L. G. Khach'erean, ed., *Yovhannēs Erznkats'i (1230–1293 t't'), Hawak'umn Meknut'ean K'erakani.* Los Angeles and Glendale: Alco Printing, 1983; Eng. trans., R. R. Ervine, "Yovhannēs Erznkac'i Pluz's 'Compilation of Commentary on Grammar'." 3 vols. Columbia University Dissertation, 1988.

————. *Kanonagrut'iwn.* Levon Khach'ikyan, ed., "Erznka k'aghak'i 'Eghbarts' miabanut'ean' kanonagrut'yunĕ" (The By-laws of the "Community of Brothers" in the City of Erznka). *Banber Matenadarani* 6 (1962) 365–377.

————. *Khrat Hasarakats' K'ristonēits'* (Exhortation to All Christians). In Ē. M. Baghdasaryan, ed., *Hovhannes Erznkats'in ev Nra Khratakan Ardzakĕ* (Hovhannes Erznkats'i and His Hortatory Prose). Erevan: Arm. Academy of Sciences, 1977, pp. 143–203; W. Arm. trans., A. Daniēlean, *Khrat Bolor K'ristoneanerun* (Exhortation to All Christians). Antelias: Armenian Catholicosate of Cilicia, 1984.

————. *Yaghags Miabanut'ean Eghbarts'* (Concerning the Community of Brothers). Ē. Baghdasaryan, ed., "Yovhannēs Pluz-Erznkats'u 'Yaghags Miabanut'ean Eghbarts'' Khratakan T'ught'ĕ" (The Exhortatory Epistle of Y. P.-E.: "Concerning the Community of Brothers"). *"Gandzasar" Theological Review* 6 (1996) 454–472.

————. *Yovhannēs Vardapeti Erznkats'woy Asats'uats Nerboghakan Govesti i Surb Lusaworich'n Hayots' Grigorios* (Panegyric Recited in Praise of St. Gregorios the Illuminator of the Armenians by Yovhannēs Vardapet Erznkats'i). In *Yovhannu Sarkawagay, Vardanay Bardzrberdts'woy, Yovhannu Erznkats'woy Nerbogheank' i S. Grigor Lusaworich'* (Panegyrics on St. Gregory the Illuminator by Yovhannēs Sarkawag, Vardan Bardzrberdts'i [read Arewelts'i], and Yovhannēs Erznkats'i). Sop'erk' Haykakank' 5. Venice: S. Ghazar, 1853, pp. 85–164; in free verse, A. Erznkats'i Srapyan, ed., *Hovhannes Erznkats'i, Bank' Chap'av,* pp. 136–199.

[Ps] YOVHANNĒS MAMIKONEAN. *Patmut'iwn Tarōnoy.* A. Abrahamyan, ed., *Yovhan Mamikonean, Patmut'iwn Tarōnoy.* Erevan: Haypethrat, 1941; Eng. trans., L. Avdoyan, *Pseudo-Yovhannēs Mamikonean: The History of Tarōn,* Scholars Press Occasional Papers and Proceedings: Columbia University Program in Armenian Studies 6. Atlanta: Scholars Press, 1993.

YOVHANNĒS SARKAWAG. *Nerboghean i Surbn Grigor* (Panegyric on St. Gregory). In *Yovhannu Sarkawagay, Vardanay Bardzrberdts'woy, Yovhannu Erznkats'woy*

Nerbogheank'i S. Grigor Lusaworich' (Panegyrics on St. Gregory the Illuminator by Yovhannēs Sarkawag, Vardan Bardzrberdts'i [read Arewelts'i], and Yovhannēs Erznkats'i). Sop'erk' Haykakank' 5. Venice: S. Ghazar, 1853, pp. 5–36.

YOVHANNĒS TSORTSORETS'I. *Hamaṙawt Tesut'iwn K'erakani.* L. G. Khach'erean, ed., *Yovhannēs Tsortsorets'i (1288–1340 t't'), Hamaṙawt Tesut'iwn K'erakani* (Y. TS. [1283–1340]: An Abridged Treatment of [the] *Grammar*). Los Angeles and Glendale: Alco Printing, 1984.

Secondary Literature

ABEGHYAN, M. *Hayots' Hin Grakanut'yan Patmut'yun* (History of Early Armenian Literature). 2 vols. Erevan: Arm. Academy of Sciences, 1944–1946.

ABGARYAN, G V. *Sebēosi Patmut'yunĕ ev Ananuni aṙeghtsvatsĕ* (The *History* of Sebēos and the Enigma of the Anonymous). Erevan: Arm. Academy of Sciences, 1965.

ADONTZ, N. *Armenia in the Period of Justinian.* N. G. Garsoïan, ed. and trans. Lisbon: Calouste Gulbenkian Foundation, 1970.

AGHAWNUNI, M. "Yovhannēs Vardapet Erznkats'i (Ukhtawor Erusaghēmi—1281)" (Y. V. E.: [Jerusalem Pilgrim—1281]). *Sion* 12 (1938) 213–219.

AGHAYAN, Ē. B. et al., eds. *Hay Mshakuyt'i Nshanavor Gortsich'nerĕ* (The Prominent Shapers of Armenian Culture). Erevan: State University of Erevan, 1976.

ALBERT, M. et al., eds. *Christianismes orientaux: Introduction à l'étude des langues et des littératures.* Initiations au christianisme ancien. Paris: Cerf, 1993.

ALISHAN, GH. M. *Hayapatum* (Armenian History). 2 vols., Venice: S. Ghazar, 1901.

————. *Sisuan ew Levon Metsagorts* (Sisuan and Levon Metsagorts). Venice: S. Ghazar, 1885.

————. *Yushikk' Hayreneats' Hayots'* (Memoirs from the Armenian Fatherland). 2 vols., 2nd ed. Venice: S. Ghazar, 1920.

ANANEAN (ANANIAN), P. "S. Grigor Lusaworch'i dzeṙnadrut'ean t'uakanĕ ew paraganerĕ." *Bazmavep* 117 (1959) 9–23, 129–142, 225–238; 118 (1960) 53–60, 101–113 (=*S. Grigor Lusaworch'i dzeṙnadrut'an t'uakanĕ ew paraganerĕ.* Venice: S. Ghazar, 1960).

————. "La data e le circostanze della consecrazione di S. Gregorio Illuminatore," *Le Muséon* 74 (1961) 43–73, 319–360 (Italian trans. of the preceding).

ANT'ABYAN, P'. "Vardan Arewelts'u Nerboghĕ Nvirvats Hayots' Greri Gyutin" (The Panegyric by Vardan Arewelts'i on the Discovery of the Armenian Letters). *Banber Matenadarani* 7 (1964) 365–397.

AWETIK'EAN, G. et al., eds. *Nor Baṙgirk' Haykazean Lezui* (New Dictionary of the Armenian Language). 2 vols., Venice: S. Ghazar. 1836.

AYVAZYAN, H. et al., eds. *K'ristonya Hayastan, Hanragitaran* (Christian Armenia: Encyclopedia). Erevan: Haykakan Hanragitarani Glkhavor Khmbagrut'yun, 2002.

BAGHDASARYAN, Ē. M. *Hovhannes Erznkats'in ev Nra Khratakan Ardzakĕ* (Hovhannes Erznkats'i and His Hortatory Prose). Erevan: Arm. Academy of Sciences, 1977.

BEDOUKIAN, P. Z. *Coinage of the Artaxiads of Armenia*. Royal Numismatic Society Special Publication 10. London: RNS, 1978.

BEDROSIAN, R. "Armenia during the Seljuk and Mongol Periods." In R. G. Hovannisian, ed., *The Armenian People from Ancient to Modern Times. Vol. I: The Dynastic Periods: From Antiquity to the Fourteenth Century*. New York: St. Martin's Press, 1997, pp. 241–271.

BIWZANDATS'I, N. *Koriwn Vardapet ew Norin T'argmanut'iwnk'* (Koriwn Vardapet and His Translations). Tiflis: Martiroseants', 1900.

BOGHARIAN (Pogharean, Tsovakan), N. *Grand Catalogue of St. James Manuscripts*. 11 vols., Jerusalem: St. James Press, 1966–1991.

_____. *Hay Groghner* (Armenian Writers). Jerusalem: St. James Press, 1971.

_____. *Koriwn Vardapeti Erkerĕ* (The Works of Koriwn Vardapet). Jerusalem: St. James Press, 1984; repr. of articles in *Sion* 56 (1982) 191–193; 57 (1983) 38–40, 87–90, 152–155, and 211–214, with an added index of the special terms considered.

_____. *Vanatur: Banasirakan yoduatsneru zhoghovatsoy* (Monastical: A Collection of Philological Essays). Jerusalem: St. James Press, 1993.

BROCK, S. "Christians in the Sasanian Empire: A Case of Divided Loyalties." In S. Mews, ed. *Religion and National Identity*. Studies in Church History 18. Oxford: Blackwell, 1982, pp. 1–19; repr. in *idem, Syriac Perspectives on Late Antiquity*. Collected Studies Series 199. London: Variorum, 1984, ch. VI.

COWE, S. P. "An Allegorical Poem by Mkrtich' Naghash and Its Models." *Journal of the Society for Armenian Studies* 4 (1988–1989) 143–154.

DIAKONOFF, I. M. *The Prehistory of the Armenian People*, trans. from the Russian, *Predystoria armianskogo naroda* (Erevan: Arm. Academy of Sciences, 1968), by L. Jennings, with revisions by the author. Delmar, NY: Caravan Books, 1984.

DOWSETT, C. J. F. "The Newly Discovered Fragment of Lazar of P'arp's *History*." *Le Muséon* 89 (1976) 97–122.

ĒP'RIKEAN, H. S. *Patkerazard Bnashkharhik Baṙaran* (Pictorial Topographical Dictionary). 2 vols., 2nd ed. Venice: S. Ghazar, 1903–1905.

ESBROECK, M. VAN. "Témoignages littéraires sur les sépultures de S. Grégoire l'Illuminateur." *Analecta Bollandiana* 89 (1971) 387–418.

ESBROECK, M. VAN and ZANETTI, U. "Le manuscrit Erévan 993: Inventaire des pièces." *Revue des études arméniennes*, n.s. 12 (1977) 123–167.

FOX, R. L. *Pagans and Christians*. San Francisco: Harper and Row, 1986.

GARSOÏAN, N. G. *Armenia between Byzantium and the Sasanians*. Collected Studies Series 218. Aldershot: Variorum, 1985.

_____. "The Aršakuni Dynasty (A.D. 12-[180?]–428)." In R. G. Hovannisian, ed. *The Armenian People from Ancient to Modern Times. Vol. I: The Dynastic Periods: From Antiquity to the Fourteenth Century*. New York: St. Martin's Press, 1997, pp. 63–94.

_____. *L'Église arménienne et le grand schisme d'Orient*. Corpus Scriptorum Christianorum Orientalium 574, sub. tom. 100. Leuven: Peeters, 1999.

_____. "The Emergence of Armenia." In R. G. Hovannisian, ed. *The Armenian People from Ancient to Modern Times. Vol. I: The Dynastic Periods: From Antiquity to the*

Fourteenth Century. New York: St. Martin's Press, 1997, pp. 37–62.

———. "Politique ou Orthodoxie? L'Arménie au quatrième siècle." *Revue des études arméniennes,* n.s. 4 (1967) 297–320; repr. in *eadem, Armenia between Byzantium and the Sasanians,* ch. IV.

GHAZINYAN, A. "Nerboghĕ hay hin grakanut'yan mej" (The Panegyric in Ancient Armenian Literature). In V. S. Nersisyan and H. G. Bakhch'inyan, eds. *Hay Mijnadaryan Grakanut'yan Zhanrer* (Genres of Medieval Armenian Literature). Erevan: Arm. Academy of Sciences, 1984, pp. 127–178.

GREPPIN, J. A. C., ed. *Proceedings of the Fourth International Conference on Armenian Linguistics, Anatolian and Caucasian Studies.* Delmar, NY: Caravan Books, 1992.

HAMBARDZUMYAN, V. H. et al., eds. *Haykakan Sovetakan Hanragitaran* (Soviet Armenian Encyclopedia). 12 vols. Erevan: Arm. Academy of Sciences, 1974–1986.

HAYRAPETEAN (Hairapetian), S. (P.) *Hay hin ew mijnadarean grakanut'ean patmut'iwn.* Los Angeles: privately published, 1986.

———. *A History of Armenian Literature from Ancient Times to the Nineteenth Century.* Delmar, NY: Caravan Books, 1995 (Eng. trans. of the preceding, revised).

HEWSEN, R. H. *"The Primary History of Armenia:* An Examination of the Validity of an Immemorially Transmitted Historical Tradition." *History in Africa* 2 (1975) 91–100.

———. "The Synchronistic Table of Bishop Eusebius (Ps. Sebēos): A Reexamination of its Chronological Data." *Revue des études arméniennes,* n.s. 15 (1981) 59–72.

HOVANNISIAN, R. G., ed. *The Armenian Image in History and Literature.* Malibu, CA: Undena Publications, 1981.

———, ed. *The Armenian People from Ancient to Modern Times.* 2 vols. New York: St. Martin's Press, 1997.

KHACHATRIAN, A. *L'architecture arménienne du IVᵉ au VIᵉ siècle.* Bibliothèque des Cahiers Archéologiques 7. Paris: Klincksiek, 1971.

KHACH'ERYAN, L. G. "Données historiques sur la fondation d'Edjmiatsin à la lumière des feuilles récentes." *Handes Amsorya* 76 (1962) 100–106, 227–250, 425–452.

———. *Gladzori Hamalsaranĕ Hay Mankavarzhakan Mtk'i mej, XIII–XIV dd.* (The [Role of the] University of Glajor in Armenian Pedagogical Thought). Erevan: Arm. Academy of Sciences, 1973.

KING, L. W. and THOMPSON, R. C. *The Sculptures and Inscriptions of Darius the Great on the Rock of Behistun of Persia.* London: British Museum, 1907.

K'IWRTEAN, Y. *Eriza ew Ekegheats' Gawaṙ* (Eriza and the Province of Ekegheats'). 2 vols. Venice: Mkhit'arean Tparan, 1953.

———. "Yovhannēs Erznkats'i." *Bazmavep* 80 (1929) 166–171.

———. "Yovhannēs Erznkats'i-Tsortsorets'i." *Bazmavep* 112 (1954) 242–245.

———. "Yovhannēs Erznkats'i Pluz ew Yovhannēs Erznkats'i Tsortsorets'i." *Bazmavep* 116 (1958) 186–196.

KOUYMJIAN, D., ed. *Movsēs Xorenac'i et l'historiographie arménienne des origines.* Catholicossat arménien de Cilicie, 1700ᵉᵐᵉ centenaire de la proclamation du Christianisme en Arménie 7. Antélias: Catholicossat arménien de Cilicie, 2000.

LAMPE, G. W. H. *A Patristic Greek Lexicon.* Oxford: Clarendon Press, 1961.

MAHÉ, J.-P. "Entre Moïse et Mahomet: Réflexions sur l'historiographie arménienne." *Revue des études arméniennes,* n.s. 23 (1992) 121–153.

MAKSOUDIAN, K. [H.] *Chosen of God: The Election of the Catholicos of All Armenians from the Fourth Century to the Present.* New York: St. Vartan Press, 1995.

MEWS, S., ed. *Religion and National Identity.* Studies in Church History 18. Oxford: Blackwell, 1982.

MNATS'AKANYAN, A. SH., ed. *Hayrenner* (Quatrains in Couplets). Erevan: Matenadaran, 1995.

NERSISYAN, V. S. and BAKHCH'INYAN, H. G., eds. *Hay Mijnadaryan Grakanut'yan Zhanrer* (Genres of Medieval Armenian Literature). Erevan: Arm. Academy of Sciences, 1984.

OGHLUGEAN, A. "Hamaṙot Aknark Hay Ekeghets'woy Vardapetakan Astuatsabanut'ean Grakanut'ean" (A Brief Survey of the Doctrinal-Theological Literature of the Armenian Church). *"Gandzasar" Theological Review* 4 (1993) 45–71.

OLMSTEAD, A. T. *History of the Persian Empire.* Chicago: University of Chicago Press, 1948.

ORMANEAN, M. *Azgapatum* (National History). 3 vols. Constantinople: Tēr-Nersēsean and Jerusalem: St. James Press, 1912–1927; repr. Beirut: Sevan, 1959–1961.

OSKEAN, H. *Kilikiayi Vank'erĕ* (The Monasteries of Cilicia). Azgayin Matenadaran 183. Vienna: Mkhit'arean Tparan, 1957.

OUTTIER, B. "Movsēs après Movsēs." In Dickran Kouymjian, ed. *Movsēs Xorenac'i et l'historiographie arménienne des origines,* Catholicossat arménien de Cilicie, 1700ème centenaire de la proclamation du Christianisme en Arménie 7. Antélias: Catholicossat arménien de Cilicie, 2000, pp. 99–112.

PALEAN, T., ed. *Hay Ashughner, zhoghovrdakan hay ergichner ew taghasats'k'* (Armenian Troubadours, Popular Singers and Song Writers). 2 vols. Izmir: Tpagr. Mamurean, 1911–1912.

PEETERS, P. "La légende de Saint Jacques de Nisibe." *Analecta Bollandiana* 38 (1920) 285–373.

POGHAREAN (see Bogharian).

RENOUX, C. A. "Langue et littérature arméniennes." In M. Albert et al., eds. *Christianismes orientaux: Introduction à l'étude des langues et des littératures.* Initiations au christianisme ancien. Paris: Cerf, 1993, pp. 107–166.

RUSSELL, J. R. "The Formation of the Armenian Nation." In R. G. Hovannisian, ed. *The Armenian People from Ancient to Modern Times. Vol. I: The Dynastic Periods: From Antiquity to the Fourteenth Century.* New York: St. Martin's Press, 1997, pp. 19–36.

———. "On the Name of Mashtots." *Annual of Armenian Linguistics* 15 (1994) 67–78.

———. *Zoroastrianism in Armenia.* Harvard Iranian Series 5. Cambridge, MA: Harvard Univ. Press, 1987.

SANJIAN, A. K. "Esayi Nch'ec'i and Biblical Exegesis." In C. Burchard, ed. *Armenia and the Bible.* Univ. of Penn. Arm. Texts and Studies 12. Atlanta: Scholars Press, 1993, pp. 185–193.

SANSPEUR, C. "Le fragment de l'histoire de Lazare de P'arpi retrouvé dans le Ms. 1 de Jérusalem." *Revue des études arméniennes,* n.s. 10 (1973) 83–109.

SARKISSIAN, K. *A Brief Introduction to Armenian Christian Literature.* London: Faith Press, 1960.

———. *The Council of Chalcedon and the Armenian Church.* London: SPCK, 1965.

SRAPYAN (Erznkats'i Srapyan, Srapean), A. "Hovhannes Erznkats'i." In Ē. B. Aghayan et al., eds. *Hay Mshakuyt'i Nshanavor Gortsich'nerě* (The Prominent Shapers of Armenian Culture). Erevan: State University of Erevan, 1976, pp. 343–352.

———. *Hovhannes Erznkats'i, Usumnasirut'yun ev Bnagrer* (H. E.: A Study and Texts). Erevan: Haypethrat, 1958.

———. "Yovhannēs Erznkats'i-Pluz." *"Gandzasar" Theological Review* 6 (1996) 421–425.

———. "Yovhannēs Erznkats'i-Pluz." In H. Ayvazyan, et al., eds. *K'ristonya Hayastan, Hanragitaran* (Christian Armenia: Encyclopedia). Erevan: Haykakan Hanragitarani Glkhavor Khmbagrut'yun, 2002, pp. 619–624.

———. *Yovhannēs Erznkats'i-Pluz, Keank'ě ew Gortsě* (Y. E.-P: His Life and Works). Erevan: Zvart'nots', 1993.

———, et al. "Hovhannes Erznkats'i." In V. H. Hambardzumyan et al., eds. *Haykakan Sovetakan Hanragitaran* (Soviet Armenian Encyclopedia). 12 vols. Erevan: Arm. Academy of Sciences, 1974–1986, 6:559–560.

STONE, M. E. *A History of the Literature of Adam and Eve.* SBL Early Judaism and Its Literature 3. Atlanta: Scholars Press, 1992.

T'AMRAZYAN, H. *Hay K'nnadatut'yun, V–XV Dar* (Armenian [Literary] Criticism: V–XV Centuries). 2 vols. Erevan: Sovetakan Grogh, 1983–1985.

TER PETROSYAN, L. *Daser Hay Ekeghets'akan Matenagrut'yunits' (E Dar)* (Lessons from Armenian Ecclesiastical Bibliography [5th Century]). Soch'i: Armenian Diocese of Nor Nakhijewan and Russia, 1993.

TERIAN, A. "The Ancestry of St. Gregory the Illuminator in the Panegyrical Tradition." *St. Nersess Theological Review* 7 (2002) 45–65.

———. "A History of Armenian Grammatical Activity: An Account by Hovhannes Yerznkats'i." In J. A. C. Greppin, ed. *Proceedings of the Fourth International Conference on Armenian Linguistics, Anatolian and Caucasian Studies.* Delmar, NY: Caravan Books, 1992, pp. 213–219.

———. "Koriwn's *Life of Mashtots'* as an Encomium." *Journal of the Society for Armenian Studies* 3 (1987–1988) 1–14.

———. "Surpassing the Biblical Worthies: An Early Motif in Armenian Religious Literature." *Saint Nersess Theological Review* 1 (1996) 117–144.

THIERRY, J.-M. "Le Mont Sepuh: Étude archéologique." *Revue des études arméniennes,* n.s. 21 (1988–1989) 385–449.

THOMSON, R. W. "The Armenian Image in Classical Texts." In R. G. Hovannisian, ed. *The Armenian Image in History and Literature.* Malibu, CA: Undena Publications, 1981, pp. 9–25.

———. *A Bibliography of Classical Armenian Literature to 1500 AD.* Corpus Christianorum. Turnhout: Brepols, 1995.

———. "The Fathers in Early Armenian Literature." *Studia Patristica* 12 (=Texte und Untersuchungen 115; Berlin: Akademie Verlag, 1975) 457–470; repr. in *idem, Studies in Armenian Literature and Christianity.* Collected Studies Series 451. Aldershot: Variorum, 1994.

———. "The Maccabees in Early Armenian Historiography." *Journal of Theological Studies,* n.s. 26 (1975) 329–341.

———. "*Vardapet* in the Early Armenian Church." *Le Muséon* 75 (1962) 367–384.

Toumanoff, C. *Studies in Christian Caucasian History.* Washington, DC: Georgetown University Press, 1963.

———. "The Third-Century Arsacids." *Revue des études arméniennes,* n.s. 6 (1969) 233–281.1

Turan, O. "Les souverains seljoukides et leurs sujet non-musulmans." *Studia Islamica* 1 (1953) 65–100.

Vardanyan, R. V. *Hayots' Tonats'uyts'ě (4–18rd darer)* (The Church Calendar of the Armenians: 4th–18th Centuries). Erevan: Arm. Academy of Sciences, 1999.

Vryonis, S., Jr. *The Decline of Medieval Hellenism in Asia Minor and the Process of Islamization from the Eleventh through the Fifteenth Century.* Berkeley, Los Angeles, London: University of California Press, 1971.

Winkler, G. "Our Present Knowledge of the History of Agat'angełos and its Oriental Versions." *Revue des études arméniennes,* n.s. 14 (1980) 125–141.

Zarbhanalean, G. *Haykakan hin dprut'ean patmut'iwn (IV–XIII dar)* (History of Ancient Armenian Literature [4th–13th Centuries]). 2nd ed. Venice: Mkhit'arean Tparan, 1897.

Index of Proper Names

References to sections of Erznkats'i's *Panegyric* are in Arabic numbers, those to the Selections in Roman numbers.

Index of Scriptural Quotations
and Allusions

Both direct quotations and explicit allusions are indexed here, along with other citations in the Commentary and in the notes to the Selections. Direct quotations in texts are indicated in bold. References to sections of Erznkats'i's *Panegyric* are in Arabic numbers, followed by a slash separating the note number in the Commentary. References to the Selections are in Roman numbers.